JOHN W. PARSONS

Wasteland Press
Shelbyville, KY USA
www.wastelandpress.net

A Journey Through Life
by John W. Parsons

Copyright © 2008 John W. Parsons
ALL RIGHTS RESERVED

Cover illustration by Barbara Tyler Ahlfield
First Printing – September 2008
ISBN: 978-1-60047-244-2

NO PART OF THIS BOOK MAY BE REPRODUCED IN ANY FORM
WITHOUT WRITTEN PERMISSION FROM THE PUBLISHER,
EXCEPT BY A REVIEWER WHO MAY QUOTE PASSAGES IN A
REVIEW TO BE PRINTED IN A NEWSPAPER, JOURNAL, OR
MAGAZINE.

This book is a work of non-fiction. Unless otherwise noted, the author
and the publisher make no explicit guarantees as to the accuracy of the
information contained in this book and in some cases, names of people
and places have been altered to protect their privacy.

Printed in the U.S.A.

Introduction

It is Sunday, Sept. 09, 2001, and I am sitting in front of my computer thinking about my next possible project since I recently completed the "Parsons-Tyler Family Tree" genealogy booklet. This booklet is the culmination of many years of research by my sister Dorothy, and I take pride in the fact that I have managed to integrate all of the information into one concise form. It is hoped that current members of the family and future generations will find the booklet a great reference and certainly informative concerning the families' records. This is my second project of the history of the Parsons and Tyler families since my retirement, the first being the transcription of Joseph and John Corning's letters to home, as they served in the Union Army during the American Civil War. About 200 letters were transcribed and organized in a book and given to each family member and a copy is filed with the Library of Congress, The Palmyra Historical Society and the Ontario County Historical Society. These projects filled many an enjoyable moment over several years of taking a few spare minutes every few days pulling together this material on our ancestors. As I came to the end of the genealogy booklet, I began to formulate in my mind the next possible project I might undertake. I remembered that when my parents passed on they had in their possession a number of diaries that my grandfather (my mother's father) Benjamin Chinn Tyler (1867 to 1936) had kept during the years 1906 to 1924. During this time he ran a mercantile store for a brief time and then took up farming with my grandmother Mary Blanche McGregor (Mazie). As I sit here, I glance at the calendar on my desk and note that today, Sept. 09, is Grandparents' Day, and take this as a positive prophecy to take on this challenge and hope that it will be successful. Unfortunately, I have little remembrance of my grandfather since he passed on when I was three years old; however, I well remember my grandmother Mazie, as we lived with her for a number of years prior to her passing in 1956. I remember her as a strong and very devout woman who had shared in the raising of eight children, several of which passed on at various early ages in life. The life that Ben and Mazie spent from 1906 to 1924 would have been, by today's standards, considered a very difficult life; however, they persevered and raised a wonderful American family of successful, honest God-fearing children. In thinking about the diaries, one thought came to mind of transcribing them verbatim and organizing them for the family, but frankly that thought did not seem to hold much appeal. My second thought of trying to write a book around their lives based on these journals, I decided would present, hopefully, a more interesting chapter in our family's history. Therefore this attempt, which I sincerely hope will offer to the family a window into the Tyler side of the family, particularly Ben and Mary (Mazie) Tyler.

Having never attempted to compose a story, I am at somewhat of a loss as to how to begin, so I have asked my grandfather to write his own story in that which follows. Certainly, he can tell us about his and Mazie's life together far better than I can.

John William (Bill) Parsons

BENJAMIN CHINN TYLER
C. 1900

**MARY BLANCHE (MAZIE)
MCGREGOR/TYLER
C. 1900**

Chapter 1

Seest thou a man diligent in his business, he shall stand before kings

This was my motto as a farmer, father and husband
Ben C. Tyler
Perry, N.Y.
12-17-1906 – 1907
(1907- Oklahoma becomes the 46th state)

I recently purchased a new ledger from the L. L. Syphers Blank Book and Advertising Company for $2 to keep track of Mazie's and my accounts as we are thinking of giving up the mercantile business in Perry, NY to take up farming, and I feel it is very important not only to record one's accounts but to keep a record of this period of our journey through life. I think I always wanted to be a farmer having come from the south, where my roots were in the soil. I left the south, specifically Prince William County; Virginia in the late 1800's to make my fortune and find the woman to be my wife and mother of my children as I always looked forward to having a large family. Since the south was so devastated during and even years after the Civil War, there were few opportunities for a young Virginian to find gainful employment in the vanquished confederacy. I therefore moved on to Bellaire, Ohio and was fortunate in finding employment and

A JOURNEY THROUGH LIFE

becoming the head of the plate-mill department of the Carnegie Steel Company. During these years, I regrettably didn't find my fortune, but I certainly found my one true love in the woman who has always been dear to my heart, Mary (Mazie) McGregor. We were married on Sept. 12, 1895 and as of this first entry in my new journal, we have four wonderful children, Robert age 10, Margaret and Dorothy, our dear twins, age 7 and Marion, age 3. No man could ask for a finer wife and four more wonderful children that the good Lord has blessed us with.

It is told to me by my mother and father, Robert Horner Tyler and Sarah Sophie (Sallie) Chinn, as passed down through many generations of my family, that I descend from royalty. One would think, if this were the case, that Mazie would curtsy as I enter the room from working in the fields; however, I have yet to convince her of my nobility in the world. Mazie has responded to my request with a number of expressions, which as a God fearing Christian woman, one would not expect to hear from her. I plan to keep working on this and hopefully, someday, she may surprise me, but I doubt if my royal heritage really impresses Mazie greatly.

The first entry in this, the first of my journals, is of December 17, 1906, finally being the time when I feel as if things are again on course and with Mazie's and our wonderful extended families' help, they will continue to be so. I must be honest to report to you that I did suffer some depression this past summer, shortly after we moved here from Ohio, and this resulted in some loss of memory and amnesia, and I vaguely remember that a few months ago in August, I found life had overwhelmed me and I lost all recollection of who I was or where I belonged. This may have been partially a delayed reaction to the loss of our dear little Helen who passed away in November of 1903. She was such a darling child and to watch, as such a little precious thing at the age of two, suffered and passed on, it was so difficult for all of us to accept for some time afterwards. We were indeed fortunate that God allowed us this sweet child for even such a short time. Without Mazie's great strength and devotion to the Good Book, I doubt if I would have ever gotten through those troubling times at all. Unfortunately, I did eventually suffer a breakdown but am back home, thanks to the strength and love of my family and we are

The first LITTLE HELEN TYLER
C. 1903

enjoying our wonderful children and our new life here in Perry. I am sure also that the recent move to Perry, N. Y. from Bellaire, Ohio and the stress related with such a move contributed to my breakdown. After I was eventually found and returned to normal (as normal as Mazie said I ever was), she would remind me that this condition was most likely caused by my royal ancestors' intermarrying between cousins. Just can't seem to get any respect from that woman. The official version of my disappearance that appeared in the **Manassas Journal of August 31, of `06** was as follows:

"Haymarket, Va., Aug. 29. — Ben C. Tyler, a well-known young Virginian and a native of Prince William County, while in an unbalanced state of mind from overwork, disappeared from his home in Perry, N. Y., on August 16 and his family and friends, after a search lasting from the time of his disappearance up to the present, have been unable to find him.

Mr. Tyler's is one of the best known families in Northern Virginia. He is the son of the late Robert H. Tyler of Prince William County and is a first cousin of W. H. Tyler of Washington, D. C., a general passenger agent of the Southern Railway.

For several years, Ben. Tyler has lived in Bellaire, Ohio where he became the head of the plate-mill department of the Carnegie Steel Company in that city. He married a young lady from Bellaire and now has a family of four children. Recently he resigned his position with the Carnegie Company to enter the mercantile business in Perry, N. Y., moving to that city on August 1. Sixteen days later he disappeared.

It is thought that Mr. Tyler has started to walk to his home in Virginia. He is thirty-nine years of age, weighing about 135 pounds, and of slight build, dark hair and eyes dark. He had a mustache when leaving home, and probably may have grown a dark beard by this time. When he left, he wore a dark gray suit, with a black derby hat."

Manassas Journal, Sept. 21, 1906:

"A private letter from Mr. G. G. Tyler, who is at Perry, N. Y. with his brother's family says that while they have no information as to Mr. Ben C. Tyler's whereabouts, they all believe he is alive and safe somewhere. They believe he has been victim of a lapse of memory or some other mental aberration."

Manassas Journal, October 19, 1906

"A telegram has been received by the family at Haymarket from Mr. Geo. G. Tyler, who is in New York, saying that Mr. Benjamin Tyler has been found. His memory is returning. When discovered, he was quietly at work on a farm near Rochester."

This was certainly a chapter in my life that I would rather forget but depression happens to everyone at one time or another and in my case it got the better of me rather than my being able to control it. Now that I am feeling in fine spirits, I must tell you that the mercantile business that we own is most likely going to be sold, and as I stated earlier, we are going to try our hand at making a living farming. Today, Dec. 17, '06, Jim Slocum called me to see if I was interested in renting Mrs. Riley Edgerlys' farm for a year beginning in April next year. Since this is just the opportunity we have been looking for, we went on over to see her and she agreed to rent it to Mazie and me for a year with the option of a second year if we were successful and wanted to continue it. She said that Mazie, the children and I could move into the house April 1st. She asked me if I would be interested in tending her stock until we move in and take it over. She has 124 sheep, two cows and a horse and she offered to pay me 50 cents a day for taking care of them. Between running the store and caring for Mrs. Edgerlys' stock, I am going to be very busy, but the good Lord knows we can sure use the extra money. It may be tough for awhile until we get settled into a routine on the farm but I always had my roots in the soil and feel that it is a place where we can grow and nurture as a family as we continue our journey through life that only the Lord knows where the roads will take us.

I went up today and fed the stock and gave them oats at 8 AM, and at 4 PM I gave them bean pods. Robert went up with me at the 4 o'clock feeding and he was a great help as he is now 10 and strong and more than willing to help out his parents whenever he can. The extra set of hands made my work a lot lighter.

ROBERT TYLER
AGE 6
C. 1903

It's Weds. and only six days to Christmas. I wrote to George Grayson (he is one of my brothers). There were 11 brothers and sisters in my family so you can see why I wanted a big family. George was a great help to Mazie and the children during my dark days and I will forever be in his debt. Extended family is so important in times of difficulty. This evening Mazie and Robert went downtown to do a little Christmas shopping. We don't have the money to buy expensive gifts but we are determined that our children will have a Christmas to remember. God has given us all our health and that is the greatest gift of all.

I always felt I was a pretty handy fellow but on this cold and snowy day I mashed my thumb pretty badly fixing a corn bin on the Edgerly's farm. I'm afraid the throbbing will most likely keep me awake all night. Even though my thumb hurts, I did manage to buy a Christmas tree from a peddler for 20 cents, a fine tree it is, too, that we can all enjoy.

It is Saturday and I am going up to the farm and partition off part of the barn basement as several of the lambs are quite weak and need to be separated from the rest.

It's Sunday and we are dressed in our Sunday best and off to church for Mazie and I and the twins. We listened to a sermon by Will, my brother-in-law who is the Presbyterian minister here in Perry. He preached about Herod the King and it was a rousing good sermon. In the evening, Mazie and Robert had the opportunity to go to a choral service.

There is a lot of excitement as we get close to Christmas. Mazie is getting ready for the big dinner and killed and dressed two big fat chickens. This evening Mazie and I decorated the tree in preparation for tomorrow's excitement with the children. Margaret and Henry, Mazie's' sister and my brother who married some time after Mazie and I, sent gifts for all and we added those to ours under our special tree.

Mazie's other sister Lucy and her husband, Pastor Will and family have joined us today, Christmas 1906, for dinner and all the children had a fine time opening their gifts. I never enjoyed a Christmas day more than this one especially since this is the first Yuletide after my breakdown.

After the recent purchases of gifts, it was appreciated today when Mrs. Edgerly paid me the $3.50 she owed me for the last seven days of work. On Friday we went to a Christmas tree festival of entertainment downtown and the twins Dorothy and Margaret recited "The Two Dorothy's" and they did a fine job. I gave them each five cents for their outstanding performance. Will preached another of his fine sermons today on, "All things work together for good to them that love God" and we went back to church again in the evening for the second service. Here it is the day before New Years and since we are going to the TeWinkels tomorrow for a nice dinner, Robert needed a haircut so I marched him downtown and he looks so much neater and it was well worth the 20 cents that it cost me. We had a delicious dinner on New Year's Day with Will, Lucy and the children. It is always great to be with family especially on holidays. After dinner Will and I went down to the store to inventory the stock. Will thinks it will fetch about $1500 but I think closer to $1300. I hope to net about a thousand dollars after paying all the bills left and collecting the money owed me from a number of customers that we gave credit to.

Will called and said that Ellsworth had agreed to buy the store's stock at 75 cents on the dollar. The money will be badly needed as I am starting to look for farming equipment and recently purchased a Bailey Fork and Hay Knife for this new upcoming chapter in our lives. It is sure getting colder and I need to get in some more coal so I called Mr. Martin and he delivered 3500 lbs. of egg coal at $6.25 per ton and also 2110 lbs. of nut coal at the same price. Cost me $17.52 for all of it and hopefully it will last quite awhile and keep us warm through these long winter months.

We heard another rousing sermon today. Mazie, Robert and the twins went in the morning while I watched Marion and in the evening Mazie and I went. Will preached on "What shall it profit a man if he gain the whole world and lose his own soul."

The children, except for little Marion, are off to school for their first day of reading, writing and arithmetic for this new year, Jan. 7. 1907. We are all excited today as Ma and my sister Tilly wrote and said they would be leaving Virginia for Perry about the 15th of this month for a visit. We are all looking forward to seeing them.

It's Thursday and I am to meet Mr. Slocum up at the Edgerly's farm, as he has to cut the horns off the two young cows.

Mrs. Edgerly also agreed I could keep our horse Kitty at the farm as long as I furnished the feed for it. I went up to the mill and got 85 lbs. of crushed oats for Kitty and it cost me $1.28. I had to attend to a few things at home later as Mazie is not feeling at all well and retired early. Robert wanted me to also order a part for his camera from the Eastman Kodak Company, which I did.

Well, we netted $700 on the store stock, things never seem to quite work out the way one would hope but that is behind us now and there is no turning back nor should we waiver on this road we have chosen to take. I agreed today to cut wood for Mrs. Edgerly from the farm if I could have half of all I cut, and she reminded me to finish writing up the contract for she and I to sign for the renting of the farm. Some mail came today from Mazie's brother, Howard, who is a zoology professor at Columbia University and he said he subscribed to a farm paper for us for the year. I probably need all the help I can get in this new endeavor so I will look forward to seeing it. He also sent $2.00 for little Marion to buy a rocking chair.

Things are beginning to fall into place this week on Jan. 13th as to the lease and the final sale of the merchandise and equipment from the store. We enjoyed church twice today, hearing Will preach on "Where sin abounded, there did Grace much more abound." We also went to prayer meeting on Thursday evening so we have done our duty this week in return for the Lord's continued blessing. The week started out with my taking the twins and Marion down to the store so Marion could pick out a rocking chair. I think she tried out every one of them in the store and we had fun watching this darling little four year old make up her mind. It cost $2.00; she helped me carry it home and was very proud of her own little rocker.

Some of the lambs on the farm are still quite weak. One dear little one died today and about ten others are very weak. The temperature of ten below is not helping the situation any. I pray we will not lose any more.

I need to begin thinking about buying seed for the spring planting so I sent today for a catalog from the W. A. Burpee Seed Co. Mrs. Edgerly and I signed the lease agreement today and we also agreed to rent our house to the Wrights starting April 1st. Everything seems to be falling in place on this new road we are about to travel. Fred Allen agreed to rent the three-deck candy case from the store for 25 cents a week and if he decides to buy it, I told him he could have it for $8.00 and any rent he paid me on it would go towards the $8.00. I have just a few more items to sell or lease and we will be clear of the mercantile store.

It is pretty cold and snowy this week of Jan. 20, 1907 and great weather for sleigh rides. It is windy also today and Dorothy is not feeling very well. I am sure the bad weather is not helping her any. I am trying to keep the house warm, especially for Dorothy, but it is hard to do with this cold and wind.

Fred Allen decided to buy the four-foot upright cigar case and paid me $6.50 for it which will come in handy. I also was paid $7.00 for the past two weeks of work from Mrs. Edgerly. It all helps, especially as we will be between careers for a month or so. The Wrights agreed to the lease for our house as of April 1st and will pay us $5.00 per week rent with four weeks' payment in advance.

It is finally warming up a little as the week progresses and Mazie decided to keep the twins home from school for a day. It seemed to help, as they are both feeling better. Heard again from Ma and she and Tilly will arrive on the 30th of the month. I wrote them and told them we would pick them up at the Silver Springs station that day. Can't wait to see them both.

Making quite a bit on delivering potatoes from our stock. I think I delivered about 50 bushels this week and we are getting 45 cents a bushel for them. Since we are taking up farming, I went to the Farmers' Institute meeting both Saturday and Sunday and got some very helpful thoughts on our future challenges. While I was there, I looked over a team of horses but thought they were a little light, only weighing 1100 lbs., but later I decided to take a chance on them and made an offer of $180 for the pair.

Here it is February and I am trying to unload the last of the store's equipment and attempting to collect what is owed us still from customers we extended credit to. Ellsworth paid me for the note I held for him for $350. He paid $352.71, $350 for the note and $1.25 was for interest plus $1.46 for 470 lbs. of coal he bought recently. Great to get this payment with the upcoming expenses. The Johantzen brothers agreed to buy the safe for $45, and said they would pay me $25 in cash and I could have the other in store credit at their establishment. Since we have the credit, I bought a new pair of shoes for myself for $2.25 and a pair for Robert for $1.25. We sure look sharp in our new shoes.

I sold the cookie rack for $1.00, the cash register to Baker and Roberts for $10 and I agreed to take the money in store credit from them also. I sold the small pair of scales to Fred Allen for $1.00 and the five-foot high cherry showcase he also wanted for $6. He has agreed to pay me 50 cents per week for 14 weeks. Watkins and McKurth will take the four boxes of Uncle Ed's Opera Cigars off my hands and they will settle up for them directly with Uncle Ed's.

What a job it is becoming to try and collect the money we are owed by persons we extended store credit to. I tried to collect from Mrs. Beeverly unsuccessfully and several other customers are questioning their bills. So much for extending credit. I decided to hire Charlie Wager to collect what he could for me and I have agreed to give him 10% of anything he collects.

It is great weather again for a sleigh ride and I took Mazie for a nice ride on the Allegheny Road. I have also taken Tilly and the twins for a couple of outings. Tilly went to the skating rink with Mr. Martin, which was a nice outing for her.

We have had quite a few doctor calls this month as Mazie's throat has been bothering her and Dr. Wright came around to the house a couple of times to check on Marion and gave her some medicine. He said she has the common croup and seems to be getting better as the weeks roll by here in February of 1907. Mazie and Tilly went to Dr. Wright a couple of times also, not sure what for, must be something secret amongst the ladies as they haven't seen fit to share it with me.

In between church services this Sunday I have been checking out teams of horses again. After communion this Sunday, Will did not preach a sermon as it was Communion Sunday so the service was a little shorter. I went and checked out Nugent's team and found the white horse a little stiff and the chestnut almost 15 years old. Since my offer a few weeks ago on a pair was turned down, I decided to offer Nugent $208 for his team. He called me and seemed upset over the offer. He felt the offer was so low it was an insult and he was upset enough to come to the Edgerly's barn where he had some equipment stored and take it all home. He probably feels that a young whippersnapper like me doesn't know anything about farming or the value of a good pair of workhorses and thinks as a shopkeeper I won't make it in the farming business. I plan on showing him and any other skeptics just how wrong they are. Some folks unfortunately are just difficult to deal with. I have looked at teams owned by Mr. Cowies and Mr. VanScooters but they want $350 and that is a little steep for me. I also am checking out Chase's and Randall's teams. For the time being I have hitched up Kitty and Mrs. Edgerly's horse Nelly and they worked well together with the rented double harness, collars and yokes that I have temporarily until I can buy my own. I also this week have checked out Chase's team, which might serve my purposes. Today I went up and checked on a team owned by Mr. Martin and they are a good team that I think I am going to make an offer on. He has given me first refusal until March 1st but the more I think about it, I plan on offering him $237 and hope he accepts it.

Today Mr. Martin called and accepted my offer for Jack and Fran. They each weigh about 1400 lbs. and I think they will make a fine team. I also bought a used wagon, yoke and other accessories that I need from Mr. Martin for $15. He has agreed to deliver them to me in good condition on April 1st. I guess I am thinking of Will's sermon on the 17th, "Remember Lot's wife." I remember she was turned to a pillar of salt when she looked back so maybe that sermon is reminding Mazie and I that there is no looking back now.

We went to a concert at the Methodist Church and then we visited with several of the neighbors for a while. It is always refreshing to get together with friends and neighbors.

I received the electric bill today from the Perry Electric Company for the period of Dec. 29th to Feb. 5th and I thought we used a little more than we should have as the bill showed that we used 28 kilowatts of electric and had to pay $3.92 for it. Sometimes it is tough to budget exactly for all expenses.

I can't say that this month didn't end on a high note as Mr. Martin called and said he thinks Fran is in foal and I agreed to pay the fees of $12.00 if she has a colt. I have to ask the children and Mazie to begin to think of a name for our new colt. Think positive.

I guess I might call this March "the month of the muddy roads" here in Perry, New York in this year of our Lord 1907. This is the month when we are going to move onto the Edgerly's farm and with the frost coming out of the ground; all the roads are muddy, rutted and almost impassable. I wonder if someday people will be able to come up with a surface for roads that will not become a quagmire every spring. It would sure make life easier.

I am still trying to collect from about 20 people who still owe us for credit we gave them in the mercantile store. As I said before, some are real deadbeats about paying, although as Mazie would say, "That is not the Christian attitude." A few, the Gagtons and the Genchoms paid me part of what they owed and Mr. Ginchoms gave me a Wyondotte rooster to cover the last 50 cents that they owed. Mrs. Gwill also paid me the $1.68 she owed. Mrs. Pavenport said she would send her son to the house this Saturday to pay hers but I wasn't surprised when he never showed up. Times are tough and I guess Mazie and I need to be understanding when it comes to our debtors.

As Will preached this Sunday on "Spiritual Cleanliness," I thought of our debts and debtors. It is hard to forgive all the folks however that still owe us, especially since we always have been faithful in paying those that we owed money to. This month seems to be filled with reminders of faith, hope and charity as we have gone to church it seems three or four times a week. Between Will's sermon on the 3rd on "And he opened his mouth and taught them," to several evangelical meetings and concerts at the Baptist Church, I feel we are fully blessed this month. Mazie might not of course agree with me, as her faith always seems to go deeper than mine. That is not to say I do not have faith, only that Mazie's is greater and deeper.

I have been fighting depression today, I am feeling terrible depressed and low spirited and cannot see why I should, but am battling against it all I can and do hope that when we get settled in the country that this will not bother me anymore. My mind is in a peculiar state these days. ***Who will win the battle in the long run, depression or I?***

My brother George back home in Haymarket, Virginia, wanted me to ship him some potatoes so today I went to the railroad office and checked on the price and found out I can ship him 700 lbs. for $1.75. Robert and I will get them together and take them over next Tues., the 12th. Harry also called and he is going to send me $200 that he will loan us for a few weeks. Family is so important at all times but especially when we are planning a big move and are in need of some temporary help.

I have been trying to get everything ready for the move to the farm and fortunately, after a few days, my depression has lifted and I am feeling like my old self again. I think sometimes when we get depressed, we think we are the only ones it happens to but the truth is it happens to almost everyone at one time or another. I have purchased some much-needed tools for the move from Mr. Nugent. He agreed to sell me a second hand hay rake for $4.00 or make me a new one for $10.00. Glenn Martin wants me to take the horses early but I told him I couldn't take them yet and an agreement is an agreement as we had originally decided I would take them on April 1st. He said OK, I think he was testing me. Mrs. Edgerly is planning on selling all her sheep and Mr. McCormick came by today to look them over. He decided to take them all and I am going to ship them out to him, half on the 26th and then remainder on the 29th. There are 10,404 lbs. total and at 7 ½ cents a lb. Mrs. Edgerly will make $780.30 on them.

I am beginning to look at cows, Mr. Courie has one for sale at $40.00 but that is just too high for me and I will keep looking. I did find a nice cow at Mr. Phillips and agreed to pay him $40.00 as the cow is with calf, so it is just like getting two for the price of one. I think I drove a pretty good bargain in this instance plus Mr. Phillips has agreed to keep them until the calf is three days old.

Well here it is the end of March and things are piling up. I got Jack and Fran today, my new team of horses, also the cow and calf and I have been moving our furniture up to the farm today. With the roads so bad it has been quite a task. Mazie, Ma and Tillie decided to visit Niagara Falls today, can't quite figure out why they choose today to be gone with all the work we have in moving, but I sure wasn't going to argue with any of them, particularly all three of them. I have a strong feeling I would have lost the argument anyway.

The twins want to move their chickens up so right after Church we gathered them up and made the move. Those chickens have kept us in eggs for quite awhile as I have had to pay Dorothy and Margaret almost a full dollar this month for the 50 or so eggs they have collected from their hen house. I had enough money left over after giving Mazie $7.50 for household expenses and Robert 40 cents for collecting what was owed us by the Allens to order delivery of the Rochester Democrat and Chronicle newspaper so we can keep abreast of the goings on in the world. It will cost us 12 cents a week, which seems high, but hopefully the news won't all be bad at that price.

Well, tomorrow is the 1ˢᵗ of April and the first or our new adventure. I am looking forward to it with great anticipation and uneasiness. With the good Lord's help, the road will be a smooth one for Mazie and I and our four children.

What a difference a day makes! We have completely moved onto the farm and my days are long and as filled as Mazie's. One thing I am finding out very quickly is that the weather is a lot more important to a farmer than it is to a shopkeeper. April is starting out windy, cold and snowing, and with the frost coming out of the ground, it is almost impossible to do any plowing or planting this early. It was good to have some much-needed help moving everything from our Lake Street home. Mr. Milroy and Jon Sullivan helped us all day and I paid them each $2.20 for their eleven-hour day. The only hitch we had, except for the weather, was that Mrs. Edgerly wanted to store a lot of her old items at the farm but Mazie put her foot down and thankfully said no.

The days are filled with laying linoleum and carpet in the house when I can't work outside. I am still trying to collect the last of the credit I extended to store customers. I bought a buggy, plow and drag from Mr. Chase for $15.00 and he owed me $4.01 on his account so he deducted that from the $15.00 and squared his bill. I called on Mrs. Gavenport, which was a waste of time as she refused to pay anything at all but I am still hopeful she will see the light at some point. Mr. Sutton still owed me $2.25 so I picked up a pair of work pants, two work shirts and three pair of socks from his store and that squared his account with me.

I am buying some livestock to add to our farming experience. I have bought several cows with calves and several calves separately. I paid $1.00 for a three-day-old calf from Bob Wright and $1.50 for a one-week-old one, which are half Jersey

A JOURNEY THROUGH LIFE

and half Durham. I also bought three pigs from Bill Douds for $10.00. Having bought the cows and pigs I was very concerned the other day when I found Jack cast in the stable and I had a terrible time getting him to his feet. He had rolled over near the wall, had his legs caught under him and couldn't get up on his own. I was worried I might have to buy another workhorse but fortunately all turned out fine. He was most likely just getting tired out as I am with the snow, cold and mud we have been dealing with all month. I think he would like to spend his day in the stall as I some mornings would like to stay in my warm bed. I am sure the weather will improve as will Jack's and my attitude, the sooner the better. To make matters worse, Jack and I were out trying to work the other day and he got stuck in the mud and in trying to get out we broke the wagon tongue. I finally got him free, Robert and I disconnected the tongue and Robert took it to get it repaired for me.

I have had to hire some help and have engaged Mr. Sherman and Mr. Rowe to trim the orchard trees for us. I agreed to pay them each $2.00 per day and they are to board themselves. I also hired Mr. Arnold to help me at $1.50 per day and we will give him his dinner. He is to work 7 AM to 6 PM. It seems like a short day compared to mine but I am feeling good and hard work never hurt anyone. It keeps my mind occupied and off my problems, especially my depression, which I hope, is history.

Here it is the 22nd of April already and finally I am able to start planting a few things. I have sowed seven acres of wheat and planted onions, lettuce, beets and radishes. Unfortunately, I broke two plow points but they can be fixed and with Mother Nature's help our crops will prosper.

I have been so busy I have neglected church. Mazie has been keeping the faith for both of us. I finally got a chance to attend today the 28th with Mazie and the children. We went in the morning and heard a rousing sermon from Will, "Rejoice in Tribulation." I think Will wrote this sermon especially for me. In the evening Will preached on "Blessed are the poor in Spirit." Maybe again he was directing this message toward me but I guess if a minister is preaching a good inspirational sermon, each member of the congregation thinks it is being directed at them.

Well, April is coming to a close and I pray that May's weather will be a big improvement over what we have been having. Maybe then Jack and I (and Fran) will face the tasks ahead of us with renewed enthusiasm. At least we had a good closure with Mr. Wright paying the rent of $20.00 on the Lake Street home, and I got the insurance bill from Jack Webster for the insurance on the furniture, which was less than I had been quoted and came in at 62½ cents for each $100 we insured. We insured the furniture for a total of $500.00 so it cost me $3.12 for the year.

It is a good thing I bought a high pair of boots when we started in the farming business as I not only need them for the mud but also for all the manure I have to haul and spread every day. Some days it seems like I am up to my you know what in manure but I guess that never hurt anyone and I am sure finding out it is a big part of a farmer's life.

Mr. Arnold is working out pretty good as a hired hand. There are a few days he doesn't show up but generally he is here and works steady when he is. I certainly don't pay him his $1.50 a day wages when he doesn't come to work so I don't imagine he will be missing too many days. With the weather the way it is with lots of rain and even some snow flakes yet, some days it is just as well he is not here as I haven't the work for him when we can't get outside.

Mazie hired Mrs. McCloud to help her with the household chores and the laundry for the six of us. I can't understand some of these folks. We are going to pay her $4.00 per week and she is already complaining about her working conditions in the laundry room. Seems like sometimes you just can't satisfy the ladies. O well, I will let Mazie deal with her as I have plenty of other things to worry about.

I am trying to get some more equipment that I need. I am looking for a sprayer for the apple and pear trees and a milk separator for getting the cream separated for delivery to the creamery. I have looked at a number of milk separators and found one I like that Mr. Reid has. I offered him $15.00 for it but he was rather indignant about that offer, so if I am to buy his I need to raise my offer some. I finally negotiated the purchase for $20.00 and since he originally wanted $25.00, we ended up compromising. I quess neither one of us won or lost which made it a good deal all around. For $20.00 I am to get it on a 10-day trial. I also bought a sprayer from Mr. Phillips for $20.00 and he is to guarantee it, come start it for me when we first use it and work a half-day with me that same day spraying the orchard.

I am finding that neighbors are gifts from God in the farming business as I have borrowed not only some of their expertise but some of their tools I have needed to get started with. As I can I will buy my own, but in the meantime, I have been blessed with those around us that are willing to help. I have shared with them my labors when possible to help repay the kindness. Seems I was wrong earlier when some of them gave me the impression that they thought I was a young whippersnapper who didn't know what he was getting himself into. I believe that our hard work and devotion to the land have changed some minds. It is a reassuring feeling.

Well, here it is already the middle of May and Robert delivered our first cream to the creamery and then he took Ma and Lucy to the train station for their trip to Bellaire, Ohio. I'm not sure how long their trip will last but I know they will enjoy the visit with family back there.

I have been missing Church again this month and here it is Sunday the 19th and I am feeling so depressed that again I plan on dragging myself out with Mazie and the children and hope that Will's sermon will lift my spirits.

His sermon was a rousing one: "There remain therefore a rest for the people of God." Made me think about all the blessings bestowed upon us by the Almighty and how he will watch over us and bring us rest. I am feeling better already.

I took delivery today of some pigs I had recently bought and also tomorrow I am taking Fran to spend a little time with the Percheron stallion at J. Coopers and Sons. I hope their visit is a successful one.

Mr. VanDresser wants to buy two of our calves, Atlantis and Dorothy so he came and butchered them and got 148 lbs. from the one and 132 lbs. from the other. He paid me 6¼ cents per lb. so I made $17.50 for the sale. I also sold some final items from the store to a fellow who is opening up a candy store downtown. He bought some jars and other odds and ends for $2.25. Every little bit helps.

Here it is already going on the end of May and I have to return Mr. Reid's separator, as it is not working satisfactorily. He was so indignant when I offered him the original $15, with no strings attached that I wonder how he will feel now. I have decided to buy a water separator and will begin to look around for one soon.

Today I have a bad toothache and we also attended Mr. Olin's funeral. I was feeling a little down with the tooth and poor Olin's funeral so I marched myself downtown and splurged on a haircut and a shave. Even though it cost me 30 cents, it lifted my spirits. Funny how the smallest of things will sometimes give a person a new outlook on life.

Finally the weather is cooperating and we are planting beans and getting ready to plant six acres of buckwheat. We are getting in 12 acres of beans after my hired hand, Mr. Arnold, spent several weeks between rainstorms plowing the fields getting ready for the planting. We have to make hay (pardon the pun) here in June to get everything plowed and planted with Fran and Jack while the weather is cooperating. Sort of a tight schedule but I believe we will get everything done that we need to.

It's great, as I have mentioned, to have such fine neighbors. We are doing a lot of bartering for equipment and manpower and helping each other out as often as we can. I borrowed Mr. Beardsly's harrow and agreed, for borrowing it, that I will help him plant his bean crop. Also Lloyd McIntire and I are sharing my orchard sprayer and we are working together to spray his and our orchard using oil emulsions to control the oil shell scale. Next to Gods' gift of pleasant weather are the blessings of good neighbors.

I took Pacific to Mr. Nevin's Jersey Bull and the Purcell cow yesterday and the Phillips' cow on Friday. Have to take Pacific back early next week as I guess she didn't find the Jersey bull to her liking. Hopefully this second time she will figure out why she is being courted by the Jersey. I also had to buy some new shoes for Jack and it cost me $3.75 for Mr. Kelly to do the job.

This has been a busy month for the family. Mazie's mother and her sister Margaret have come for a visit from Bellaire, Ohio to spend some time with us and with Will and Lucy. Mrs. McGregor lost her husband Robert, Mazie's father, a year ago this past March so it is nice for them that they can make this trip and spend some time with family here in Perry, New York. Since they are here, we can take advantage of their looking after little Marion while Mazie and I take the time to drive over to Mt. Morris to dicker with the used buggy salesman at the buggy dealership. We are interested in buying a new or used surrey to replace our old buggy. If there is anything I hate, it is having to dicker with these people over the cost of a new vehicle and the value of our trade-in. Maybe some day people will find an easier way to buy their wheels without always thinking they are getting shafted. We finally settled on a new surrey. I actually think the salesman wore me down and Mazie was so taken with it that we agreed on the price. He gave us a $12 trade-in on our old one and the difference in price is $78 so I gave him a check, hooked up the horse and we were off to home in our proud new purchase. When we got home, Mazie's brother Howard from New York was at the house and had come unexpectedly to pay us a short visit and be here also to visit with Mom and Margaret. Howard and I spent about a half a day planting rose bushes for the ladies to the great delight of Mazie, as she always loved them. In full bloom, they give us all great pleasure. There are so many wonderful natural blessings abounding on this earth if we only take the time to stop and enjoy them. These are the kinds of things that help keep my depression at bay along with taking the kids fishing on occasion, as we are going to do tomorrow. We all got up early, Robert, the twins and I and went fishing in the inlet and we had a fine fish dinner in the evening as a reward for our labors.

We enjoyed church as usual on the 30th. Will preached on "systematic giving" instead of the random Sunday collection contribution that the congregation had been used to. He convinced us, as Will usually does, and many of the congregation pledged on the spot following the guidelines of the Presbyterian Church U.S.A. General Assembly. We decided to pledge 75 cents a week to be divided up as follows as they recommended.

33% for home missions	33% for foreign missions
5% for education	5% for Sabbath School work
5% for Church erection	5% for disabled ministers' fund
5% Freedmen	5% for college fund
3% for Bible Track Society	1% for temperance

In the afternoon I went out and did some work in the fields with Fran and for the first time I noticed that she became wind broken. I sure hope this is only a temporary condition and she will be able to work as well as ever soon. We sure don't need any problems like that at this point. This condition could, if not temporary, render her almost useless for working in the future. I checked with the vet and he seems to think Fran will be OK. I sure hope he is right. He was not sure why she was getting so winded.

Now that we are into July, I was hoping it might not be so wet, but we have had some pretty heavy rains. It has been hit and miss as far as cultivating the acres of beans we have, however we did manage with some hired help and good old Will's help to get through the cultivating of all of them once around. I really appreciate Will's help, it isn't often that your minister, even though he is my brother-in-law, comes out and works in the fields with members of his congregation. I guess you could say Will is tending to his flock not only on Sundays but also throughout the week.

We have also started haying between the rainstorms. If I was in charge of the world, and Mazie often says I act like I think I should be, I would have made every day a sunny day and every night with light rain. But then again the Lord didn't ask my help and frankly I am sure doesn't need it. Robert, who is eleven years old now, runs the horse rake for us when we are haying and I am very proud of him as he does it as well as any grown man. We keep breaking some of the slings on the haying equipment, especially with the hay so wet and heavy, but that is the way of a farmer, always something breaking down and always something to fix.

I paid Mr. Nevins several times this month for the use of his bull for servicing the Phillips' cow and the Purcell cows. I paid him $2.00 each time so I sure hope it all works out OK. I don't want to keep shelling out good money if Nevins' bull is shooting blanks. I also took Fran over to visit the Cooper's stallion on four different occasions this month, on the 6th, the 13th, the 20th and the last visit on the 29th. Her being wind-broken has cleared up but after these four different dates with the Cooper's stallion when she did not take we began to wonder about her. Cooper checked her out carefully and said he thinks she is in foal and that is the problem. Can't understand how she got in foal and I may have to have a little talk with Jack! Cooper probably thought I was a pretty incompetent farmer not to know that my horse was with foal. Well, I never said I was the smartest farmer in the world, only the hardest working.

Our farm population is ever increasing with the purchase of three pigs from Perry Chappel for $9.00 and we had 15 chicks hatch out on the 15th. We are getting lots of eggs from our chicken coop. Dorothy and Margaret are kept busy collecting them and cleaning out the coop. It gives them some spending money and also those very important chores around the farm that each of us has, makes them feel as they are part of this entire enterprise and they are such a big help.

Church has been hit and miss here in Perry in July of '07. With all my work, I only managed to attend one regular service but we did go to the Baptist service one Sunday evening and we also went to a Methodist service one Sunday also. I must say that the Baptist minister sure is a hellfire and brimstone preacher, must be something about the Baptists that really put the fear of God in them and they sure want to pass that along to anyone that will listen. I enjoy more the temperate preaching of Will's in our Presbyterian Church. It seems us Presbyterian's are a little more reserved, but then to each his own.

It was nice to have so many of the family here this month off and on and especially to the picnic we had to celebrate the fourth. Mrs. McGregor, Margaret, Tillie, Howard and all the TeWinkels joined us for the feast. It is great to watch all the youngsters have so much fun with each other. Children are truly a gift from God.

Not too much else happening of consequence although I did have to give testimony at E. J. Webster's law offices in the matter of George vs. the Carnegie Steel Company. In my previous job as foreman there in Bellaire, Ohio, I had information they wanted involving the case. I think I would rather be cultivating beans or bringing in hay or even slopping the hogs as having to give testimony. I guess as long as I tell the whole truth, which I always do, I cannot get into any problems over the matter. Seems the only people that ever appear to make out in these lawsuits are the lawyers anyway. O well, maybe this time it will be different.

Well, we are finally getting a chance to harvest some of what we have sown this past spring. We are cutting hay, oats and wheat when the weather cooperates. I even had my first dish of fresh peas from the second planting. Why is it that they always taste better when they are home grown? It has been a busy month with all the farm work, sometimes it seems backbreaking but I feel good in the evenings knowing that I have accomplished something during each day. I was particularly tired the other day when I weeded part of the acres of beans by hand; it is a good thing I have a strong back. Old man Hoyt worked some this month for me and several days he spent his time cutting grass with a scythe. That is also backbreaking work for an old man but he never complains and always carries his load. It was the way that his generation was brought up, never looking to try and get out of work but always being in there doing more than their share. It is a pleasure to have him as a hired hand. Our orchard of apples and pears is also coming to harvest time and Mr. Knowlton came by, looked it over for me and he estimates that we should get 300 bushels of apples and 15 bushels of pears by the time we are finished picking them all. I called C. H. Toan to give me a price on the pears and he said he would pay 3 cents per lb. for the first quality ones and 1½ cents per lb. for second quality. Frankly this is not enough and I plan on getting some other quotes elsewhere.

Mrs. Edgerly asked me to take her mare over to Charlie Shepherd's stallion, "Bonita Boy" but it was a no go. I did take Kit to the other of Charlie's stallions, "Peter Corning," everything worked out fine and I plan on leaving her there over night to make sure. Hope Peter has a fully loaded gun this time.

Since the children are out of school for summer vacation, Robert has been a great help to me on the farm. I have been paying him only a little less than the hired hands and he is saving his money for a buggy. In fact, he is trying one out that J. Naultin had and he has let Robert take it to see if he wants to buy it. These young folks can't seem to wait to get their first set of wheels. Just like the new surrey Mazie and I bought recently, he will be very proud of his purchase if he decides to get it and I am sure he will take great care of it. Mazie and I are enjoying the surrey, and have taken several long rides in the evening around the countryside and enjoyed the warm summer evenings out with our surrey with the fringe on top.

I have written a few times this month to Ma. She has been alone for several years as my father passed away in 1902. My father was a Captain in the Confederate Army and was decorated for bravery for his part in the battle of Balls Bluff. He also spent many months in the Old Capital Prison in Washington, D.C. He was imprisoned with General W. H. F. Lee, the son of our famous leader during the Civil War, General Robert E. Lee. They had both been captured and imprisoned together and were to be executed by the Union if the Confederacy executed two Union prisoners that they had taken, Captain Sawyer and Captain Flyn. My father and General F. Lee had been chosen by the Union forces as the two officers that would be executed if the South carried out the death sentence against Capt. Sawyer and Capt. Flyn. Needless to say this was terribly nerve racking for my father and as he told the story in later life that he said he lost 40 lbs. while in prison waiting any day to be taken out and shot. When General Robert E. Lee was asked to intervene and save his son Fitzhaugh and, of course, my father, by commuting the sentence of Sawyer and Flyn. General Robert E. Lee's response, as my father told the story, was that he would not set aside the death sentence for the two Northern soldiers and if it was his son's fate to give up his life for his country's cause he should commit and comply to it. Fortunately, when General Lee refused to intervene, President Davis was besought to intervene and he did and commuted the sentences of death of the two northern prisoners so that my father and General Fitzhaugh Lee were spared. I guess I owe a great debt of gratitude to President Davis, if he had not intervened; I would not be here to write my story today.

Church has been hit and miss this month of August in 1907. Tillie managed to get to the Episcopal Church on several Sundays but with all the farm work, the rest of the family neglected our obligations to the Lord. We all feel bad about it so we managed to all go on the 25th. Will preached a sermon entitled "My Church" and it was very impressive. Mazie and I were so impressed that I feel I would like to repeat his sermon message which was organized around the following as written by William Henry Boddy, D. D.

"Before I was born *MY CHURCH* gave to my parents ideals of life and love that made my home a place of strength and beauty.

In helpless infancy *MY CHURCH* joined my parents in consecrating me to Christ in baptizing me in His name.

MY CHURCH enriched my childhood with the romance and religion and the lessons of life that have been woven into the texture of my soul. Sometimes I seem to have forgotten and then, when else I might surrender to foolish and futile ideals of life, the truths *MY CHURCH* taught become radiant, insistent and inescapable.

In the stress and storm of adolescence *MY CHURCH* heard the surge of my soul and She guided my footsteps by lifting my eyes toward the stars.

When first my heart knew the strange awakenings of love *MY CHURCH* taught me to chasten and spiritualize my affections; She sanctified my marriage and blessed my home.

When my heart was seamed with sorrow, and I thought the sun could never shine again, *MY CHURCH* drew me to the Friend of All The Weary and whispered to me the hope of another morning, eternal and tearless.

When my steps have slipped and I have known the bitterness of sin, *MY CHURCH* has believed in me and wooingly She has called me back to live within the heights of myself.

Now have come the children dearer to me than life itself and *MY CHURCH* is helping me to train them for all joyous and clean and Christly living.

MY CHURCH calls me to Her heart. She asks my service and my loyalty. She has a right to ask it! I will help her to do for others what She has done for me. In this place in which I live, I will help Her keep aflame and aloft the torch of a living faith.

It might serve us all better if every now and then we reminded ourselves of the above words of the importance in our lives of our church and of our faith. We all get so caught up in the hustle and bustle of our busy lives that we too often forget who we are and what our purpose on this earth is.

These months seem to roll around so fast, particularly when you are getting up at 4 in the mornings and not getting to bed until 10 or so. It seems there is so much to do on a farm that there is little time to think about anything else. Well today Sunday Sept. 01, 1907, we all took a break and went to Church to hear Will give another of his rousing sermons. We were so moved that in the evening we decided to attend the new Methodist Church that recently opened here in Perry, New York. Now I certainly wouldn't be one to say anything negative about our brethren in faith, the Methodists, but I didn't think the sermon held a candle to the inspiration that Will puts forth from the Presbyterian pulpit every Sunday. Of course one might say I am a little prejudiced since Will is my brother-in-law and Mazie and I are old-time Presbyterians. It's not that we think there are no other true believers but then again who is to say? Tolerance of all peoples' faith and religion should be a goal for all of us.

Little Marion is starting Sunday School this month and looking forward to it. She will have Old Mrs. Johnson for a teacher and she sure will be filled with hell, fire and brimstone from her. Nothing against her but she has been teaching Sunday School here for longer than anyone can remember and setting many a young mind on the road to a spiritual life. The other children, Robert, Dorothy and Margaret will also be starting school this month and it will be good for them to get on with their studies. They are all looking forward to it enthusiastically and even though I will miss their helping hands around the farm, particularly Robert's, school is where they belong during these formidable years.

There has been a lot of rain off and on this month so it has been hit and miss as far as harvesting the buckwheat, oats, apples, pears, etc. Old man Hoyt has been helping me a lot and I have been paying him $1.25 a day for his help. Would you believe he asked to borrow a $1.00 in advance on his wages today? I can't figure out what that man does with all the money I pay him. He and I both have been trying to plow the hill lot and clear it of stones but the soil is so hard there that it is a trying job with backbreaking work, but then again what did I expect as a farmer? I have talked to C. H. Toan about buying the apples in the orchard and he has looked them over and offered to pay $2.00 per bushel for the 1st and 2nd grade ones. He will furnish the crates and I will furnish the labor of picking and packing them. I wonder how come I always furnish the labor! I think I will try and get other quotes on them for the work involved. I would think I could get more than $2.00 a bushel.

MARGARET & DOROTHY
C. 1908
8 YEARS OLD

Harold Phillips of the Phillips Brothers' Fruit Co. came by and said they would pay $2.75 per bushel and take them all. I called Toan but he wouldn't match the price so they are sold to the highest bidder for the $2.75. Am I a shrewd businessman or what? The Phillips Company will furnish the crates and I am to pick them and take them to the station for loading. Now if I was really shrewd, I could get $2.75 for them, have them furnish the crates and have them pick them. Oh well, maybe next year. I think it best I draw up a contract between myself and Mrs. Edgerly and the Phillips Fruit Co. and will ask Mazie what she thinks of the following and see if she has any suggestions. Mazie is not only a great mother and farmer's wife but she also has a head for business matters, pretty too.

"Mess. Phillips Bros., Castile, N. Y. Gentlemen: Referring to the offer that your Mr. Harold Phillips made me this afternoon for our apples, I will say that I understand it to be as follows. You will give me $2.75 per bushel for all of the apples in our orchard. You will furnish the crates and deliver them at our barn as needed and I am to pick the apples and put them in the crates, but not sort or face them, and deliver to cars in Perry. You are to load them in cars and you are to have the cars ready to load as the apples are crated and ready. Competent judges estimate the orchard as good for 300 bushels and I would ask that you pay me $300.00 down when we sign the contract. Mrs. Adelle Edgerly has an interest in the apples and I want a contract to show her just how the matter is. Hoping that the above is satisfactory to you and asking for an early reply". Yours Truly, Ben C. Tyler.

After sharing this with Mazie and getting her stamp of approval I sent it on to the Phillips Co. and trust it will be favorably looked upon by them.

Here it is already the 25th of Sept. and Old Man Hoyt and I have been picking apples it seems for an eternity. If I never see another apple it will be too soon. The Phillips Company came through fine and the money will come in handy as we have saved almost enough from our milk, apple and pear sales and other crops and livestock sales to pay off the final mortgage payment on the Lake Street home that we are renting out right now. I owe the bank $1,344.20 in principle and interest and when the apple check comes in I will go down to the bank and pay it off. We have worked hard and lived frugally and it is slowly paying off. Maybe with continual hard work we will be able to enjoy a little more free time and less back-breaking work, but only time will tell on that score.

As a celebration of all our efforts, Mazie and I took all the children to the county fair and a fine time was had by all. I think the children would live at the fair if we let them. Robert particularly seems to enjoy it so much. Maybe he is also beginning to look at all the pretty girls that are there. We had to keep a close rein on him though since we were concerned about a possible risqué side show that he seemed to always be interested in seeing. If Mazie ever caught me in there, I would be spending the next month sleeping with the cows and I can't imagine what she would do with Robert.

Well here it is the end of Sept. in `07 and we are all sitting around the stove I put up in the living room and enjoying a nice quiet wood fire on this chilly evening. It sure is hard to heat a large old farmhouse like this one with the coal furnace and this stove should add to our creature comforts as the fall and winter approach. I sure am not looking forward to winter and pray it will be an easy one for us, and a healthy one.

Talk about being tired of seeing apples, here in October I think we have been picking apples morning, noon and night and also in our sleep. I have had little time to become depressed which maybe is the answer to that problem, keep yourself so busy you don't have time to worry about yourself or feel sorry for all your perceived problems. Whatever, it is a good feeling to have that on the run.

I hired Frank VnScooter to help Old Man Hoyt and I in the picking, as it seems we are going to easily surpass the 300 bushels I had estimated we might get from the orchard. I agreed to pay Frank $1.75 per day and board for the apple picking and $1.00 per day of any other kind of work. The two of them picked all day for a couple of days and then VnScooter quit, he wasn't much of a worker anyway so it was good riddance. I think he must have told Old Man Hoyt what I was paying him for picking because today, the 12th of October, Old Man Hoyt got mad and quit. He didn't say what he was mad about but I would guess he found out I was paying Frank a little more per hour. Oh well, there are a lot of farm hands out there looking for work so I will just hire someone else. Maybe I should remember to pay them all the same so I don't get into that problem again. It sure seems like $1.25 to $1.75 per day is a lot of money when I appear to always out-pick the hired help by about 2 to 1 in bushels. I guess that is why I am the boss and they are the hired hands. I better stop thinking about it or I will start getting depressed again.

Today on Sunday we were all going to attend Church but there was a problem with the furnace in the Church and the smell of coal gas was so strong that it had to be cancelled. Maybe this Sunday was truly a day of rest since we didn't even have to go out and we just stayed around the house and enjoyed the children, each other and spent some time just talking amongst ourselves, something we too seldom do in all our busy lives. The Lord works in mysterious ways to bring us closer together.

I settled with Parris Andrews for the 640# of milk we had delivered from the 23rd of Sept. to the 12th of October, and the $8.63 came in handy since we have a few bills to pay and haven't gotten all our apple money yet. As soon as we wrap up the final few bushels of apples, the Phillips' brothers settle up with us, and Mrs. Edgerly and I settle up, we will have a little cushion in our bank balance. I think I will get those sheep I have been thinking about buying and raising, and contact L.A. McComber to work out the details with him.

I bought 125 lambs from him and their total weight was 7820 lbs. I have to pay $6.15 per 100 weight plus 4 cents a head for shipping and 5 cents a head for dipping plus a commission of 10 cents a head to McComber. I think it will be a good investment and look forward to raising them.

Here it is the end of October already and right on schedule the first snow and hard frost of the season is upon us. As I have said before, I sure hope this is an easy winter and the Tyler family has a healthy and wealthy winter season.

We have been renting the farm from Mrs. Edgerly now for over 7 months and Mazie and I have to decide if we are willing to commit to another year in the farming business. We decided to sit around the second stove I recently installed in the dining room and talk about the ups and downs of a farmer, his wife and family. The warmth of the stove on this snowy Nov. Sunday helps us to have clear heads in making our decision. Mrs. Edgerly is pressing for a commitment for the next year, 1908, so I guess there is no reason to put off deciding at this point in time. You might wonder why we are not in church on a Sunday but as it turned out there was some trouble with the electric lighting in the building and so the services have been cancelled. As I said before, the Lord works in mysterious ways. When we weigh all the pros and cons we decided to make a commitment for another year. It is hard work for all of us but it is sure a healthier life than being a shopkeeper and certainly beats having to deal with all those customers with credit issues all the time. The big advantage that Mazie and I discussed along with Robert who is now old enough to contribute to the family decisions is that I am so busy that the old Tyler depression gene is kept at bay since I seldom have the free time to start feeling sorry for myself. That one thing in itself is enough of a reason to keep going in farming. Mazie, Robert and I all agreed to stay the course. The twins and little Marion aren't old enough yet to offer any judgment, at least any opinion that we would listen to on such an important determination. It is probably a good thing that we are staying as I just bought all those lambs and they are going to keep me very occupied for some time to come.

Next Sunday, the good Lord willing, we will all make church services and ask the Lord's blessings on our decision. We are all asking the Lord's blessings on our continued success and good health everyday as it is, but there is something special about asking in the Lord's house. We have to go, as we have to pay our systematic pledge for this month of 75 cents that is divided between the various causes that the church has set forth.

Here it is Election Day on Tuesday, Nov. 5[th,] and after Mazie and I voted (can't divulge whom we voted for since it is a secret). We went shopping and bought some gumshoes for the twins and for Robert, and Mazie bought a hat for herself. She sure looks like a pretty sharp lady in that new hat. It cost me $5.00 for the shoes and the hat but it was worth it to see the happy smiles on everyone's face. I also decided to buy 2 sets of long underwear for myself and 2 nightshirts, one for Robert and one for myself. These cost me another $7.00 but it will be appreciated on those cold winter days when I am working in the barn and also appreciated during those long winter nights when everyone is so tired, including myself to go stoke up the coal fire and we all crawl a little further under the covers to try any keep Jack Frost at bay. Robert particularly will enjoy the new nightshirt, as his bedroom has no register to allow any heat to rise up to it during those long winter nights. He is a solid tough young man, however, and much better suited to those difficult conditions than his sisters. We are blessed, as he is such a support and help to his mother and I and to his sisters and never complains but always does what is requested of him. If only all families could be blessed like Mazie and I with loving and obedient children.

Mazie has been pressing me to get her someone to help her with the children, with the housework and the chores that she has to do around the farm, so to keep peace in the family, I have decided to honor her wishes and take a trip into Rochester to see if I can hire someone to help. It is always best to try and keep the ladies happy, as I am a firm believer in the old adage that you can't live with them and you can't live without them. As any one who knows me well will attest, I am only kidding as I am devoted and still in love with Mazie as much or more than the first day we met.

I decided to go to Rochester on Thanksgiving afternoon after we all enjoyed a fine Thanksgiving dinner and after we made out some of our Christmas list and wrote out an order for Sears and Roebuck. We had a great time, all looking at the pictures in the catalog and dreaming about what we would like and then being a little more practical in actually deciding what we would order. There is a wide gap between one's dreams and one's reality. I left on the train in the early afternoon and went to the Sturges Employment Agency and they suggested an older women named Mrs. Gage who had done this work for some time and was currently unemployed. I agreed to take her on and pay her $2.00 per week and board. She is to start tomorrow. While I was in the city I decided to take in a movie, have dinner and buy some special candy to take home to the children. All in all it cost me $1.00 for the train trip, 60 cents for dinner, 10 cents for the candy, 05 cents for the movie and I had to pay the employment agency $1.00 commission for their efforts. Great trip. If I was independently wealthy, I would do it once a week and take the whole family with me.

November of 1907 has come and gone, never to be seen again. Unfortunately it did not end on a high note since Mrs. Gage left on the train to go back to Rochester. Seems she either didn't like the work or the pay, or more likely didn't care for being stuck out here in the sticks with us hicks, which is what some of the city folks think we rural farmers are. I still choose the country over the city any day of the week. I just have to try and find some different help for Mazie to keep her happy.

The Christmas season is almost upon us here in December. In looking back over 1907 I would say all in all it has been a good year. Our family is healthy, we are a little bit wealthier than a year ago and my depression has been kept at bay.

It is the season of giving and receiving and the first thing that happened is that we received the shipment of Christmas gifts that we had ordered from Sears, Roebuck and Co. on Nov. 18th. Even though it took over three weeks to get the gifts and cost me 56 cents for shipping, there is great excitement in the household from Robert and the twins Dorothy and Margaret and, of course, we cannot forget little Marion. I am afraid they will just have to wait until the big day to see what was delivered. In the giving area, Mazie and I and the children put together several boxes of apples, pears, carrots, parsnips and cabbage and we sent some to the TeWinkels and some to Mazie's mother in Ohio. It feels good to share earth's bountiful harvest with others. Will TeWinkel said that he as our minister feeds the soul and we as his relations feed their stomachs, which seems like a fair exchange to me. Will often calls on us in his capacity as the Presbyterian minister as he makes it a rule to call on all his parishioners at least once a month. I think that is a great service to his flock and all ministers could well learn from his example. He is truly a devoted Christian.

Robert and I and our current hired hand are spending most of our time this month repairing such things as the plows and ladders and painting everything that isn't moving. Between taking care of the lambs and the repairs necessary to get ready for spring, there is little break in the hectic life of a farmer especially compared to the pressure during the good weather of the planting and harvesting season.

Old Man Winter sure is breathing down our necks. It has been cold and I added some insulation strips around all the house windows trying to cut down on the heating costs of coal and wood and make the house a little more comfortable for us all. Winter seems a time to enjoy the out-of-doors so we decided to buy a bobsled and Robert is cleaning it all up and painting it for his and the girl's use. He has done a fine job as he always does.

On Christmas day I drove the surrey into town, picked up all the TeWinkels and everyone came to dinner. We all enjoyed the chicken and lamb that Mazie prepared. I have to say that we did ample justice to the meal. The children all opened their gifts, as did Mazie and I and William and Lucy, and everyone was very pleased with what they received. Will led us in a prayer of thanksgiving for the bountiful gifts of all of 1907 and for the continued health, happiness and prosperity of both our families plus the extended family of our neighbors and friends here in Perry, New York. I also added a little silent prayer to keep that always-lingering depression away in 1908.

We finished up the month with church services on Monday night and went to the children's performance of "The Christmas Tree." The twins and Marion were all in it, and Mazie and I were the proudest parents and thought our children had by far outperformed all the other children in the activities. Just for being so vain, I had to make a little extra contribution to the church in the hopes that my vanity wouldn't be registered in that big ledger in the sky. I can't believe the good Lord would take issue with parents being so proud of their children's performances. What is life if it isn't being absorbed in your children's activities and enjoying their every moment?

Chapter 2

1908

Wilber Wright flies 30 miles in 40 minutes

Can you believe it, 1908 already? I had high hopes for this year for the Tyler family of Perry, New York and already they have been dampened with literally a pain in the head. I have tooth trouble and neuralgia and both are interconnected and both are very unpleasant. It is difficult to concentrate on anything else and I will most likely be forced to bite the bullet and see Dr. Reads who advertises as the "pain free dentist." Now if you believe that maybe you would also believe that someday man will fly from one place to another in a flying machine. Wilber Wright and his brother Orville should stick to bicycles. If man were meant to fly, the good Lord would have given us wings.

I dragged myself in to see Dr. Read in between hauling manure from the barn to the fields and orchard. I have to say that hauling manure sure beats going to the dentist. As you can tell there aren't many things that I dread more than the possibility of having my teeth drilled. I wonder if someday they will have something they can give a patient to dull the pain when working on your teeth. I sure hope so, as it is most uncomfortable. Dr. Read says I have a cavity and another tooth next to it needs to have a porcelain cap put on it. I dread to think what all this work will cost. I have to go back in a few days for the work to begin and in the meantime he said to try and keep my mind off the discomfort. That's easy for him to say.

A JOURNEY THROUGH LIFE

In trying to keep my mind off my problem, I wrote Governor Hughes the following letter as I and a number of my farming friends have been concerned about this looming problem. "Dear Sir: I have watched with a great deal of interest the charges the Rural New Yorker makes against F. E. Dawley in regard to his fraud in the sale and registry of Jersey cattle. I see the Rural New Yorker has asked you to look into the matter. I know that you stand for a square deal, so please investigate and let the farmers know the truth for they are all watching this case. Yours respectfully, Ben C. Tyler."

We will see what kind of a response, if any, I will get. Unless it is an election year, I may not hear back at all.

Mr. Macomber wants to buy 80 of the sheep that we are raising between Mr. Edgerly and Mazie and I. He is willing to pay 7 cents a lb. and it seems like a fair offer so I am going to take him up on it. We are going to ship him the 80 and they weighed in at 7,140 lbs. and when you take off 160 lbs. for shrinkage, that leaves 6980 lbs. at 7 cents a lb. for a total of $488.60. We will split that with Mrs. Edgerly and our half will come in handy. Hopefully I won't have to spend too much of it on my teeth work.

I went back to "painless" Dr. Read today and he drilled the one tooth and ground the other down so he could put the crown on it. If I were a drinking man I would have gotten smashed beforehand so I wouldn't have been so uncomfortable. Now I have to live with the hole in my tooth and the other pointed tooth for another week before I can go back and have the rest of the work done. He again told me to try and keep my mind off of the discomfort and at least now some of the pain has subsided.

I decided to butcher a pig we have and it dressed out at 184 lbs. We shared it with the TeWinkels and some of the other neighbors. That's one thing about farming in a rural community, you get to know your neighbors well and share with them some of your bounty as they share with you some of theirs.

A few other things that I have to do are pay the state and county tax this month and it is $16.38. I can't imagine what the state and county do with all that money and they seem to always be raising the taxes and finding more things to spend the money on, or should I say, waste the money on. By the way, I did get a letter back from Governor Hughes and I must say it sure seemed like he was piling it on even a little more than I pile it on the fields and the orchard. Hopefully, if enough of us write him, he may become involved in the investigation if he needs the votes.

It is so cold this month, 6 below today and going to 10 below tonight that I have had to buy extra coal to keep us warm. I bought about 2800 lbs. from Fanning and Company and it cost me $15.52. Hopefully it will last a little longer than the last coal I bought. We are sure going through a lot of coal this winter, as it is colder than normal. Margaret has been ill and missing school so I must keep the house even warmer than normal than when only Mazie and I are here during the day.

Back to Dr. Read and he filled the cavity with gold and put the porcelain cap on the adjacent tooth. He wants me to come back again in a week to see how I am doing and if they need any grinding down. I think he keeps having me come back so he can charge me more but I have an ace in the hole when the bill comes due from him.

Will TeWinkel called and asked if I would pick up the substitute minister at the railroad station for his preaching on this coming Sunday. I agreed even though Mazie and I are concerned that the reason Will is going to preach in Troy, New York is that he may be considering leaving his flock here in Perry to move up to the larger church there. Of course being family we would be the last to know. I picked up Reverend Fales at 6:15 PM and took him to the manse and he will be holding forth tomorrow at church.

All hands were at church to hear Reverend Fales and he preached about the "Good Samaritan." He gave a fine sermon but certainly didn't hold a candle to Will who can really get the congregation engrossed in the sermon like no other minister I have listened to. We are most likely prejudiced since Will is of course married to Mazie's sister but I truly believe he is much more inspirational than others I have heard are. There is a gift to being a good preacher and it is something they are born with and don't necessarily learn in seminary.

I am finishing out the month with my fourth visit to Dr. Read. It is a good thing I went back as the porcelain filling fell off last night and I almost swallowed it. He will have to refasten it and I hope it holds this time. Can you believe he charged me $13.50 for the filling and cap but I got him back for all the

A JOURNEY THROUGH LIFE

discomfort in the end as he still owed me $8.67 for items he had bought from our store when we owned it. After deducting that, I paid him $4.83, bid him a fond farewell and told him I hoped I didn't see him in a professional capacity for many years. Now it may sound as if I don't like Doc but he is a fine fellow. It's just his profession I fine fault with. Would you believe it today after settling up with Doc. and getting his old account squared away, I ran into C. B. Houghton and he paid me the $4.17 he still owed me for the items he had run up a tab on from the mercantile store. I am on a roll as the month of January comes to a close.

Mother Nature is releasing her full fury here in Feb. with snow, snow and more snow. There is so much snow that it has stopped the trains and that does not happen very often. I have been taking the children to school in the cutter since Kit cannot pull the surrey through the heavy snow. The 2-mile walk for them with the remnants of this recent blizzard is just too much to ask even of Tyler children. Under better weather conditions I firmly believe it is not only healthy but also a character builder for the children to have to hike that far twice a day to school. Hopefully the weather will clear soon and they can get back to their character building. The drifts are so high that I even turned over the cutter on my way to Perry Center to check on a girl to help Mazie with the children and housework. Fortunately no one was with me and the snow cushioned my fall so all's well that ends well. It didn't hurt Kit or the cutter either so we got it righted and went on our way more embarrassed than hurt. I visited with Thomas Campbell and his daughter. Anna is looking for employment and seems like a fine young lady so we are going to give her a try. Sure hope she lasts longer than Mrs. Gage did. Since she is a local girl and of good farm stock rather than a soft city woman I have high hopes for her and Mazie hitting it off.

My health continues to give me some problems with another tooth that needed filling and Dr. Wright came to the house and has diagnosed me with an ex-opthamatic goiter. He is recommending that I contact Dr. C. L. Myers of Buffalo to see what he would recommend as far as treatment is concerned. Hopefully it can be treated and surgery will not be necessary. Unfortunately there are so many conditions that affect humankind with various afflictions that one never knows what lies ahead.

When we have our health there are few other blessings that the Lord can bestow upon us that are more important.

We have a steady stream of money coming in from the creamery for our milk and cream sales and that certainly comes in handy. I also closed another deal on the mercantile store with F. D. Allan, working out a payment schedule on the display cabinet from the store. He is to pay me $1.00 per month for 5 months. Slowly but surely, the old accounts are getting resolved. Patience is a virtue. We also have sold the remainder of the sheep at a nice profit so that also has come in handy and Pacific had a bull calf so our farming business is on schedule and moving along as we planned. Of course, in the business of farming anything can happen at any time but we will count our blessings while we can. With this blessing we are taking some extra clothing, food and a few other things to Mrs. Donaldson who is being helped through the combined efforts of Will and the church. She is in desperate need for help and the congregation and community have pulled together to help her in her hour of need. It makes one feel good to reach out and help those less fortunate.

We all recently attended a revival meeting in Rochester put on by the Reverend Gillam, the travelling evangelist, and Robert who is now 11 years old stood up and signified his intentions of coming into the membership of the church. Dr. Gillam also is scheduled to preach in the Perry Presbyterian Church and Robert is planning on his confession of faith at our church where he will be joining. He has made his parents proud and we are so pleased he has chosen to join the family of Christians and lead his life in such a way as to please the Lord. Dr. Gillam preached his sermon on "The Palm Tree Christian." The title of the sermon speaks for itself and those Christians who we only see in church on Christmas and Easter should take heed from it. Dr. Gillam has really struck a cord with Robert who attends his meetings every opportunity he has and has really found Christ in his life. It shows how a gifted speaker can easily get into the mind of a person and in some cases this can be dangerous, but in this case we support the effort with all our hearts.

Slowly here at the end of winter she is giving up her grip on the earth, the snow is melting and the weather is improving. I have been able to get into the orchard and start to trim the trees in

A JOURNEY THROUGH LIFE

preparation of the coming of spring and the rebirth of the earth. As a sure sign of Spring I have sent for a Burpee Seed catalog and also signed the contract with Mrs. Edgerly for another year's lease on the farm with the option of an added year after that. The other day one of our neighbors asked me if we would be interested in buying his farm but at this point I think we will stick with the lease since we are not quite ready to take on the responsibility of full farm ownership. I would hope to learn even more about farming in the next couple of years before we consider taking on that responsibility.

This Sunday, April 5 in this year of our Lord 1908, Robert officially joined the Perry Presbyterian Church along with 51 other new members. Will is bringing them through the doors and hopefully we will see a continuation of this growth in the future. The Church is an anchor for anyone who chooses to enter its doors and particularly in times of trouble. Anna Campbell also went home today and I hired Nellie Henry to help Mazie. Did I mention, while being so wrapped up in my busy world, that the reason Mazie needs help is that we are expecting a blessed event to happen to the Tyler family very soon. This will be our fifth child unless of course Mazie has another set of twins. As I have often said, children are a true gift from God and we have been particularly blessed with wonderful children. Neither Mazie nor I will of course ever forget little Helen, who sadly passed away at 2 years of age in 1903. We are praying for a fine healthy baby, all else being secondary.

There is a threat of a possible cooling pattern of weather coming and we are all worried about the possibility of a devastating ice storm. I can't fathom the damage to our apple orchard if we do get such a storm that Mother Nature may send our way. I can remember back when I was a youngster at "Ben Lomand" in Manassas in Prince William County, Virginia. It was about 10 years after my father, Captain Robert Horner Tyler, returned from his imprisonment as a Confederate prisoner in the Civil War. We were finally getting back on our feet from the devastation left in that area from the fighting, the aftermath of the slow reconstruction and unrest after the war was over. As I remember it happened when I was about 8, early one evening in April of that year, that the freezing rain came and by morning it was hard to fathom the devastation. This was particularly difficult because in that part of the country freezing rain is very rare. Thinking of the tremendous efforts we all had to put forth and the depression it left us with, I certainly pray we don't experience the same wrath of Mother Nature as happened then.

As it turned out we were blessed and the weather warmed just enough to give us rain instead of the freezing rain we were so worried about.

Having spent so much time worrying about the weather I had almost forgotten that I am a farmer and I must tend to my farm. Not good to be such a worrier especially with my tendency to become so depressed, so I went out and butchered 2 hogs at 183 and 171 lbs. respectively and sold the meat for 7 cents per pound. What a great way to get over depression! With another mouth to feed shortly the money will come in handy. I even took our mare to visit with Peter Corning, Charles Shepherd's stallion, but to no avail, Peter said we will (or they will) try again in 3 weeks. Maybe they will be in the right frame of mind then. Fran has gotten sick and I am quite worried about her since she recently gave birth to a little colt. Dr. Mills stopped by to check on her and he drenched her and he is coming back tomorrow to check on her again. Doc. says Fran is still not doing well and he will try drenching (tube feeding medicine directly into her stomach) again. I hope she recovers but it does not look promising.

Unfortunately she did not make it and I will have to begin to look around for another horse to take her place. She was a fine animal and I will sorely miss her but everything comes to this eventually and she did her duty well while a part of our farming life.

We all decided that the children and I would take a day off after Fran's passing, and go to the woods, spend some time with nature and pick some wild flowers for Mazie. She is due any day now and we think the wild flowers will lift her spirits. I also took the surrey into town and brought Lucy and the children out to spend some time at the farm and keep Mazie company.

Here it is April 30th and Mazie is going into labor. Mrs. Gledhill, a midwife and Dr. Brownell are here and assisting. The children and I are anxiously waiting what we all pray will be a strong cry from their next little brother or sister. Mazie's labor fortunately was not too long having already given birth to 5 children and for the small-framed woman that she is that is a blessing. Well, we have a fine son, Howard Alexander Tyler. We named him after Mazie's brother Howard and Mazie's grandmother's maiden name. He is a fine strapping baby and the children and Mother and I are all very proud and excited. Thank the good Lord for this new blessing to our family and may he lead a long, healthy, prosperous and productive life. Lucy and Mrs. Gladhill will be staying for a few days to help out until we are all on our feet again.

I have bought a new mare for $150, she is guaranteed not to be over 6 years old and sound in wind and limb. It will be tough for her to follow in the hooves of Fran but I have great hopes for her. She will need to be strong for here in May of 1908 we are having heavy snow, rain and more rain. I have started, in between rain showers and snow, to plant, and we are putting in cabbage, corn, onions, falsify, carrots, parsnips, radishes, lettuce and beets.

Heavy snow again last night and in fact it is so heavy that I will take the children to school in the cutter. By this time of year one would hope for more pleasant weather but alas the Lord decided instead to try our metal but again. If I were in charge of the weather I would have it sunny and pleasant each day and a light rain at night. The last I checked however, God had not put me in charge. Some say that the Lord expresses his pleasure or anger though the weather, wonder what we have done to deserve this heavy snow in May.

Mazie is getting quite a bit of help from the neighbors and Lucy has come out as often as she can to help. Also, of course, Mrs. Gladhill has been here for several weeks and she has been a tremendous help. Mazie, being the strong woman that she is, has gotten back on her feet and decided that she can manage without Mrs. Gladhill so I paid her the $27.00 for her work and she is going home. With the girls, Dorothy and Margaret, and Robert to help and, of course, I pitch in whenever I can so it should get easier for Mazie with a little time. If this weather doesn't improve, I think I will be in the house most of the time and be able to help her often. Also Dr. Brownell is keeping tabs on both the mother and baby and that is reassuring. I had to pay him of course $10.00 for his services but I guess it is well worth it. I can't believe what doctors charge for their services nowadays.

Here it is Sunday already, the 17th of May, and all hands except Mazie and little Howard are off to the services and also to Sunday School. It is a bright and beautiful day, a day the Lord has made. It is a great day to be alive and it has lifted my spirits immensely. I find myself thanking the Lord for such a fine day, a beautiful wife and a wonderful family. I have been blessed. To top the day off a Jewish peddler came by at the end of the day and he and I haggled over some items. I ended up giving him some old rubbers and I took a tin bucket and an enamel dipper in return. The fun thing about dealing with these peddlers is that after all the haggling everyone seems to feel he got the better of the deal. That is the way things should be I guess.

We finally closed the deal on the lot we owned on Cherry Street and sold it to the Newmans for $400. It will sure be nice to put that money in the bank as a nice little nest egg for a rainy day. As it sits there, we can also get a little interest on it, although the banks certainly seemed to be a little tight fisted when it comes to giving out a little interest on peoples' money. O well, where else can we put it but under the mattress and it sure doesn't get any interest there.

I have taken the Phillips' cow over to Beardsley's Guernsey Bull a number of times this month all to no avail. They just don't seem to be attracted to each other. Maybe I will break out a bottle of wine next time and see if that helps. Also I have taken Kit to Peter Corning, the Shepherds' stallion, and they seem to hit it off right away. Maybe that proves once and for all that horses are smarter than cows. I decided to sell Pacific and Phillips' calves to T. H. Commisky for 6 cents a pound and we netted $16.80 on the sale. This money will come in mighty handy since we have another mouth to feed, even though it is a small one at this point. Another blessing this month, the sow had 12 little pigs. One of them unfortunately was dead but the other 11 are doing great so one must believe that 11 is a luckier number than 12 anyway. This is like money in the bank for me since if I get depressed someday I will have all these hogs to butcher to get over my depression. What a weird way of curing ones depression, but I guess if it worked it was worth it. Maybe the secret of overcoming depression is just to get your mind occupied on something different, whatever it might be.

I hired Henry Walther to help me on the farm and he worked one hour and quit. Must be a new record, guess this just isn't his kind of work. I paid him the 25 cents that he had coming (I think) and he was on his way. I have Clarence and Willard who are helping as I need them and they are very dependable so I should be in good shape. We finished spraying the trees in the orchard and we are setting out all sorts of goodies for the farm to sell and for all to consume once harvest time comes around. We are planting oats, beans, beets, tomatoes and cabbage along with other things in Mazie's garden that she likes. We worked so hard, especially in this wet weather that I went through the pair of gumboots I had and went to town and bought a new pair at Cole's & Sons and had to pay $3.50 for them. Inflation is just going wild it seems. Robert helped me bag up 6800 pounds of beans and we took them to the processors where we received $195.88 for the account of Edgerly and Tyler. I can't imagine bagging them all myself and am so grateful for Robert's help that I paid him $5.00. I wish I could have paid him more but we need all the money we can save in the hopes someday of owning our own farm. Robert is such a strong boy and so willing to help when he is not in school. We also need the money for we have another mouth to feed and even though it is a small one it still will take more cash to keep our growing family strong and healthy.

Speaking of needing all the money we could come by, I worked up the following agreement with J. Albright for the rental of our home which we still own on Lake and Center Street in Perry. I have to believe it is a fine arrangement for the both of us.

" This agreement made this day of June 1908 between Ben C. Tyler party of the first part and J. Albright party of the second part witnesseth the party of the first part agrees to rent to the party of the second part" (sure a lot of party's and parts) " his house, barn and lot connected with same on the corner of Lake and Center Street for the rental of $5.00 per week, to be paid in advance for 4 weeks at a time. The term of the lease is for one year from June 1st, 1908 with the privilege to the party of the second part" (there are those party's again) " for one year more from June 1909."

Who says I needed a lawyer to draw up such papers. I dare say this seems as confusing and with as many words as any lawyer would have done and certainly it was a lot cheaper. Thinking of renting out our home brought to mind the home I was born in and its importance in my life. The old homestead was in Prince Wm. County in Virginia about 30 miles south of Washington City, near the village of Manassas and in a section of the county made famous by the fact that two of the great battles of the Civil War were fought there, the 1st and 2nd battles of Bull Run. My father in the late 50's took three of his slaves with him and went to Memphis, Tenn. where he had a position to teach in a college; the slave boys he hired out and drew their wages. Today it seems like an abomination to think of one man being a slave to another, but we cannot judge those that have gone before and we must remember that in the south in those days, slavery was an accepted way of life even though I find it of a wicked nature when one thinks deeply about it. When the war arrived in the 60's, he returned to Virginia, helped organize a company, went into the war with them as a 1st Lieut. and later was promoted to Captain. As I recently mentioned, twice during the war my father was imprisoned by the Union and was fortunate to have survived as he was scheduled to be executed with General W.H.F. Lee, the son of our most famous leader, General Robert E. Lee. When the war closed, he was still a prisoner of war at Johnson's Island in Lake Erie, having been a prisoner earlier at the Old Capitol Prison in Washington. He was in some ways lucky and unlucky at the same time as a soldier for the Confederacy. He was unlucky to be captured twice; however, he was lucky that if he were not in prison at the time of the great battle of Gettysburg, he would most likely have been killed. Most of the captains and many of the soldiers that were in that battle were casualties and never returned to their homes.

Several months later, my father was released and returned to his home in Manassas and, of course, found things in terrible shape. The armies had burned all the fences, the stock had all been driven away or eaten and all that was left was the land and fortunately the buildings. Other veterans returning home were not as fortunate as their farms had been burned to the ground. On his return home my father had come into possession of an old horse and shortly thereafter another horse wandered onto the farm, let loose he supposed by some straggler returning home. He made these two animals his farm team and immediately started to try and rebuild his life. He and my mother Sally Chinn cheerfully went forward to begin to rebuild their lives after the devastation of the war. It took many years of hard work and stressful times but eventually Ben Lomand became the beautiful productive farm that it had once been. Those that survived the war and rebuilt their lives after all the devastation are truly admired, along with my mother and father for their fortitude and courage in the face of overwhelming odds.

Enough reminiscing, it is time to get back to the realities of today and the joys and hardships that we must face every day. June has been an active month in a number of ways; we are still planting a little bit of everything with an especially wide variety in Mazie's garden. She enjoys having all the various fruits and vegetables to choose from at harvest time and beyond, and she makes sure her husband spends a certain amount of time planting and tending to her garden. You would think I could call it my garden but she will have none of that, and being the strong willed woman she is, I certainly am not going to argue the point with her. I'll call the entire farm my garden and concede to her that the garden for the family's fruits and vegetables is her garden.

We have had an active month in the church activities, going each Sunday, having communion and enjoying the Children's Day exercises. We were especially proud of the fine presentations of Robert, Dorothy and Margaret during the service. We also enjoyed a fine day at the church picnic at the Silver Lake assembly grounds at the end of the month. Mazie's brother Howard came from New York City to spend some time with us, also made the picnic, and we shared the excellent food and the many friends with Howard. Mazie insisted before the picnic day that I get my hair cut so I went to the local barber and he lowered my ears for the exorbitant price of 20 cents. What a price for a 10 minute haircut, but I should be set for another couple of months as I don't think it is necessary to get one's hair cut too often.

Old Mrs. Edgerly's mare died and I told her we would bury her in the orchard. Charles Green and I dragged her out there on the sled and dug a deep hole and put her to rest. She was a good horse and I am sure Mrs. Edgerly will miss her. I may help her look for a new one shortly. Mr. Beardsley called also and asked if I would help him butcher some hogs so we set about at the task and did seven of them. I wasn't even depressed so I should have saved the task for another day, but he wanted the help right away. This time of the year I don't seem to get as depressed since we are so busy with the farm work and planting and trimming, etc. that I seldom have time to think about anything else. As I have said before, keeping one's mind occupied is one of the best defenses against depression.

We are planning on expanding the farm some and Mrs. Edgerly has agreed to our building a 20-foot by 32-foot lean-to so that we can store the equipment out of the weather. I hired Charles Green to help me on the farm on a regular basis and pay him about $10.00 a week for his help, depending on how many hours he has worked and what he has been doing. He is starting to dig the foundation and I will pay him $1.75 per day for this and charge it to Mrs. Edgerly since the lean-to will be on her property and she has agreed to this. It is hard work for Charles; hopefully we can use some of the horsepower to help dig the foundation.

We have been thinking about possibly buying a farm of our own since things seem to be going well in this newest endeavor in our ***Journey Through Life***. We had looked at Mrs. Steadman's farm and were in the hopes that she might consider selling it to us at what we would consider a fair price. I met with the lawyer, Johnson, who represents Mrs. Steadman and he said that she is not willing to think about selling at this time. She said that she would remember us if she changes her mind later on. It did seem like a good idea at the time when we gave up running a mercantile store and went into farming to rent a farm so that if we were not successful or found it not to our liking that we would not have such a large commitment to walk away from. Renting from Mrs. Edgerly seemed like just the ticket but now that we have seen some success, it does not make sense to share the profits with her. She has been a wonderful landlady and certainly carried her entire load of this endeavor, but maybe the time has come to take the big leap on our own.

With all the planting, cultivating and harvesting of early crops and hay I shudder to think about the possibility of moving. I wonder if there is a good time to move and a bad time to consider moving. Maybe the winter months would be better for this decision since at that time the outside work has come to a halt and one would have more time to devote to uprooting and pushing on. I guess the thing to do is just make the decision no matter what time of the year it is and then just do it. After it is all done and time has moved on I am sure we would look back and wonder why we agonized so long over moving.

Charles Green is helping me keep up and Will and Mazie's brother Howard are also pitching in. And of course I would be amiss if I didn't mention the wonderful help from our oldest son Robert. As I have often said, he is strong and willing and of such a good nature. Will has certainly been a big help, sharing his strength with us on the farm as well as his strength in the pulpit. I think there is a definite advantage to having your pastor as a family member in many ways. Mazie's brother Howard, who as I have said, is an anthropology professor at Columbia University is also very talented as an amateur artist. I have put him to work making a fancy sign for us to place by the road announcing that we have pigs for sale and he also has painted our name and some decorations on the mailbox for us. I dare say we have the fanciest mailbox in Perry.

Mazie has finally given in and bought me a pipe and tobacco to enjoy. I did smoke one before but it has been 14 years since I gave it up and Mazie was never very fond of the smell of the burning tobacco so I relented and didn't even sneak a smoke in the store or barn all these years. She must be mellowing as she has decided that I can try it again. Who says she rules the roast? I must be in the driver's seat since she has finally relented after only 14 years. Am I kidding myself or what? I certainly don't think smoking would do anyone any harm and the pleasure one gets from it is indescribable. It also seems to calm my nerves when I am getting uptight and should help keep that old nemesis depression, at bay.

We certainly enjoyed the Sunday service here on this beautiful day, the 12th of July in 1908. Will preached on the value of sharing and we were moved so by the service that we went home and dressed a chicken and took it to the widow Donald who needs all the help she can get at the present time from friends and neighbors. In the spirit of giving, we decided to hook up the horse and take a trip to Canandaigua to visit my brother Hans and family. We left Perry about 2 PM and arrived there about 6:30 after the 40 mile drive. It took us a little longer than I expected but Jack got winded and had a tough time over some of the terrible roads in the area. We got there just in time for supper (could we have planned it that way) and Hans and Virginia were gracious enough to invite us to their table. We all enjoyed a fine feast and catching up on the news. They did ask us to spend the night but since I am such a homebody and wanted to be in my own bed, we decided to head out about 8:30 and make the trip in the dark. We took our time and got home about 1 AM and the bed sure felt good. I went to bed thinking that someday mankind will most likely have surfaced roads and some means of travel between towns that are not connected by rail where it will only take minutes rather than hours to get from here to there. I can dream can't I?

One thing we sure look forward to in the summer months are the ecumenical church services where the Presbyterians, Methodists and the Baptists all combine their services so that they can accommodate their ministers' vacation schedules. I would also believe it is because there are so many parishioners that decide that they only have to attend church in the fall, winter and spring to be good Christians. I never felt that way as I think ones commitment should be year round and not a seasonal thing. By combining the services, the Sunday service is much better attended than if it were each individual church holding their own. Even though I think that Will is a fine preacher (outshines them all) it is eye opening to get the perspectives of other ministers on occasion. I will have to admit, however, that I am never quite sure about the Baptist minister as he seems to have been blessed with just a little extra hell, fire and brimstone, and certainly can get carried away on a Sunday morning. When you do listen to a good preacher you can easily get caught up in his message and forget your own problems even if for only a short time. My mood swings, which I believe everyone has, are much greater on some Sundays when I hear stirring words from the pulpit. A doctor who has treated me for depression once told me that everyone has the mood swings and in some people they are much more severe than in others, and they not only occur over a period of days or weeks but also even during the waking hours of a day. When one knows that many other folks are having the same anxieties that you are it sometimes helps you to cope better with them. Of course some people show it more openly and others keep it well hidden. I have to think now that when I disappeared for some time after little Helen's untimely death it was because I was keeping my feeling bottled up inside until they reached a boiling point. I now have learned to share them more with Mazie and Will as the need arises.

On to more pleasant things and we are celebrating Robert's 12th birthday here on this beautiful day on August 12th. We had an enjoyable family get-together and Will and Lucy and the children came out and joined us in a fine feast and a big cake to help us honor the occasion. I gave Robert $1.00 and I hope he can make it last awhile. We also received a surprise visit from Hans and Virginia from Canandaigua and they gave Robert another 50 cents so he is riding high with all his gifts. We invited them to join us at our table and we discussed their interest in having us look at a couple of farms that are for sale in their hometown of Canandaigua. As I have mentioned, we are starting to think about this move more and more.

It's hard to find the time to go farm shopping with all the things that are going on at the present time. I have been building fences to keep the hogs out of the oats and working on the new shed. The foundation is complete so we will soon see the structure start to take shape. Also I have had to tend to the horses Kit, Maude and Jack and all of them have had to have new shoes recently. In between all this I have been cleaning out hedgerows and cultivating anything that doesn't move. This is a very busy time of the year for a farmer and his family. We also are cutting oats but every time we get started, the equipment breaks down and we lose some time getting it fixed. In addition, the weather doesn't always cooperate and we have been getting some heavy rainstorms, which hold us up. I have to be watchful that I don't get too anxious over all the work to be done and have that old nemeses, depression creep back into my life.

**Reverend
William TeWinkel
c. age 39
c. 1909**

**Lucy McGregor TeWinkel
c. age 37
c. 1916**

The Bartlett Pears are ready to be picked and I hired Willard Nevins, Frank Aimie and Jon Hensey to help me. I am paying Willard and Frank $1.75 each for their days' work since they are boarding themselves and I will pay Jon $1.50 since we are furnishing his dinner.

We finally found the time to go to Canandaigua and look at three farms that Hans thought we might be interested in. They are the Matther's place and the Metcalf place and if you can believe me, the Outhouse Farm. I think if I was blessed with that name I would seriously consider changing it. We did like the Matther's farm but found out they have given another party a 30 day option on buying it so we will have to wait on that one. We constantly worry about taking on full ownership of a farm especially since we just got the tax bill for 1908 on the home we still own on Lake and Center Street and it was a whopping $21.67. I fail to understand what these politicians do with all the money that they are raising from these high taxes. Maybe they could use a little of it to fix up some of the terrible roads around here.

Mrs. Edgerly and I decided to invest in some more lambs so I ordered 125 of them from L.A. McComber at a cost of $3.40 each. They are to be delivered in good shape via the railroad and should arrive hopefully on the 17th. This is a big undertaking especially if we were to decide to move on but I would assume Mrs. Edgerly could find someone else to run the farm and take over the operation if we were not here. Isn't it human nature to think that we are indispensable and then we always find out that we are not after all? Maybe it is one of God's mysteries to bring us back down to earth on occasion as we start to think to much of ourselves.

Mazie's mother Mrs. McGregor has been visiting us from Bellaire, Ohio and has been helping a great deal with baby Howard. Unfortunately she received a telegram from Margaret advising her to come home, as Uncle Harry is not at all well. We are all going to say an extra prayer for his speedy recovery. I drove Mrs. McCregor to the railroad station and saw to it that she was settled in on the 8:30 AM train to Bellaire. We will anxiously await word from Bellaire on Harry's condition. Life is so tenuous that we sometimes take it all to easily for granted when it can be over in a heart beat, as we found out so sadly with little Helen.

I have been planting a lot of winter wheat with the help of Charles Green and also the generosity of my neighbor J. Nevins who was kind enough to loan me his planting drill for the time we are needing it. I in turn am planning on helping him fill his silo in exchange for his generosity. It is always uplifting to receive help from one's neighbors and also to give assistance in return and both were completed by Monday the 21st of August.

Time sure flies when one is busy. Seems like only yesterday that I was waiting for the icy clutch of winter to give up her grip on the earth and here it is going into October already. All in all we have had a good season with our milk income, sale of produce and the great price we received for the pears of $1.50 a bushel. We managed to pick and ship hundreds of bushels and the money will keep us in food and warmth for the winter. Our greatest blessing, however, this year has been our health and the blessing of little Howard who we are all doing our best to spoil.

We have decided to make an offer on the Metcalf Farm in Canandaigua and I contacted the agent who is handling the property, Church and Church. I offered them $65.00 per acre for it and we will see what comes of it. I shudder to think of all the problems we would have with moving since over the years one accumulates so many things. I am sure much of what I have gathered isn't worth keeping and certainly not worth moving but I will have a difficult time parting with anything. One never knows when something you have set aside will someday come in handy, especially in the farming business.

We all made church here on Sunday, Oct 4,1908 and heard another rousing sermon by Reverend Will. I paid our pledge of 75 cents to the Systematic Beneficence Fund. It was good to get some time off from the farm work and especially picking of pears. I have hired three hands to help Robert and I, and so far we have picked and sorted several hundred bushels. I am seeing pears in my sleep. It was also a big day as little Howard was baptized Howard Alexander Tyler by his uncle Reverend William TeWinkel. After the service we decided to have a small party at the TeWinkels' to celebrate this blessed event. A fine time was had by all.

We finally have received a response on our offer on the Metcalf farm from Church and Church. They said that the

Metcalf's would not consider our offer of $65.00 an acre. We will just have to keep looking. Sometimes the good Lord moves in mysterious ways and maybe it is meant to be that we don't buy their farm. Neither Mazie nor I were too upset about the rejection, and we are not going to raise our offering price, so I guess it really wasn't in our hearts to buy it.

All of our lambs arrived here on the 15th of Oct. and I bought several gallons of sheep dip, Daytholeum, to dip them in and I hope it is enough to treat them all. It's going to be a lot of work tending to all these sheep and hopefully they will grow, stay free of disease, and Mrs. Edgerly and I will turn a nice profit on the investment. I broke down the cost of Mr. Nevins' help and the cost of the sheep dip and it cost of 2-3/8 cents per head to dip them. Now I think that is keeping pretty detailed records but when one is running his own business, which operating a farm is, one must keep good records or else.

Church time here on Sunday and we all went to hear the Reverend Cowles of the Anti-Saloon League preach on the evils of alcohol. He referred to the users of this devil's brew as "rum soaked, whiskey swilled, Satan faced rummies". The sermon was so inspiring that I pledged 25 cents per month for one year to support the Anti-Saloon League in its efforts. I wonder if someday Reverend Cowles and his organization will be successful in having a prohibition put on the making and selling of alcoholic beverages. I also wonder if it ever happened, how successful it would be. Mazie and I are certainly in his corner on this issue but I must admit that some of the wine I make from the few of the fruits that have fallen to the ground and bruised sure tastes good on a cold winter's night. I don't think I will mention that in front of Mazie as she thinks alcohol in any form is a demon. We all have to have a few of our own little secrets now and then. Of course I must admit it also helps to ward off the depression that always seems to be lurking just around the next corner. I would expect if a prohibition ever comes that most folks are ingenious enough to get their devil's brew anyway so maybe Reverend Cowles is fighting a losing battle, but fighting he most certainly is. It always seems like the noisiest ones are those whose issues are listened to and the great majority of those of us that keep to ourselves and don't preach how others should live generally are ignored even though we outnumber the small very verbal few. It always has been that way and most likely always will until the majority finds their voice.

Mazie and I, Marion and little Howard went for a nice ride in the buggy here on this second to last day of October. We expect some snow tomorrow and it was nice to take a break from the farm work, deliver some apples and pears to Mrs. Edgerly and just relax and forget one's cares for a while. Robert has been drawing coal from Fanning and Co. so he was unable to join us today but hopefully he will be able to next time. We also have cut up and split a few dozen cord of wood to help keep Jack Frost from our doorstep this winter. We will need all we have, especially with the baby in the house and his needs for comfort. It sure is a lot of work to cut up and split all those cords of wood and I wonder if someday someone will invent a way to do it with less effort. Of course, if that happened, then we all would become fat and lazy.

Can you believe it is already November and I am awaiting the bean thrasher to come by and thrash our bean crops for us? They arrived a little later than I would have expected, about 10 AM (banker's hours) but they went right at it and finished about 2 PM. We got 117 bushels of beans from the 40 acres. Along with doing this, getting Maude's shoes replaced and tending the sheep, cows and hogs, I am one busy fellow. If it gets any busier I may have to take a little bit of that "devil's brew" to give me the energy I need.

The money keeps coming in from the sale of produce and milk and of course it keeps going out just as easily, if not more so. Mazie's mother sent her a check for $50.00, which was a blessing, and Mazie decided to loan it to me to help with the farm expenses. I will have to pay it back, most likely with interest, as she always reminds me that what is hers is hers and what is mine is ours. You would think a smart farmer like me could figure that out but I'm not sure the "weaker sex" hasn't worked out a plan amongst themselves to make us fellows just _think_ we are in charge. We even splurged a little and Mazie and I took Robert to the Auditorium to see Hadley's moving pictures. Robert and Mazie thought it was fascinating but I don't think anything will ever come of motion pictures. On top of that it cost us $1.05 for the three of us to see the show.

We have expanded our area to consider the possibility of buying a farm. I have corresponded with a Mr. Sharp from Buffalo who owns a farm he has for sale about 15 miles west of here. We will have to find out a few more of the details and decide if we want to travel up there and check it out. Before we take the time to go, I have to get the beans to Belden and Co. and with Mr. Nevin's help and Robert's, we got them all together. We weighed them in at 2,228 lbs. but when we got there they only came to 2,108 lbs. Isn't it always the way that the final count is less that you expect it should be? Sort of like the butcher resting his thumb on the scales when he is figuring out the price of that cut of beef you are buying. I can't believe they cheat at all and is most likely is my overly suspicious nature.

With Christmas only a little over a month away we can use any extra cash we can muster to help buy some gifts for everyone. With Robert, Dorothy, Margaret and little Howard and, of course, Mazie and I, we have quite a few to consider and it all adds up. I expect we can trim our list as far as little Howard is concerned since he isn't old enough to realize what giving at Christmas time means. Mazie and I have put together a shopping list of gifts and I sent it off with a check to Sears and Roebuck. Hopefully all will be here in plenty of time for Christmas.

We all looked forward to a great Thanksgiving dinner and get-together with the TeWinkels here on this Nov. 26th. We were not disappointed, as it was all that we had hoped for with a fine turkey dinner and all the fixings prepared by the ladies. Will led us all in a Thanksgiving prayer, before we partook dinner, to thank the Lord for all the blessings he has bestowed upon us. After our feast we all decided to get the cutters out and take an early winter's ride to check out the Sharp farm. He told us he wants $8,000 for the 72 acres and the house that is on it. It sure was a brisk ride and even though we all bundled up good we were huddled when we got home. Too bad they don't have heaters in these cutters. I think the asking price is a little steep, the house would need a tremendous amount of work and I don't know how I would find the time to fix it and farm also. Mazie thought the farmhouse was also a little small for our growing family, which we also have to consider. If we were independently wealthy we could stay here and hire someone to fix it up and then buy it and move. That is a dream that I don't believe will come true.

We received our packages from Sears and Roebuck in plenty of time for Christmas since it is only Dec. 1st. Pretty good delivery as it took less than two weeks to get them. I imagine the children will have a hard time not peeking at them between now and Christmas morning.

Mazie's sister and mother were here again visiting and I had Robert haul their trunk to the railroad station and then he took them in the surrey to catch the 5:05 PM train to Bellaire. He had to make two trips as the trunk was so large Jack would have been tired out hauling it and all the passengers at the same time. Ladies sure like to pack a lot of things when they travel. I was too busy as I helped Mr. Beardsley butcher and dress six hogs and he helped me with three of ours. Mine weighed out at 109, 113 and 124 lbs. and I sold two of them to Mr. Hodges for 7 cents a lb. and I will need to deliver them tomorrow. It helped to get my mind off my mood swings as it usually does when I get really busy. I should probably seek some professional help but then again it is hard to admit you can't handle your problems on your own.

I finally have taken pen to paper and written Mr. Sharp about the farm. "Dear Sir: A few days ago my wife went with me to your farm and we looked the house over. After talking it over and thinking about it we have concluded that the house is not large enough for our family. At the price you have placed on the farm, any addition to the house would be out of the question for us so I guess we will have to say we cannot consider your proposition."

Yours Very Truly,

Ben C. Tyler.

I spoke to Mr. Chapin and he told me of two more farms for sale, the Cattin and the Tabor farm. When we have time we will take a look at them and get some of the details.

Well Christmas is just around the corner and we received a box of gifts today from Bellaire. We also bought some gifts for Mazie's family in Bellaire, I packaged them up and it weighed 10 lbs. and cost me expressage of 85 cents. We have received some very bad news. Carrie contacted us and Uncle Harry Tayloe died last Friday night, the 18th of December. We wrote back to Carrie and sent her a copy of the Tyler pedigree. It is always sad to lose someone but it seems even sadder at this time of the year. We all wish Carrie and the family in Ohio the best.

Robert and I drove the sled out and cut a beautiful Christmas tree and we all set about to trim it on Christmas Eve. I had also taken Mazie into town to buy her a gift this afternoon so it has been a full day of preparation. The children woke us from a peaceful slumber at a very early hour so we decided to get to the festivities and let the fun begin for the day. We all opened the box from Bellaire and it was a well-filled one. Mrs. McGregor sent me $3.00 which I appreciated, and she sent each of the children $1.00 each in addition to some toys and clothes, including little Howard. The children spent some time playing with their gifts before we had a wonderful duck dinner. It is a bright and beautiful day that God has made. It was sad that the TeWinkels could not celebrate this blessed day with us but they had gone to Belaire to be with the family during this sorrowful time of Harry's passing.

Here on this last day of December in the year of our Lord 1908, we have decided to renew the lease for the farm with Mrs. Edgerly. I do believe she would be willing to work with us if something comes along that we decided to buy. What a difficult decision this is becoming, but life is full of difficult decisions.

Chapter 3

1909

(William Howard Taft inaugurated as 27th President)

The TeWinkels arrived home from Bellaire here on this first day of January in the year of our Lord 1909. They filled us in on the details of the passing and arrangements of Uncle Harry. Will preformed the service for him and I am sure he did a fine job. It is a sad time for those that are left to deal with Harry's passing and all the associated things that must be dealt with. We all pray that Harry is in a better place.

On a more pleasant note, Mazie took baby Howard to Olin's Photo Gallery to get his picture taken. I am sure it will be a fine picture as Mr. Olin does wonders with his Eastman Kodak camera and Howard is such a handsome baby, as are all our children, that he will photograph well. On another happy note Marion started kindergarten today as they allow children to either start in Sept. or in January depending on their age at the time. She will be a fine student and I am sure she will learn a lot and be a pleasure for the teacher to have in class. The time certainly flies, as it seems like yesterday that Marion was brought into this world to bless Mazie and I and her brothers and sisters.

It seems farmers are always a little short of cash until the crops come in or we sell some stock or something else, whatever that is, that brings us in some money. Since I have to pay the exorbitant town tax on the Lake Street property of $20.26 and the fire insurance on Lake Street of $17.20, I had to go to my brother Harry and ask him if he would loan us $75.00 until some money comes in. As usual Harry came through and the money will go for the above plus whatever else I need to cover in the short term. I told Harry it is just for a month or so and I would be happy to pay him some interest but he said he wouldn't hear of any such thing and to pay him back whenever. There isn't anything more important than family. I am even so short of cash that I gave up smoking my pipe for the month of January to try and kick the habit and of course the cost of pipe tobacco at 5 cents a package is prohibitive. I can't believe smoking the pipe is hurting me any but Mazie says I should try and cut back. Actually it helps to calm my nerves so I am not so sure it is a good thing to cut back on. Sometimes things look up when the mailman comes as Mazie received $50 from her brother Howard for her birthday so that she could take a trip to Bellaire to visit her family. She is looking forward to it with a great deal of anticipation. I will have to have a lot of help with little Howard while she is gone and I know that Dorothy and Margaret, Marion and Robert will pitch in so that Mazie can go and relax and know that he is in good hands. It is always nice to get away and I have written to the ticket agent for the BRTP Railroad to see what it would cost to buy tickets for a train trip to Washington, D.C. for all of us. Maybe when the time is right and the money is there we can all see our nation's capitol. It would certainly be something that the children would remember all their lives. I hope, the Lord willing, we can do it someday soon.

We all made church here in mid-January except baby Howard and Mazie and Will gave another of his inspiring sermons. I always come away with my spirits lifted after the service and that is the way things ought to be. I have to admit that I said a little prayer for the Lord's help on my dream of taking the family to Washington would come true. After church when we got home baby Howard was coming down with a cold so Mazie got him some skunk grease to rub on his chest from Mrs. Beardsley and if that doesn't cure him I don't know what will. I guess I will not ask her what is in that concoction and I am sure the fuss that the two ladies and his sisters and brother are making over him will also help cure him. Since the baby was feeling under the weather, Mazie decided to stay home for the evening from her sewing circle at Miss Dibble's. That was too bad as it gives her an out away from the routine of the family. No one is a better wife and mother than she is but everyone needs a little time to break the routine and be with other folks, if only to share your hopes and dreams with them and, of course, maybe a little gossip.

**HOWARD TYLER
1914**

The picture to the left is Howard in c. 1916 and then above in adult life.

A JOURNEY THROUGH LIFE

It has been a busy month on the farm with the animals. Mrs. Edgerly and I decided it was a good time to sell the 120 lambs we had acquired some time ago. L.A. McComber offered us 7 cents a pound for them and he said he would take them next week. Next week rolled around and he called and said the price had dropped a quarter of one cent in Buffalo for sheep and he was hoping we would hold on to them awhile longer. Since a deal is a deal I told him we would not and he will have to absorb the quarter cent drop. That is what you get when one speculates in the markets, sometimes you are a winner and sometimes you lose. The total income from the sheep came to $602.70, and split between us we received $301.35. I sure needed the cash. I paid the bank $200 on the note that was due and I sent Harry $75 to pay back the short term loan that he had given us. As I said, he would not accept any interest on the money that he loaned us. I also owed $42.72 on my life insurance policy for the year and I didn't want that to lapse. It is too important to the wife and family that I have some life insurance coverage in case anything happens to me. I certainly don't anticipate anything since I am generally feeling well but one never knows when the Lord may call you home. I also spent the ridiculous sum of $1.00 to order the <u>Democrat and Chronicle</u> newspaper from Rochester for six months. At that price, I sure hope there is some good news in it for a change. I don't need to read only bad news all the time and get myself down.

Beardsley helped me butcher the last of the hogs that were part of the lot born on May 22, 1908 and they weighed in at 192 lbs. and 447½ lbs. We kept part of them and sold the rest at 8 cents a pound. I spent a couple days here at the end of January making lard and sausage from the part we kept for the rest of the winter months. Sometimes I wonder if all that lard and sausage is good for us; only time will tell. Since we sold the lambs and butchered the hogs I decided to buy some wethers and we bought 74 of them at $4.95 per 100 lbs. By the time we pay for shipping, weighing and the commission for the broker, we end up paying $5.887 per 100 lbs. Nothing is ever as cheap as it might seem at first since all the extras have to be added in. Hopefully they will stay healthy and grow and turn us a nice profit.

It is very cold and wintry as we start February of 1909. I am forced to work mostly in the barn, as I cannot get out to do any of the spring work. I must be dreaming that it is spring already. I should enjoy this time while I can as the workload increases tremendously in the spring when I get up at the crack of dawn or before and am usually asleep in my chair when I get in late in the evening. This is a momentous month; Abraham Lincoln was born 100 years ago this month and the Perry Presbyterian Church under the able leadership of William has just decided to build a new church. It will require a great deal of sacrifice by all of the members but it is growing and since it is the anchor of our community of the faithful we need to invest in a larger facility. Mazie and I will certainly do our part in helping to see this come to completion.

My sister Mary, who is now 34 years old, arrived from Virginia to spend some time with us and even though she is part of the family we cannot hold it against her that she wanted to go to the Episcopal Church. I think Mazie may well work on her while she is here visiting and if I know Mazie she may well convert her. We did get her to go to the Baptist Church with us and listen to the Reverend Creighton of Buffalo preach on the question of temperance. It was a rousing sermon so full of hell, fire and brimstone that when I got home I had to sneak out to the barn for a little shot of the special homemade wine I keep stashed there. I have a feeling that if prohibition is ever the law of the land, a lot of people will be sneaking out to the barn and a lot of money will be made on illegal booze. We will watch and see where this all leads. Reverend Creighton is certainly in the corner of outlawing the devil's brew. I wonder if he has a secret stash in his barn?

Mazie has had a few outings this month and also has had Lois and Helen out to spend some time with her and baby Howard. She has gone to a reception at the Mattisons and also spent an evening with the ladies at their sewing bee. It helps to get out and also to have visitors this time of year to overcome cabin fever, which always come along with the winter blues. Robert drove Mazie and Mary down to the railroad station to get Mary's trunk, which finally showed up several days after Mary. Wouldn't you think when you get on the train for a trip that they would put your trunk on the same train? We finally learned that it sat on the railroad platform in Virginia for several days before they finally put it on another train for Perry. Hopefully someday when travelling becomes more efficient everyone's baggage will end up getting to the destination with the traveler. I can only hope for this, as do many other travelers. Fortunately Mazie is about the same size as Mary so she was able to borrow some of her clothing while we patiently waited. She even made me go down to the barber shop and get my ears lowered in honor of Mary coming to visit, and it cost me the exorbitant sum of 20 cents.

Mazie reminded me that her brother Howard had sent her $50 so that she could travel home to Bellaire and visit her family. We went to the railroad station and got the tickets for her and Marion and baby Howard to go and they left on the 17th of the month for an extended stay. Extended stay means until the folks in Bellaire get tired of having them there or Mazie gets homesick and wants to head back to Perry. I pray that their trunks will arrive with them because they will surely need all of baby Howard's things as soon as they get there. I will miss them greatly and will try and keep busy with the farm work to keep my mind off their being gone for awhile. I had to hit Harry up for another loan so Mazie would have a few extra dollars and he sent me $100 and said I didn't have to pay it back for two months. It will come in very handy. Family is sure important for many reasons, the least of which is when they can be a banker for you. We appreciate it very much.

The wethers are growing rapidly and I am now giving them about 50 lbs. of corn at each feeding. A couple of them were scratching so I got some sheep dip to treat them. Hopefully it will stop any problems before they start. I even went out and started to trim the trees in the orchard to keep my mind off Mazie, Marion and the baby being away. I plan on writing them every day and hopefully she will write to us every day. Robert plans on writing often too and enclosing pictures that the twins have drawn for them. It is hard to realize how much you miss someone until they are away even for a short time, or at least I hope a short time.

I am helping a couple of my neighbors get in some straw and also to draw some much needed firewood as the weather is already below zero several days this month. As I have said, good neighbors are a gift and here in March of 1909 several of them are helping me do some trimming of the trees in the orchard. It is a pleasure in a way to be outdoors and trimming trees rather than cooped up inside or hauling loads of manure to the bean lot. If manure were gold I would have the mother lode. Mr. Beardsley also helped me take the meat out of the brine and begin the slow process of smoking it. I returned part of the favor when I happened to notice that he had a small fire started in his barn and Robert and I and another neighbor were fortunate to get to it and extinguish it before any major damage was done or before any stock was harmed.

We have had several calves born this month and I sold them for 7½ cents a pound for a nice return. The wethers also are growing rapidly and weigh an average of 127 pounds apiece and Mrs. Edgerly and I are thinking about selling them if we can make a decent return on our investment. We were offered 5¾ cents a pound but I think being a shrewd business man that we can get 6 cents a pound for them. Robert Gregg has expressed an interest and I think he is willing to pay that so we are going to make a deal with him. Robert and I delivered the wethers to him and I calculated the following accounting for Mrs. Edgerly for the sale for Edgerly & Tyler. The cost of 74 wethers bought from Gregg & Abbott on Jan. 21 1909 was 5.483 cents per pound. The other costs involved were shipping them via the railroad at .253 cents a pound and commission to the seller's agent of .151 cents a pound for a total cost of $5.887 per wether. Our total investment, less my time, and the feed and care came to $435.64. We sold them for 6 cents a pound and they weighed in at 9590 lbs. We had to allow for shrinkage and that amounted to 3 lbs. per animal so our end total receipt on the sale came to $562.62. I think this worked out quite well for a novice farmer who is still learning the ropes and I sent Mrs. Edgerly a check for $281.10 for her half. This income will sure come in handy as we are so short of cash that I have had to write to the Penn Mutual Insurance Co. and borrow $100 against my life insurance policy to tide us over for awhile. It isn't too wise to borrow against my life insurance since that could mean less for Mazie and the children but hopefully I will get it paid back soon. For all the trimming I am doing in the orchard this month I calculated about 90 hours total at a cost of my labor of 20 cents per hour so I deducted half the total of $18 from Mrs. Edgerly's check. This seems only fair as she has never complained and I sure hope she doesn't this time.

With some of the receipts from the sale, I sent Harry a check for $50 on our loan and I sent Mazie $8.00 to help tide her over. I also spent some of it on buying two loads of coal from Fanning and Co. or a total of 3800 lbs. at $6.00 per ton. I paid them the $11.40 and it is a good investment in this weather to help keep us comfortable. We are also taking in a little money on our continuing milk sales every week.

I am a little surprised but pleased that Mazie and Marion and baby Howard are staying so long in Bellaire. She is writing every day so I guess she still loves me and hopefully misses me. In her latest letter she said the baby had come down with the measles. I am extremely worried about him and hope he gets over them quickly as I could not face another loss of a child after what we went through after little Helen died. With my losing my way in life and leaving those that I loved so much even for a short time was to say the least overwhelming. I never want to have to deal with that kind of deep depression in the future. Fortunately a few days later Mazie sent me a telegram, which set my mind at ease and said baby Howard is getting much better. I worried for nothing but worrying certainly comes with parenting.

The remainder of March has been filled with church goings as I paid Robert 50 cents for two tickets to the dinner at St. Patrick's that he was helping one of his catholic friends sell. The meal was excellent, even for the Catholics, but maybe a little steep in price. I am only kidding as I enjoy seeing our Catholic friends and sharing supper with them at any price. I even had enough money left over to splurge on two new pair of boots, one felt and the other rubber. I bought them at Cole and Sons at the ridiculously high price of $1.50 for each pair. What is this world coming to?

To end the month, we all attended an evening service in the church to hear Mr. Sherman and also to see his stereopticon views of his mission work in Colorado and Wyoming. It certainly looks like beautiful country and I hope he is successful in converting some of those that live there to the Presbyterian faith. The Presbyterian Church in the United States is growing and with missionaries like Mr. Sherman, hopefully it will continue to expand.

JOHN W. PARSONS

April is even more of what those of us in the farming business call a transition month when one's work, even more than in March, moves from inside projects to the fields. I have been trimming more of the apple trees by the day whenever the weather permits and then I finally think I am finished with Robert's help and we burned all of the trimmings that we could. There is a lot of smoke from our fire and it's good we are out in the country away from the Village of Perry, as all those city folks wouldn't appreciate all that smoke if the wind was in their direction. Someday there will most likely be restrictions on what a person can burn but fortunately such is not the case yet. I'm sure all that smoke cannot be good for people to inhale but out here it just seems to blow away. After getting it all cleared and burned it is time to plow the orchard so Maude got behind the plow that I had borrowed from Mr. Nevins and we went to work. I don't think Maude had her heart in it as she stepped on her left hind foot and went lame and I had to put her in the barn and hook Kit up to the plow. Kit is much more dependable; those lady horses are something like our ladies and can be finicky at times. I guess I still don't know how to handle either one too well. If I live to be 150 I am sure I still won't master that art. This reminded me that Mazie, Marion and baby Howard are still out in Bellaire and don't seem to be in any hurry to return home. I wonder if she is purposely avoiding coming home too soon to have to put up with me. I just can't believe that is the case as "perfect" as I am.

Robert is getting into the farming business in earnest and sold the Phillip's cow calf to Cominkey for 7 and ½ cents a pound and since it weighed in at 155# he made $11.62 for all his hard work in taking care of the calf. He also was given a lamb to raise by Mr. Nevins and hopefully will turn a nice profit on that venture. As hard as it is to be a farmer with the long hours, back breaking work and the constant weather to contend with, I am not sure I want my children to end up in this occupation. As I have said before I believe hard work never hurt anyone and being outside so much must be good for a person, but there has to be easier ways to make a living. Robert is such a smart boy that I believe he will end up being a doctor or a lawyer some day. We always hope that our children through their upbringing and their education will end up doing better than we, having an easier time of it and I am convinced that will be the case with all of Mazie's and my wonderful children. That is the way things should be.

In our daily letters I finally received the one that I had been hoping for and Mazie said they are coming home tomorrow on the 8:30 A.M. train. I have sure missed them and it will be great to be all united again. It worked out well as Mazie's brother Howard is also coming from New York City. He has a short time off from his professorship at Columbia University and is arriving on the 6:15 P.M. train. Robert and I will be making several trips to the train station to pick them up and hopefully their luggage as well.

We celebrated their return by all going to church in our present building and having the last communion in this structure. The new church is well under way and moving along much faster than anyone had expected. The Lord works in mysterious ways. I gave our systematic beneficence of $1.00 and also we made another contribution to the building project. We all want to feel that we are part of this new and growing Presbyterian Church of faith here in Perry. After church we all took supper at the TeWinkels and I took the chicken I had recently prepared which weighed 3-½ lbs. We all had a great meal. I even had my hair cut again for the extravagantly high price of 20 cents. It doesn't seem that a person should have to get their hair cut more than once a year but Mazie will have nothing to do with that. She says 20 cents or not, "you hook up old Kit and drive yourself down to the barber shop or else." I have never dared ask her what else meant and I don't think I want to find out. The TeWinkels even paid for the milk we had been selling them for the month and gave Robert 20 cents for delivering it. That boy is going to be better off than I if he keeps it up.

Mrs. Edgerly asked me to give her an accounting of the business for the period from April 1, 1907 to April 1, 1909 and since I keep such meticulous records that was not a problem. In figuring it all out I noted that she still owed me $5.21 for one of the last year's transactions and when I showed it to her she paid up immediately as she always does. This has been a good partnership for the both of us and at the present time it looks like it may continue since we have not thought anymore about buying our own farm. It must be my lucky month since F. D. Allen also ran into me and paid me $1.00 he still owed on the display case he brought from the mercantile store. Even though it is a year or so late and he still owes me $1.50 balance, it is appreciated. As I have often said, every little bit helps.

Here at the end of April we have had several blessings and some very bad weather to contend with. We have had a hard frost and lots of snow, which really has slowed me down. I have managed to plant the Timothy Seed and fortunately I had just finished planting 22 rows of 26 hills of potatoes with lots of manure and even the stove ashes from the winter mixed in for good measure. That should be a combination that grows the biggest potatoes in this county. Our old cat even had 4 kittens that the children will have fun with and also have to come up with names for all 4 of them. The Purcell cow had a bull calf, which was also a blessing for our continued success in the farming business.

To top everything off for a great month in which Mazie returned, the new church is moving right along and I even received the garden seed that I had ordered from the Henry Field Seed Co. The best was kept for the last. Baby Howard had his 1st birthday on the 30th of the month and we had a great celebration with a fine cake with one candle in the middle of it. Since we couldn't get baby Howard to blow out the candle we called upon Robert, Margaret, Dorothy and Marion and believe me they put a great deal of effort into it. It is hard to believe baby Howard is 1 year old already. Time sure flies by especially when you are busy which is certainly best for my mental well being. We all said a prayer for little Howard that he lives a long, healthy, prosperous and productive life as I am sure all my children will. Thank the Lord for all His blessings.

We are moving along nicely with the farming and the family as we enter May of 1909. It would be nice if the weather cooperated as it has started out with heavy rain and then snow. I am happy that I had already gotten the oats sowed with all the mud that is around to contend with. This time of year should be warming with sunny days so a farmer can get his fields plowed and his crops planted. It is so wet I haven't even been able to draw the manure out to the orchard. It is very hard on Maude who certainly doesn't like to work in this weather and even old dependable Kit balks at having to try and pull a plow or pull a load of manure out to the field. Maybe the good Lord should have been a farmer rather than a carpenter and then He might have had more sympathy for us farmers when it comes to the weather. I am of course only kidding as the Lord has blessed us with a fine family, a good farm that we have the privilege of renting from Mrs. Edgerly and we all have our health at the present moment. I am even so busy I don't have time to feel sorry for myself and when I think about it I have no reason to feel sorry for myself. The mind however works in mysterious ways. I'm afraid if the weather were perfect all the time with sunny days and a light rain at night as needed we would become a nation of fat and lazy folks. That certainly is not a possibility as hard as Mazie and the children and I work and as hard as most of my neighbors work to put a roof over their families' heads and food on the table. And of course hopefully have a little left over for a few of the pleasant things in life.

This Sunday I stayed home from church with baby Howard and let the rest of the family go. In the evening Robert and I went to the Episcopal Church and listened to a fine sermon by a travelling evangelist. Robert had gone to our church in the morning but wanted to go again in the evening and was not disappointed. The reverend gave a rousing sermon to all assembled. I think we all walked out the better for it. On my way out I ran into Fred Allen and he paid me another $1.00 on the 3 deck candy case he bought from our mercantile store. He still owes me 50 cents but he is getting it paid off. I might have thought the reverend's reference to it being better to give than to receive may just have moved old Fred a little bit. Whatever moved him the dollar was appreciated and I thanked him from the bottom of my heart.

It is so cold that the water pipes in the kitchen running from the cistern froze and I had to spend some time working on them. It's funny how they don't freeze in the middle of the winter when it is so much colder, but they wait until there is an enormous amount of outside work to be done and then they tie me up inside for a day. With the weather as bad as it has been we can't do much outside anyway. The roof also has started to leak on this old farmhouse and I talked to Mrs. Edgerly about it. She said she would send over Will Austin to take a look at it and hopefully fix it. If it can't be fixed then she said they would replace it. Fortunately I will not have to do that since it is her house. That at least is one of the advantages of renting rather than owning. When I talked to her, she said she was interested in extending the lease another year from April 1st 1910 until April 1st 1911. Mazie and I are not sure we want to commit ourselves that long at this point as we still have our hearts set on a place of our own, bad roofs or not.

It finally has cleared up some and the mud is not quite as deep as it was a few days ago. I think Maude thinks it is still too muddy to work in the fields but I didn't give her any choice. I told her if she didn't pull her weight she was not going to visit Charlie Shepherd's stallion again and that seemed to get her attention. I haven't seen her pull the plow with so much enthusiasm in a long time. It is amazing what a little incentive will do even with a horse. Now if you believe all that I have a bridge in Brooklyn I would like to sell you. Since we are able to get out, I hired Floyd Wilcox to help me and we spent a day and a half spraying the orchard. I paid him 75 cents a day and gave him supper and the second day we only worked half a day so he did not get supper that day. Fortunately I did even though Mazie was a little upset with me. She was upset since Nellie has had to leave our employment and go and live with her aunt who has rheumatism. That is a debilitating disease and she is needed more there than with us. Mazie has been on my case to hire a replacement to help her with the children and the house but they are difficult to find, especially a dependable one and I really don't have the time now to spend looking for someone. Mazie will make sure shortly however that I do find the time and find someone to help her or I may be sleeping in the barn with the cows.

We have had some money coming in from the sale of milk and the sale of cream to the Jeff. Co. Creamery. It all helps but even so I had to hit up my friendly banker Harry for another short-term loan of $50.00. As usual Harry came through and I told him I would repay it in about 30 days. It seems farmers never have enough money to keep them going between selling crops or livestock. Even on top of all this, the old Wizard Plow that I had bought from old man Chase a couple of years ago has broken down after so much work and is no longer repairable. I sometimes wonder why the equipment breaks down but I seem to be able to keep going. Muscle and bone is sometimes stronger than steel. I went out and negotiated with the farm coop to try a new Leroy

Plow for a couple of days to see if I want to buy it for $10.00. Harry's loan will come in handy as I certainly have to have one and hopefully this will be a good one that will last a little longer than old man Chase's did. At least there is some good news as Mrs. Edgerly has hired Mr. Austin to replace the roof and he is starting as the weather allows. It will be nice to get it replaced as it had been giving us trouble. Baby Howard is not feeling well and we certainly don't need a leaky roof in the house where we are raising our children, and especially one that is so vulnerable as the baby at this stage of their life. Mazie has been so worried about him that she called Dr. Brownell to come to the house and look at him. As it turned out it was just a very bad cold and hopefully with some skunk grease and rest he will soon be good as new. As a parent you always worry that something bad has taken hold of your loved one and it is such a relief when you find out from the doctor that it is nothing to worry about.

This month did not end on a high note. We sold the Atlantis Calf to Commiskey who butchered it and he reported to me that he could not use it, as he was sure it was badly infected with Tuberculosis. Since this can be passed from cows to humans I was terribly concerned and immediately wrote to V. C. Beeby in Arcade, NY to inform them. They oversee the farming business for this area for the State Agricultural Dept. I sent them the following letter: " Dear Sir, One of our local butchers bought a calf from me today and after dressing it he said that it was badly infected with tuberculosis. I have 6 cows and this is the first indication of anything being wrong with them, but thought it best to notify your office at once. Yours Truly, Ben. C. Tyler.

Being a good citizen I most certainly want to follow all the necessary procedures when it comes to keeping a healthy herd of cattle and especially since the milk could be infected and pass the disease on to humans. It seems they are also concerned because I heard from them almost immediately and they requested that I send a certified and notarized letter to Albany indicating our findings. The state government has a program whereby they immediately investigate and if a herd is found to be infected they are destroyed and the farmer is reimbursed by the state. Since some unscrupulous farmers might not report sick cattle if they thought they would suffer a financial loss, the program insures that all livestock owners will comply. I am not concerned about the loss, only about the safety of the herd and the milk we are selling, and of course that even our own children are consuming.

The state has decided to send a veterinarian out to investigate and if the herd is found to be sick, then we will have to round them up, shoot them all and burn and bury the carcasses. I am not looking forward to that. After awhile one becomes somewhat attached to the animals and each one seems to have a personality of their own. Any such minor attachment, however, is out the window when it comes to something like this. In the interim time, while I await the state veterinarian, I will have to dispose of all the milk in the proper fashion so that it does not fall into the consumers' hands. This will set us back some but the financial setback is the least of my worries. I may have to end up going back to the well, Harry, for another loan. Even though the state will reimburse us, it may take awhile to get the money and in the meantime we will be shorter than normal.

Since I sometimes wonder if Harry gets a little tired of being our banker, I decided to write my brother Robert and see if he could help us out some over this rough time. Unfortunately he wrote back and asked for a loan from me so I guess he is not in a position to help at this time. Harry will have to be our bank of choice. I am making sure we all attend church as often as possible here in June of `09 as all the prayers we can muster are needed now in the hope that our cows are not infected. As I mentioned, it would be a setback even though the state would eventually reimburse us. As tough a father as I am though, I couldn't force Dorothy to go this Sunday as she had a sprained ankle and even though the cows are important, her getting well is so much more important. As I have often said, family comes first and foremost always. The rest of us did attend and heard a rousing sermon from the Reverend Dibble who preached on Elijah's discouragement. Just the kind of sermon I needed to lift my spirits in these trying times. Talk about Elijah's discouragement, what about Benjamin's discouragement? I decided not to go back to church in the evening but Mazie, Robert, Marion and Margaret went and I stayed home with baby Howard and Dorothy and we all pitched in and fixed a fine supper for the family. Mazie was pleasantly surprised and even commented how good everything was. I am sure it was not as good as Mazie's cooking but she was gracious enough to let on that it was a fine meal. It is nice to be able to reap the benefit of all those things that we planted and stored in the root cellar and that we are planting again this year in the garden. I don't believe there is any seed that we have not planted so we will be getting a wide variety of all of our harvest again this year as we have in the past.

I received a letter from Albany that they will be sending out Dr. Smith from Arcade to check on the health of the cows. In the meantime, I sold the Purcell Calf to Mr. Hodge for 7 cents per pound and he is to take her after Dr. Smith comes out and hopefully gives them a clean bill of health. Mr. Hodge said he had every confidence that the rest of the herd was clean and he wasn't worried. Since worry is my middle name, I wish I could be as sure as he is. The calf weighed 200 lbs. so the money will come in handy if the deal goes through.

I have a surprise birthday present here on my 42nd birthday on June 15. Dr. Smith showed up and he and I took the temperature of all the cows at 3-hour intervals this afternoon. If someone were to ask me what the least enjoyment would be on my birthday it would most likely be taking the cows' temperatures every 3 hours for the day. However when you are in the farming business, either the weather or the animals dictate your time and you have little choice otherwise. After we took their temperatures and recorded them, Dr. Smith injected each of the cows with a modified form of tuberculin. This was made from cultures grown from samples taken from infected animals. He said if an animal was infected with TB he would get a reaction at the injection site of a large, hot lump, and the animal would spike a fever within 24 hours. He and I then checked their temperatures again, at 12:30 AM, 2:30 and again at 4:30AM. He left for Arcade the next day and told me to take their temperatures again, at least a couple of times, and report to him my findings. He felt there was no infection in the herd and that certainly lifted a heavy weight off my shoulders. With the stress and the lack of sleep, I have been very concerned about falling into a depressed state but as it turned out, the good news was certainly an anti-depressant and the best kind of medicine. On top of all that, Snooper had a bull calf today. Now if you think I don't become attached somewhat to the cows, as I previously mentioned, how come I would name one Snooper. I don't dare tell you what the girls have named the others.

I have finally gotten some much needed rest and Mrs. McGregor and Mazie's brother Howard have come for a visit and to help me celebrate my 42nd. I certainly don't feel 42 years old and I think the hard work of farming keeps me feeling young. Howard went into town and brought all the TeWinkels out with another big surprise. The big surprise turned out to be ice cream and strawberries and you would have thought none of us had eaten in a month as we totally devoured the treat. It is surprising that some of the simplest things in life bring us so much pleasure. People seem to always be searching for life's pleasures when all along they are with us in the smallest ways. I had a fine birthday and am looking forward to many more with the good Lord's help. As an added bonus, I took the children fishing in the outlet and we caught about a dozen sunfish and 8 bullheads for a fine meal. We all had a great time and it was so much fun watching the girls pull in what they considered such big fish, another of life's true pleasures.

I have been helping my neighbors out this month as they have been helping me. I worked two days with Mr. Needham, drawing beets for him and he insisted on paying me $4.80 for my help and the use of my wagon. I told him I didn't want any pay and valued his friendship but he insisted, and we could also use the money. He is quite well off, it is rumored, so I guess he won't miss it and I appreciate his generosity. I borrowed Mr. McIntire's bean planter to drill and plant the bean crop and when I finished with it I told him I would take it to George Brown who also wants to borrow it to get his bean crop in. Fred Sherman also asked me if I would help him spray his 3 acres of oats, which have mustard in them, and he wants to try and kill it off. We used my sprayer and I helped him and it felt good to help out a neighbor as they are helping us.

Since I am hopefully finished this season with the drag, I took the opportunity on a rainy day to clean it up and paint it so it would be ready for its next assignment. I also started to paint the wagon and I wanted to get a new spoke put on one of the wheels. Robert took it over to J. Ireland's repair shop and he will install the new spoke for us. I also found a broken wheel on the cultivator and unfortunately it could not be fixed so I had Jay order me a new one. I hope it doesn't cost me too much but one has to keep his equipment in good order if he is to be a successful farmer.

A little more income is coming in this month with Lucy TeWinkel paying $1.80 for the 30 quarts of milk we furnished them in May and the Jeff. Co. Creamery paying $9.31 for the one hundred and fifteen and a half pounds of cream we sold them in May. Even though Commiskey couldn't use the meat from the Atlantis calf that had tuberculosis from the umbilical infection due to navel poisoning, he did want the hide and paid me $3.00 for it. At this rate I may not have to hit Harry up again for awhile. On top of this, Mrs. Jillette has expressed an interest in buying our property on Lake Street. We were hoping to hold off on selling this until we found a farm we wanted to buy so that we would have a good down payment on the new place. We do have some equity built up on the Lake Street home and if we could get the right price for it, we might sell it and put the money in the bank. The bank is paying so little interest that I hate to put any money in there. It almost seems it would be better off buried in the back yard. These bankers can sometimes be thought of as highway robbers without the masks. I guess though they can only pay interest as conditions warrant; otherwise they wouldn't be in business very long. Since there aren't many alternatives for our money if we sell the property, I guess it will be going in the bank after we settle our outstanding bills.

The month ended on a sad note as old man Brigham passed away and we all went to pay our respects to the Brigham's home where he was laid out in his finest in the parlor. It was a sad time for all and Mazie helped the ladies in the kitchen prepare some food for the rest of the family during this difficult time. They are very religious folks and so we are sure their faith will see them through this arduous time. Mazie commented that she was sure that he was in a better place with his God, as he had been a faithful Christian and family man all his life. He will be missed and he leaves a large hole in our community of the faithful.

The Wrights are planning on moving out of our Lake Street house in Sept. so we are seriously going to put it on the market. Several folks have expressed an interest in the property, including Mr. Jillette who has made a tentative offer of $4800.00 for it. We are not sure if that is enough and plan on having someone appraise it for us. That seems like a lot of money but with the rising real estate market of late I certainly don't want to sell it for less than it is worth. If we manage to get around $5,000 for it that will seem like we are millionaires for a period of time since we have not seen that kind of money in years. I would be interested in holding the mortgage for whoever buys the property except we are going to need the money for a down payment on a farm if we can find one that we like. It would be great to hold the mortgage as it would give us a steady income each month so we wouldn't have these high and low points all the time in our cash flow or lack of cash flow. We decided to take a look at the Marrow and Beardsley's farms, which I think could be bought, but neither one of them were what we really wanted. Time will tell and that is one thing we have plenty of. We can take all the time we want to see what is out there and make sure we do not make a mistake when the final decision is upon us. I have talked to a few folks over the years that have rushed into buying a property only to be disappointed later on and wish they had waited. With the good Lord's help, the right place for us to raise our family and continue our farming will come along.

I never realized just how busy I would be when I went into farming. This time of year is filled up with cutting hay, drawing hay, cultivating and still planting. It is a better medicine to keep one's mind occupied than all the cures all the doctors in the world could come up with. When your mind is filled with all these responsibilities, you just don't have time to feel sorry for yourself. Even the Reverend Will helped me cultivate beans and it was so great to have our minister helping and of course as my brother-in-law he is always ready to pitch in. Will never had any problem with depression so it must not run in his family. I sometimes envy him that he is so upbeat all the time. That is the way the Lord intended our ministers to be. Can you imagine going to church on a Sunday and listening to someone preach who is continually downhearted? I guess in His infinite wisdom He made Will a minister and I a farmer.

Robert is a tremendous help with all the work around here in July. Being off for the summer from school, he can spend a great deal of time helping me keep up with things. They always said that farmers have big families so that the children can help out in keeping the farm going. Our reason for having a fairly large family was certainly not for help on the farm as we had most of the children when we were shopkeepers. Our reason was that we wanted a large family to love, nurture and enjoy every day as they grew and matured to adults and of course to have their love and companionship when Mazie and I grow old. Robert is even finding time to hire out to several of the surrounding farms and pick up some money for himself in doing so. He is a hard worker, as I have said, and is getting paid 12 ½ cents an hour for his efforts. It seems like a lot of money per hour for a young fellow to be paid. I of course don't pay him and I am sure he would not expect it from his own family. Now if I was a wealthy man, I might see fit to pay him but since that is not the case, our love for each other will suffice.

We have added to our livestock here lately with Maude recently giving birth to a colt and the old sow had twelve little piglets. The girls were very excited about all the births and think that the twelve little piglets are the cutest. Twelve little piglets' sounds like a song title. Maybe I should give up farming and write songs. There is lots of money in that if you are successful, but alas I have no talent in that territory.

Church has been hit and miss this month. On the 18th we all attended, even little Howard, as it was the last regular service in the old church. We even all went back to the evening service to hear Will preach a fine sermon and reminisce about this church building and all the fine things that have happened here over the years. All the baptisms and all the weddings, and of course the funerals for those who have gone to a better place. There are so many memories it will be hard for us all to leave here for the last time. Will is bringing them in the door however, and we needed the extra space. That is the price of progress. I have always been someone who likes to cling to the past and the old ways and fortunately there are others that see the brightness of the future and are willing to take the necessary chances to see the brotherhood of the faithful grow. Mazie and all the children also enjoyed a fine church picnic down at Crystal Lake this month. I could not make it as I had to draw more hay in so Kit and I spent the day working in the fields and a beautiful day it was. It would have been even more beautiful at the lake with the family but it was pleasing to know that they were all also enjoying this day with so many friends. At the end of the month we all attended the Baptist Church while some finishing touches were being put on our new building and we heard a rousing sermon by the Reverend J. Addison Jones. Now that is a great name for a preacher and he sure could preach. He almost had my hair standing on end as he blasted away at all the sins of the world. When I got home I needed to sneak out to the barn for a little nip of that wine I have stacked out there.

We are broadening our search for farms and it doesn't seem any distance is too far to look. I am going to take the train up to Colchester, Conn. and look at a farm up there that a Mr. Backus has for sale. I heard about it from a mutual friend and he said he thinks it might be something we would be interested in. Mazie and I are not mentioning it to the children, as they would be upset to leave their school and their friends even though they would very quickly make new friends, I am sure as smart as they all are that they would adjust rapidly to a new school. Mazie insisted that I go down to the barber shop and get my ears lowered before I go as she said I should look presentable when I am travelling and representing our family and our community. I shelled out the usual exorbitant amount of 20 cents and did her bidding. I left on the morning train and met Mr. Backus at the station in Colchester, Conn. and they were gracious enough to put me up for the night. I think after looking over the farm that it may be something that we would be interested in if the price were right. Mr. Backus was even kind enough to take me on a side trip to New London and I spent a few hours there taking in the sights before taking the night train back home.

I have been trying to catch up with things around here from the time I missed from being away, and with the daily milking, delivery of over 70 pounds of milk a day and the cutting, cultivating and planting I can't find much time for anything else. I did sell Snoopers' calf. That is one of the names the girls and I named our cows and a fine name it is. Mr. Commiskey bought the calf and it weighed out at 143 pounds and he is to pay 7 cents a pound for it. He also bought 3 hogs, which weighed in at 133, 132 and 103 pounds and he will pay me 9 cents a pound for those. In addition, he took 20 hens and his total bill came to $52.85. The money from the calf and the hogs goes into the Edgerly and the Tyler account and since the hens are the girls, that money will go into the Tyler account only. I have even had Maude out working in the fields dragging the cultivator and it is the first time she has worked since she had the colt. I think that almost a month off from work after the ladies give birth is more than enough time. Some might think me harsh but the work never goes away, is always staring us in the face and we certainly don't want the ladies to get the idea that life is too easy. Speaking of giving birth, Pacific had a calf today and Robert and I are taking Snooper and Atlantic to Mr. Nevins' bull to see if we can continue on our string of successes in adding new stock to our farm. We were sidetracked on our trip however when we saw some dogs attacking Ed McDonald's sheep. They had killed one before we managed to drive them off. Ed was grateful for our help and asked me if we would go to town with him the next day and help identify the dogs that were responsible. We did go into town and found that one of the dogs belonged to the Turvillings and the other was a dog that the Kensers kept. We notified the local police and Ed agreed that as long as the dogs were kept confined that they did not have to be put down. The police said they would agree to that but told the owners that if they got out, they would then be put down. The problem of course with dogs is that once they become aggressive with sheep or any other farm animal they seem to have it in their blood and want to repeat their attacks. Ed was very forgiving in this case and I have a feeling if it were me I would have demanded that the dogs be put down or I would have taken matters into my own hands. All was not wasted that day however as we ran into F.D. Allen and he paid me the last 50 cents he owed on the display case. It is great to have that behind us.

I decided to take the train to Dover, Delaware and looked at several farms for sale there so I made a quick trip and checked them out. I didn't think it was in any way as good a farming area as was Colchester, even though it looked promising, and decided not to pursue that area anymore. I got home early Sunday morning in time to go to the Methodist Church and hear the Reverend Jones of Albany give a fine inspiring sermon. In the afternoon we decided to write to Mr. Backus and make him an offer on his farm in Conn. Mazie agreed with me that she would trust my judgement on the farm and it had better work out because if we buy it and move there and she does not like it I will hear about it forever. I am convinced it would be a fine home and farm so I wrote the following letter to him.

" Dear Sir, Your letter of the 6th inst., enclosing sketch, came to hand safely and I thank you for same. I went down to Delaware and looked at several farms there and found a fine farming country there. If you will consider an offer of $6500.00 for your farm and outfit I believe we might do business. I doubt whether we can leave here before April 1st next but if we can bargain I can pay you a reasonable sum down to bind same and we can arrange the other details. If you are willing to consider such a proposition kindly let me know and I will arrange to come to Colchester and go over the matter with you. With kind regards to Mrs. and Miss Backus and thanking you for your kindness to me while with you. I am, yours very truly, Ben. C. Tyler, August 10th, 1909."

We shall see what comes of this. When it gets right down to it, and you have submitted an offer, I already find I am getting cold feet and wondering if I have down the correct thing. I guess we will just wait for their response and take it from there. As I have often said, what will be will be. The Lord works in mysterious ways and we have always put our faith in Him.

Since we are getting serious about buying, I put our house on Lake Street in the hands of E. J. Webster to see if he could sell it for us. In the meantime, Mazie has gone to check out the Marrow Farm and I drove out to the Sopers farm to see if that would be anything we would want. After talking it over, we decided not to pursue either one of those and wait to here from Mr. Backus in Conn.

Church is becoming more and more a hit and miss proposition this summer what with the new construction and as busy as we all are. We did get a chance to go to the Baptist Church and hear the Reverend Waite Edgar Baggs preach. That is a fine name for a preacher and his sermon and delivery lived up to his name. It was almost as inspiring as hearing the Reverend Rust speaking from Rochester. I am sure if I thought about it for awhile I could come up with something about the Reverend Rust's name as a preacher and the sermons he could preach around his name. I believe there are some passages in the Bible referring to "turning to rust" but I would have to talk to Mazie about that, as she is by far the expert in the family on the Bible.

As the days move on here in August I am beginning to get cold feet about the Backus property. I can't imagine anyone putting in an offer on a piece of property and not having second thoughts about it after they had presented the offer. Is it the right thing to do or is a terrible mistake?

Mazie and I talked it over and decided to write Mr. Backus again since we had not heard from him yet and August is rolling to a close. "Dear Sir, Your letter in reply to mine asking if you would entertain a certain offer for your farm has not been answered promptly. As I have been obliged to change my plans somewhat and have been thinking over the matter. As things stand with me now, I cannot make you an offer, and do not see any way clear now to move from this section for some time to come. Thanking you for your kindness, I am truly yours, Ben C. Tyler."

Now that we have backed out of that one, I am sure I will wonder if that was the right thing to do. I find it so difficult to make up my mind, especially on such a big decision. One day I think we should move in a certain direction and the next day just the opposite. I will need to be on my guard not to get depressed over all this. I think everyone that we know and those that we are dealing with are beginning to wonder if we are really serious about moving or not. I guess I really don't care what they think as this is a big decision and we will not be rushed.

Mazie wants to look at Dr. True's farm in Castile so we decided to take a Sunday afternoon ride on this beautiful day and see if we could catch the good doctor at home as we have heard he is looking for a buyer for his property. Unfortunately no one was home so we came on back and I decided to write him the following letter. "Dear Sir, We called at your farm on our way home from Castile but there was no one at home there so we did not get to see the farm or house. Cannot get away now for some weeks as have so much work to do now, but will try to see your farm later. Would you rent for a year with an option to buy? Mr. Nevins, your cousin, can tell you about me. Yours truly, Ben C. Tyler."

We shall see what comes of this letter and if he would be willing to let us try it for a year to see if we want it after that. I am sure it would cost us a fairly large option to do it that way and I can't even decide if that is the way we should go. Sooner or later, with the Lord's help, we will settle on something. I need to get back to farming and get my mind off this tremendous decision on buying and possible moving. It seems it is the only thing I can think about all the time. That is not healthy to constantly dwell on one thing so often. I work all day thinking about it and then I go to bed at night and think about it some more and it keeps me awake.

I hitched up Maude to the plow and we dragged all day on the 20-acre lot and it helped me a great deal. The fresh air and hard work seemed to clear my mind. Even Maude looked like she was enjoying the work and the outing on such a beautiful day. I also spent several days picking pears with Willard Nevins helping me and we delivered over two thousand pounds of them to Pavilion and received $54.25 for the account of Edgerly and Tyler. Robert picked up all the fallen ones and went into town and sold them for $3.77. That boy sure has a good business head on his shoulders. Harry was here with his family and they also helped Robert with the sales. It was good to have them here and I hated to see them leave on the train on the 5:05 special to Virginia. Maybe Harry came to check on his money that he is always loaning me, make sure it is in good hands and I am not spending it foolishly. Seriously, it is great to have them visit and I am sure my suspicions about his checking up on me are misplaced. At least I hope they are.

Can you believe I also hired out as a helper to Willard to help with the thrashing of his oats and wheat and then I paid the thrashers $14.05 to thrash 185 bushels of oats and 345 bushels of wheat for me? I like to keep meticulous records, as you may have surmised by now, so the following is the breakdown of the wheat sales.

Statement of 345 bushels of wheat sold Sept. 1909
Used for seed 22 bushels
Sold to Tomlinson & Son-282 ½ bus. @ $1.03 = $291.06
Sold to Peter Nugent – 20 bus. = $20.60
Sold to Wm. TeWinkel – 5 bus. = $5.15

Screenings (551 lbs.) – 11 ½ bus.
Shortage to make threshers measure – 4 bus.
Total = 345 bushels ---- $316.81
Check enclosed to Mrs. Edgerly for ½ of amount = $158.42

Every time I do the accounting and send a check to Mrs. Edgerly I wonder why I am giving half of everything when I am doing 99% of the work. Now don't get me wrong, she is a wonderful landlady and has been very agreeable to work with but it sure makes me think again about getting our own place and then all deposits would be to the account of Tyler & Tyler. That sort of sounds good to me.

We have managed to make church on a regular basis this month and we paid our systematic beneficence for the month. We all attended church on the 26th as the TeWinkel girls who are only 5 and 7 years old are headed for India with a group of folks from a neighboring church group. I think they are a little young to be heading off to another part of the world but alas, Lucy and William didn't ask my opinion. Most likely I am a little jealous that we cannot afford to send our children also. It should be an exciting time for them. I can only dream of places like that. I have always suspected there is a little old family money on the TeWinkel side since Will certainly doesn't make enough money as our pastor to be able to afford this type of trip for his children. The girls are very excited about going. I would be a nervous wreck if it were I going that far from home. I envy their composure.

Here, near the end of the month we are getting back to looking for farms and thinking about moving. We decided to put the Lake Street home on the market for sure this time and the realtor advised that we ask $4300.00 for it. I should have taken Mr. Jillette up on his offer of $4800 a month or so ago but I got greedy and thought it was worth more. In the meantime he went and purchased another piece of property. The Wrights have paid their rent in full and have moved out so it is sitting empty. They tell me that it is always harder to sell an empty house as compared to one that is being lived in. George called and told me he had heard about a farm or two for sale in a little town north of here called Palmyra. I took a little time and caught the 6:45 AM train and arrived there about 10:30. I checked out a couple of places and caught the 3:30 train and arrived home at 7 PM. I thought it was a nice farming community and found one farm that I really liked. Mazie will have to take a trip up there and check it out also. My only concern with Palmyra is that it was the birthplace of the founder of the Mormon Church, Joseph Smith, and Mazie has always frowned on any religion outside Presbyterian as not a really true religion. Only time will tell whether the Mormon Church attracts more converts than the Presbyterians and only God knows which ones are the true religions of Christ. My best guess is that all believers regardless of church affiliation are good people in the eyes of our Savior. I think maybe I will just not mention anything about this to Mazie at this time. We will see where this road takes us. It is time to take a break from all this anyway. Mazie and I have decided since I had a fainting spell here at the end of the month, that maybe I had better slow down a little. We think it is from stress, overwork and constantly having this decision on my mind. Stress is a surefire road to health problems. Doc. came out and checked me out and said I was as fit as a horse. I wasn't sure if he meant in mind or body.

I could well say without exaggerating that Oct. is the "Month of the Apple." Between Robert, when he is not in school, and myself I have never seen so many apples picked by so few people in such a short time. I must admit that I hired Mr. Sharp and Mr. Lockwood to help us, as we are overwhelmed with apples this year. Here I am complaining when we have a bumper crop. You would think I would be grateful and not complaining. I would say it is a farmer's lot in life to never be satisfied with the way things are at any given time. This is particularly true of the weather, as I have often said. I will be grateful when we sell them all and I have time to rest my weary bones from all the picking. We are doing about 100 bushels a day and it seems to go on and on. We pick a tree bare one day and the next it seems to have flourished all over again. I'm sure what I am seeing is another tree, as they all look the same by this time. Maybe I should name each tree, like I did our cows, so I can keep track of which ones are picked. Pick Anne this day and Penelope tomorrow and so forth. I guess that isn't such a good idea since there are so many of them and I would be spending all my time naming them instead of enjoying their fruits.

We have contracted with Mr. Bert to take them all after we finish picking and packing them and he is to pay us $3.00 a bushel for the first and second quality ones. Even Reverend Will came out a couple of days and helped us and it is certainly appreciated. I never knew that ministers were pickers of fruit as well as being pickers of men. Will does both equally well. We are taking the fallen apples to the evaporator in Perry and getting 50 cents per 100 pounds of them. We have delivered several thousand pounds of them already and have more to pick up.

So much for harvesting since there are other things going on in our lives this month. Unfortunately not all is well as Dr. Brownell came out and checked on Margaret and he announced that she has the measles. He also checked me out again and said everything was fine and I should learn how to handle stress better. Easy for him to say. We are hoping none of the other children come down with the measles. She is quite sick and we are doing all we can to keep her comfortable. Someday maybe mankind will be able to eradicate all these diseases and they will not be such a worry. I sometimes wonder if mankind is successful in eliminating some that others may crop up in their place that no one have ever heard of. We all went to church except Mazie and Margaret and said an extra prayer for Margaret's speedy and full recovery. I paid our $5.00 contribution to the new church building fund as well as our regular pledge.

Mrs. Edgerly and I have decided to buy 100 lambs as an investment for the winter months so they were ordered and should arrive later this month. I also sold the pacific calf for 8 cents a pound and received a check for $13.84 for Edgerly and Tyler accounts. I used some of my money to go to town and buy a pair of gum boots for $3.50 and two shirts for 90 cents and I even bought a package of cigars for 5 cents. I will have to keep them well hidden from Mazie but I find an occasional cigar calms my nerves so I will sneak one when I am alone out in the fields. If she caught me smoking again she would tan my hide. I guess if that is my only sin I am not doing so badly. She would, I am sure, not see it that way however.

We have rented the home on Lake Street to Mr. Wiltse for $5.00 per week. We have had no offers from anyone to buy it so I decided it best to rent it out for the time being. We also received a letter from Mr. Griswold and his wife, Romana in Palmyra about the farm I looked at. Mazie and her mother decided to take the 6:45 A.M. train to Palmyra and look at the farm for themselves. They arrived back on the 7:30 P.M. express and said that they liked the farm very much and I was to proceed to purchase it. Just like that, the ladies made up my mind about where we are moving. I have almost driven myself to drink and illness worrying about this decision, and the ladies make one quick trip and come home and the matter is settled. Maybe that is for the best because I could not go on forever struggling with this decision on where and what to buy. Will said he would go with me so we took the early train to Palmyra and I signed the deal to buy it for $4,500.00. The deal should close, hopefully, sometime early next year. When we got home, we all went to church and Will led us in prayer for success in our new endeavor. We will surely miss the TeWinkels and the church here in Perry but it is time to move on. It isn't that we are moving so far away that we cannot visit often and we will even try and get here on occasion to hear Will preach. It may be quite awhile before we move anyway so I guess I will not worry about things like that at this point. I do need something to worry about though or things would not seem normal for me.

It sure will be good to see our labors go to the account of Tyler and Tyler instead of Edgerly and Tyler. I didn't mention to Mazie the fact that Palmyra was the home of Joseph Smith and the birthplace of the Mormon religion as I am sure Mazie will most likely unearth that soon enough and then we can deal with it. She did check out the churches on the main four corners in Palmyra and did find the Presbyterian Church, which made her feel right at home. I am sure all the Mormon neighbors will be most kind and considerate and the type of neighbors a family would love to have. In fact, this farm we are buying is right next door to the old Martin Harris farm. Martin Harris was the follower of Joseph Smith that furnished the money to print the Book of Mormon for the first time in Palmyra. Here I am going on and on about this and you might wonder if I was thinking about converting. If that ever happened I would be a single fellow so quick that I wouldn't know what hit me. As I have said, Mazie thinks the sun rises and sets on Presbyterians only. Not to misunderstand me, she is a fine, God loving woman who would be a great asset to any church she was affiliated with.

Nov. of 1909 has dawned bright and clear and I pray it is a precursor to a fine, healthy and happy month for our little family and the people of Perry, New York, New York State, this great United States and the entire world. There, I guess I have covered it all. If only I had the power to make it all come true. Since things are starting out so fine I decided to place an order with Sears, Roebuck and Co. and amongst other things we ordered was a first suit for Robert. He is excited about getting it and can't wait for it to arrive. In fact, I am feeling high in spirits, and I sure wish I could feel this way all the time so I suggested we all go chestnutting for half a day and stock up on some horsechestnuts. This was followed be a delicious roast pig dinner at the Baptist Church in the evening. We all came away with our stomachs filled as provided by our Baptist brothers and sisters. Now as Mazie would say when everyone else was out of ear shot: "it is all well and good for our Baptist brethren to fill our stomachs as long as they don't try and fill our minds and souls with their brand of beliefs." As I have previously said, Mazie is a true believer in the Presbyterian faith.

The apple picking, packing and shipping has just about been rapped up. It was a successful year with the apples and the weather cooperated during the harvest, but I am just as happy to see it over with, as it is backbreaking work. I certainly could never have done it without all the help from Robert and Will and I do not want to forget S. O. Sharp, a fine worker who worked for me a number of days. I want to tell you that there is much good in everyone as proven today when I ran into Mr. Sharp at the Baptist dinner and he paid me $1.00 which he said was an overpayment I had made when I gave him his wages for his help in picking apples. A person as honest as he is will have a special place in heaven. That small gesture of kindness and honesty made us all feel that we were proud to be part of this community with it's honest God-loving people.

Now that the apples are finished, it is bean time and we have drawn, sacked and delivered so many sacks of beans that I have almost lost track. I am sure as you read my story you realize that I try to never lose track of anything we do. I have a record of every last sack of beans delivered and sometimes I am tempted to keep track of every last bean but even I admit that would be going too far.

Our home on Lake Street is taking quite a bit of my time as the furnace is broken down and I need to fix that and some of the plumbing in the kitchen is also in need of repair. Our tenants are not shy about calling whenever there is a problem and I guess I can't fault them for that since they are paying $5.00 a week for the rent. I am sure they feel that means everything is to be in working order. Sometimes I do wish however, for the small things, that they would just pick up their toolbox and fix it rather than call me. Speaking of fixing things, Mrs. Edgerly has been talking to me about her well water as it not tasting just right and she asked me if I could clean it out for her. It would be hard for me to refuse her since she has been such a great landlady. Therefore I undertook that little gem of a job here on a cold miserable day. It is not easy to crawl down a 30-foot hand-dug well and make sure your feet do not slip from one rock to another. Since I am not a very big fellow in girth, I managed and was down it in no time, it wasn't too long before I found her problem. She had two dead rabbits in the well and I am sure they were not adding a great deal of good taste to the water. Once I got them out and she pumped a lot of water from it to clear it, the water seemed fine, although I let her test it and took her word for it. I want to say that the old expression, "colder than a well digger's ass," is rooted in fact. Anyone who has climbed down into a 30 foot deep stoned up well in November to clean it out knows what I am talking about.

Our Sears' order finally arrived and you could not imagine the pride in Robert's face when he modeled his new suit that we had bought him. He will certainly have to fight the ladies off now, as he is a handsome young man at age 13. I do hope however that he waits a few more years before he becomes too interested in the young ladies. What an experience awaits him as he starts that part of his journey through life. As I look back on those days I wish I could repeat them but alas it is not the way of things.

Getting back down to earth, I have had to take Maude and Jack to the blacksmith to get new shoes put on all around. For the 8 shoes, it cost me $2.80, but I think it is a good investment on these fine steeds. Old man Huningtonn came by and wanted to look at Jack, maybe buy him and said he would be back with an offer. I am not sure if I could part with Jack as we have worked so hard together for so long we are almost attached at the hip. When he did come back, he brought his blind mare with him and wanted to trade me his blind mare for Jack. He must have thought I was born yesterday, or had recently been kicked in the head by a mule, to agree to such a trade. At least it was good for a laugh between Mazie and I after he had left with the blind mare. Maybe he can find someone else to trade him with but not this fellow.

Mrs. Edgerly and I have decided to invest in Wethers again so I ordered 75 of them and hopefully we will be here in Perry long enough for me to fatten them up so that we can sell them and make a nice profit. With the Palmyra farm on the horizon, I wonder how long we will be here. I can't just sit back and not do any work or invest in new animals or crops since the time line is unknown at the present. That would be an absolute path to bring back that old nemesis, depression, if I even slowed down even for a little while. I will keep moving full speed ahead and hope that the big "D" stays away. We also took Pacific to Mr. Nevins' bull and I was to pay him $2.00 for the bull's service but instead he asked me if I would work a couple of days helping him cut wood in exchange for the servicing of Pacific. Frankly I think his bull got the better half of this deal but I agreed and we spent 12 hours over two days cutting wood. I even broke my axe handle and had to buy a new one. Someday I certainly hope that job becomes easier. Maude's foot was hurt while we were helping Mr. Nevins haul some of the wood we cut so I had to get Dr. Davis to come out and he ended up blistering her foot. Hopefully that will take care of it and she will be fit as a fiddle shortly.

For a month that started out so great, it ended on a down note. I had to go to our "painless" Dr. Crocker and have one gold filling and three silver filings put in and Mazie had to have a gold filling put in. After drilling in my mouth until I could hardly stand it, and filling the teeth, Doc. had the nerve to charge me $4.00 for the five fillings. You would think enduring the pain would be pay enough. I guess even dentists have to make a living. On top of all that, Howard was threatened with an episode of the croup that we had to deal with. Mazie took him outside in the cool air in the night when it happened to help alleviate the problem while I rushed over to Dr. Brownell's for some medicine for him. Mazie sat and rocked him in the cold on the porch until his throat became less restricted, his breathing became easier and finally his cough eased up after we gave him some of Doc's medicine. The image of a mother sitting on a porch in the cold of a November night and rocking her child who is sick paints a wonderful picture of the true meaning of love. Fortunately by morning, with tender loving care, he was fine again. Those are scary times, no one needs them, and hopefully they are few and far between.

We cannot end this month without a wonderful Thanksgiving meal with the TeWinkels and I dressed a couple of 8 pound turkeys, we all feasted and had a wonderful time celebrating and being thankful for all of God's blessings on this day of thanksgiving. The meal was A-1, and that is tops in my book. We ended the month at a symbolic service of laying the cornerstone for the new church. We paid our last $5.00 pledge toward the new building and that finished our $25.00 commitment that we had agreed to. The month started on a high note, had a few potholes along the way and ended on a high note. What more can a man ask for in this life?

Earl Jenkens has contacted our lawyer E. J. Webster to see if we would consider trading our house on Lake Street for his house on St. Helena Street. I hope this isn't the same kind of deal where old man Hunningtonn wanted to trade his blind horse for Jack. We are not familiar with Earl's house and will have to find some time to check it out. I am not sure I want to get involved in such a deal since we will not be in Perry too much longer. It is a small house near the Tempest Knitting Mills and we will think it over carefully. I plan on keeping our options open. It's bad enough to pay the town tax on the property that we do own on Lake Street. Maybe the smaller house would have fewer taxes; however, I am not sure it would be worth as much as our home on Lake. I did just get the town tax bill for that house and it came to a whopping $12.93. Even though it was down considerably from last time it is still too high. Politicians love to find ways to spend our money and those politicians in Perry are no exception.

Mazie insisted I get my suit cleaned for the Sunday services so I took it to H. S. Penn, the dry cleaners and they did it for me for $1.25. Maybe I should be a dry cleaner, as it seems there is pretty good money in it. Mazie said it looked fine so we all went to church with me in my newly cleaned suit and enjoyed a fine sermon by Will. In the afternoon we went back and partook of communion and in the evening we all went to the Baptist Church and heard a rousing sermon by the Reverend Waite Edgar Baggs. That man can make the walls rock with his sermons. I'm not sure if I agree with him always and frankly like the more reformed and less robust sermons that Will gives. It seems that Will can move us without all the screaming and thumping, but the Baptists here in Perry are famous for their fiery sermons. One thing one will never do is fall asleep during one of Reverend Baggs' sermons. About every 5 minutes he will yell out "HELLO" and if anyone was nodding off they sure will wake up fast. We also attended a fine children's Sunday School program for the Christmas celebration. Robert played a part and the twins performed as usual with dignity and grace. Maybe we should have named them Dignity and Grace instead of Dorothy and Margaret.

Brother-in-law Howard sent me a subscription to the farm encyclopedia and I have read it with a great deal of interest. You farm for a few years and think you know all the answers and then you get something like this, read it over and realize you don't know hardly any of the answers, let alone the questions. It is good to get a reference like this as it makes you think rather than just do things the same way time after time. I was so impressed with the book that I decided to take a day and attend the local farmers' institute and it was a great program with speakers and demonstrations from the local, county and state representatives. I think I will try and become more involved in this type of educational program when we move to Palmyra.

It has been a fairly busy month with the milk sales and I also sold some hogs for Mrs. Edgerly and Tyler at $5.00 each. I had to have new shoes put on Jack also. The biggest problem I had with the animals this month was when Jack got cast in his stall and panicked and I had a devil of a time getting him calmed down and freed up. That is a scary situation, and not being able to comprehend their situation, they easily panic. After getting Robert to help me, we finally got him freed up and he seemed no worse for the ordeal. It is pretty hard to try and move an animal weighing hundreds of pounds when he doesn't want to move but Robert was very good with him, seems to be able to talk to him calmly and Jack seemed to respond to him. That is a gift that few people have.

Mrs. Edgerly is starting to get inquiries into renting the farm when we leave. We have had Mr. Austin come by and check it out and also Mr. Hillflicker called to look at it. I can't imagine any one of them being as good tenants as Mazie and I and anyone being as hard a worker as I but time will tell. It is always nice to think of yourself as at the top of your game and I am sure Mrs. Edgerly will miss us as we will surely miss her. She has been a kind and considerate landlady and we will always be in her debt, figuratively, not literally I hope. I decided to spend some time weather stripping and sealing all the windows since I am sure we will not be moving for a month or so. It has gotten really cold and we need to seal up for the season and keep old man winter outside.

Robert bought some traps and the other day he caught a skunk in one of them. I don't think we will skin it and eat it. I suggested to him that he abandon that trap for good and hope his others produce something that is edible and not as fragrant as this creature. Even the TeWinkels' children wanted to see the skunk but decided it was a little fragrant even for their curious minds. They are staying with us while their papa and mama attend the Whitenack and Cole wedding. I am sure, even though Will is not doing the service, he will be called upon to say a prayer or make some other remarks as he usually is.

As the last month of 1909 winds down, Mrs. Edgerly called and said that she was renting the farm to Mr. Hillflicker. I think she made a good choice and I hope that their relationship will be as fine as ours was. I wrote to Mr. Griswold to see if we could settle on a date to move in to the new place in Palmyra and said we would like to make it the first of March. Hopefully that will work out for everyone. I also wrote to Aetna, and Mutual Ben. Life Ins. Company to see how much money I could borrow on my life insurance polices. I also wrote the Penn Mutual to see when I might expect the check from them for the money I borrowed on that policy. I think we will need every penny we can get our hands on when it comes time to move and get started in our own farming business. I may even have to hit up my favorite banker Harry for a short-term loan. Harry always comes through.

Here it is almost Christmas time in 1909 and Mazie and I and the children gathered together the gifts we had purchased for Mazie's Mom in Bellaire, packed them up and sent them out. The box weighed eight pounds and it cost me 85 cents to send it express. We also sent a box of gifts to Mazie's brother Howard at Columbia University in New York City. We also all went on our annual Christmas tree-cutting excursion, even pulling baby Howard on the sleigh. We cut two fine trees, one for us and one for the TeWinkels. The children are all excited as we received a box of gifts from Bellaire and also one from Howard and they can't wait to open them. Along with the gifts that Mazie and I bought the children, I think they are in line for a great treat on this day that the Lord has given us to celebrate the birth of the Baby Jesus.

We waited until Christmas Eve to decorate the tree and I also dressed two turkeys for tomorrow's festivities with the TeWinkels. None of us were disappointed as the box from Bellaire held 42 presents including $5.00 that Mrs. McGregor sent me plus a knife, and the children all received fine presents that they were very excited over. I also received a shirt from Harry and Margaret and will wear it proudly. We all gather around the pot-belly stove after such a fine meal and Will led us in a prayer to thank the Lord for a healthy 1909 and a prosperous, successful and healthy 1910. This next year holds a great deal of adventure for Mazie, I and the children as we will be moving to our own farm and taking up residence in a new and unknown community. Let us pray that our decision was the correct one.

Chapter 4

1910

Halley's comet returns after 76 years
Mark Twain dies at 76 yrs. of age

After 76 years we are now experiencing Halley's Comet in the skies. This is the best known of all comets and appears every 76 years. Many people are upset over its reappearance but it has been coming around every 76 years since they have calculated around 240 BC. There is a lot of speculation that it is a bad omen but I look at as just another great mystery of the universe and the world God has created for us.

So much for my incite into the universe, my opinion of the influence of Halley's Comet most likely will not be listened to in the scientific field so I guess I will just keep it to myself and go back to farming and raising a family. These are the important things.

Mazie has not been feeling very well these past few days with bad headaches. I sure hope there is nothing seriously wrong. We all attended church and left Mazie home to recuperate and we decided to take Howard with us so that she could have some quiet time for a while. In the evening I drove Will to Castile in the cutter so that he could fulfill his preaching duties at the Presbyterian Church there. The Reverend Pearson is out for awhile so other pastors are filling in for him. We didn't get home until 11 PM and it was, to say the least, a very cold ride as it is seven below zero out. Someday maybe they will have heaters in the means of transportation people use. I suppose then that people would tend to get soft and not stand up to the elements as we have to. It sure would be nice though.

Margaret, Dorothy and I took the train into Rochester and Dr. Bissell gave her an eye exam and determined that she needs glasses. He charged $5.00 for the exam and gave us a prescription for the glasses. We stopped at the eyeglass store and they said they would fill the order tomorrow and send them to us. It cost me the exorbitant price of $3.00 for the glasses but it is best she gets them as she was having some difficulty doing her school work and that is so important. I took the girls to the Jackson Temperance Hotel for supper and that cost me 35 cents for each of us. The girls were thrilled going out to a big hotel for supper so it was well worth the money. We arrived home tired but happy on the 7:15 train. It is so satisfying to spend the day with the children; I don't do it often enough. On top of the glasses our medical bills keep adding up, as Mazie had to go back to "painless" Dr. Crocker for some additional fillings. Mazie doesn't seem to mind the drilling and filling like I do. She is made of stronger stock I guess, or she has a higher tolerance for pain than I do. I think it is one of the most unpleasant experiences to get one's teeth drilled.

The weather here in January has been cold with a lot of snow. It has kept me confined to working around the house and barn most of the time. It is hard to keep as busy as I would like to this time of year with this weather so my depression has returned. I have been trying to keep as busy as possible, driving the children to school in the cutter and I even did some work for Miss Nevins, cutting, hauling and stacking wood for her. I worked 6 and ½ hours for each of two days and cut, hauled and stacked 10 cord of wood for her. She paid me generously for the work and if the truth were known I would most likely have been willing to do it for nothing just to keep busy. Dr. Benjamin Tyler (???) has determined that the secret of keeping depression from your doorstep is to keep busy. Maybe I should hang up my shingle, give out advice on such mental problems and take advantage of my personal experiences in this area.

I have ordered 1630 pounds of coal from Fanning and Co. and it cost me $4.89. They charge $6.00 per ton delivered. It is well worth it this cold weather even though we go through it very fast when it is below zero out. After I took delivery of the coal, Nevins asked me if I would help him drive his sheep to the railroad station and I jumped at the chance to occupy my time. Of course he could have taken a couple dollars off the coal bill for the help but alas he did not. It's too bad that some of the work that is always there in the spring, summer and fall cannot be spread into the winter months also. That way I could stay busy all year round but not be so swamped in the good weather.

We have had a couple of people express an interest in the Lake Street home. Mr. Towne and Mr. Austin are working up an offer and I agreed to sell it to them for $4,000 if it were cash and $4,100 if it were not. I even told the realtor that I would pay him an extra $25 on top of his commission if he could get it sold for us. You may recall that we had the offer awhile ago for $4,800, which I decided was not enough at the time and here we are thinking of selling it at $4,000. What a great real estate tycoon I would make. At the time, Mazie said we should grab that offer but I, thinking I was so smart decided to hold out. I can't understand why I don't listen to her more often. She is so much smarter than I am about so many things. Of course I don't let on to her that she is or I would hear about it all the time. She has the grace not to remind me that I held out for more than the $4,800 offer, which was a big mistake. I am sure she thinks about it but is too much of a lady to rub it in.

Talk about a mistake, I would have to classify February of 1910 as the month of frenzy for me. The old adage "we grow too soon old and too late **shmart**" sure holds true for me. I am so worried that we will be moving to Palmyra and not have sold our old home on Lake Street. I am putting a lot of pressure on our lawyer, Mr. Webster, to find a buyer or buy it himself. As the local lawyer and realtor, he should be able to come up with something. I now realize that all the potential buyers are figuring, rightly so, that our backs are up against the wall since we are moving, so they are holding out to squeeze the price as low as they can. This is not the way it should be and if I were smarter I would have sold it before anyone knew we were moving. You would not think that all these old "friends" in Perry would try and take advantage of us since we are moving but alas money is a great motivator. I think sometimes friendship goes out the window when it comes to the almighty buck. Here I am blaming our friends and neighbors when it is really my fault and mine alone. It is enough to drive me to drink.

I have shown the house to Miss Bullen but she told our lawyer that the tenants gave the furnace a bad name so she was not interested. Can't blame them I guess since they have had some problems with it. It is very cold here in early Feb. and the thermometer has been as low at 18 below, and it has stayed in the minus zero category a number of days. They all know that I do not want to own this house in Perry when we move as the maintenance on it would all have to be contracted out since I would not be here to do it and that would cost us a fortune. Hawleys said their top price would be $3500 and I said I would not let it go that low. I offered it to the Eatons and also the Websters for $3800 but they are not biting. Mr. Webster finally offered us $3500 and I have countered at $3675. This is sure a far cry from the $4800 we could have gotten for it a few months ago.

All this fortunately hasn't driven me to drink but it has driven me to church. I really shouldn't say driven since the church calls me rather than my being driven there. We attended church on the 4th, 5th, 6th, 7th, 8th, 9th and the 13th, 14th, 15th and 16th this month. We also made it on the 20th for communion and went back to hear the Baptist minister in the evening. I wouldn't think it would be hard for you to imagine what I was asking the Lord's help with in all these church services. Will has been comforting me somewhat in this time of trial and with his help I think we will eventually get through it. It is stressful enough to think that we will be leaving here shortly to start a whole new life in Palmyra without having sold our house on Lake Street. Maybe this is the Lord's way of letting us go from this place without so much regret to leaving, after the hassle we are getting from old acquaintances over the home. The Lord works in mysterious ways and one should never question Him.

There are a few other things going on this month with heavy milk sales to Hubbard and Waite and we also sold the Phillip's cow to Mr. Beardsley. The Wright heifer had a calf and I had to have a new shoe put on Kit. These small things remind me that life goes on even through difficult times. We should always look ahead and never backwards. We cannot change the past but we can certainly influence our future and we should never lose sight of that.

Mazie, the children, when they are not in school, and I are beginning to pack up things for the upcoming move. It is a good time of the year for a farm family to move if any time is a good time as there is not so much fieldwork facing us in the middle of the winter. I even took the train to Palmyra, went to the auction at the Griswold's farm, and purchased quite a few items. It is a good thing that the First National Bank of "Harry" came through again as he just sent us a check for $200 as a loan to help tide us over until we get moved and settled in. What a kind and considerate brother Harry is. We will always be in his debt. Well, actually I hope not always if you get what I mean. Seriously Harry is truly a gem and a brother in the true sense of the word. The Griswolds were kind enough to invite me to spend the night. I was grateful and enjoyed their company and came home the next day on the 7:15 express.

As the month draws to a close, we are reminded that our days here are numbered as the Hillflickers are starting to move things into the home we have occupied for the past several years. We still haven't been able to sell the house on Lake Street and I have nightmares that as we board the train for Palmyra, Mr. Webster or someone else will come running up to us and offer us about $3000 for the house. We will be forced to take it, under the circumstances, but I am in the hopes that we can get more than that before we have to leave. If I ever trade in real estate again I hope I have learned an expensive lesson. Lord; help us out of this predicament that we find ourselves in at this point.

Several more families have looked at the Lake Street home but no one seems to be able to make up their minds on whether they want to put in an offer or not. I am hoping this nightmare will be over soon. Mazie has me hanging the rugs out, here in early March, and spending my days beating them clean. Every whack I take at them I imagine hitting myself for my stupidity on the real estate deal. Mazie says it is great therapy to be out here in the cold and beating on the rugs. She always knows best.

Halalulia, Mr. Webster called and he said that Mr. Donnelly has decided to offer $3,625.00 for the property and Mazie and I have jumped at it just to get that part of our "Journey

Through Life" over with. He is to pay us $200 down and the remainder in 10 days. Hopefully the bank will see fit to loan them the money and there will not be any more roadblocks thrown in our way. I had to pay Mr. Webster $47.50 in commission for selling it for us and Mazie and I signed the deed in the hopes it would seal the deal. Would you believe it after all this mess, Chief of Police Butler served me with a summons filed by Mr. Austin who claims that we owe him the sale commission on the property even though he was never able to sell it for us? Talk about nerve. I have paid L. A. Walker $10.00 to handle this for me since of course we will be moving shortly. I can't believe he has a leg to stand on. It sure tells you who your friends are when it comes to the almighty buck.

Mrs. Edgerly and I are settling up accounts and I paid her $123.59 to date and that should settle it all. She was kind enough to give me her half interest in the white sow, which we owned together, and so I am naming it Lady Edgerly. She also said we had been very satisfactory tenants and from her that is quite a compliment. I also told her she had been a very satisfactory landlady. We said our good-byes and we moved in with the TeWinkels for a few days prior to our move. Since the TeWinkels didn't have quite enough room for all of us, Robert and the twins moved in with the Nevins for a few days until we can get on the way. I received a letter from the Griswolds that they are moving out of the farm on Maple Avenue in Palmyra on the 14th instant and so we can move in any time thereafter.

We have most everything packed and I went to the Silver Lake Railroad Station and rented two rail cars for the move. One will carry the furniture and the other the livestock. The rail car for the furniture will cost me $26.40 and the livestock car will cost $44. Our plans are to load them up on the 15th and then I will head out, get some things settled in Palmyra, and the stoves set up before Mazie and the children follow. I have sent ahead to the First National Bank of Palmyra a check for $3500 to be deposited in a new account for us subject to a check on our character.

Well, here it is the big day and Mr. Nevins and his son and several other kind neighbors are helping me move the furniture, fixtures and the livestock to the rail siding. It is a cold and snowy day to be doing it but we have managed with a lot of hard work to get the job completed. Nothing worthwhile ever comes along without hard work and sweat. We all went to one last church service to pray, with Will's leadership, for our safe and successful trip in this new road that we have decided to travel.

I have said my fond farewells to all those kind neighbors and friends that we have here in Perry and I climbed aboard the 1:20 PM train and headed out with our possessions and stock for Rochester. We arrived in Rochester at 7 PM and had to spend the night there until we could hook up my two rail cars for the trip to Palmyra. I feel a little like Noah and his ark with all our stock. We loaded the 3 horses, 2 colts, 1 calf, 2 cows, 1 sow (Lady Edgerly), 28 chickens, 3 rabbits and a dog and a cat. What an uproar that many animals in one boxcar can make. I can't imagine how Noah did it.

I finally left Rochester at 5 AM after having paid 5 cents for a cup of coffee to sustain me and we arrived in Palmyra at 7 AM. I had made acquaintance with Abe Haak when I was in Palmyra before and he met me at the rail siding and helped me move everything to our new home. I got the stoves set up and the furniture in the house, contacted Mazie and told her I would meet her and the children in Rochester on the 19th and bring them all down to Palmyra. I am sure there will be some sad good-byes for Mazie and the children as they leave their friends in Perry but they are strong, will soon make new friends and adjust easily.

When I got to Rochester and found them, they were all quite excited about this new adventure so we headed out. Mr. Haak met us at the railroad and said he had supper all prepared for us all and we were to join them. He has been very kind and helpful and I tried to pay him for this help but he would have none of it. We had a wonderful supper with our new friends and then settled into our new home for the night. We all pitched in, set up the beds and I don't think it took us more that 2 minutes to all be asleep after a tiring but pleasant day.

It is Sunday morning in Palmyra but we are all too busy getting things organized to make church on this first Sabbath in Palmyra and we will thank the Lord for a safe trip here in our own way in our new home. Hopefully next Sunday we will be in attendance and we are looking forward to it. We did manage to get to town, which is about a mile from our farm. We bought groceries from Bowman and Sons, we bought some meat from

Thrasher's and we bought our bread from Parsons. I even received a check from the Penn Mutual Insurance Company for $609.87 on the 20-year endowment policy that I cashed in. This money will all be needed as we settle in here.

The animals all made the trip fine and we have them bedded down in the barn, with the dog and cat having taken over the house. I am putting up curtains, laying carpets and all sorts of household chores. Mazie and all the children are pitching in the best they can with the exception of Baby Howard who is mostly supervising. We also bought some post cards and are sending them to those folks in Perry who we already miss. It seems like we have been gone from there for some time when it has only been a few days.

I sent Robert on a mission into town to try and find someone who we could hire to help Mazie for awhile until everything is set up. He came back and said that Mrs. Martin would be happy to hire out with the condition that she can bring her young son with her. We don't think that will be any problem as one more set of feet around here will hardly be noticed. She is a good worker and Mazie certainly needs the help

I worked a full day with Mr. Griswold figuring out how much hay and other feed there was in the barn and then we made a list of the feed and tools we will be buying from him. I paid him $381.90 for the entire list. It had come to $481.90, but being the gracious fellow that he is, he decided to forgive $100 of it. I also gave him a check for $300 as the first payment on the house. After that Mazie and I had to go and meet them at the office of George Tinklepaugh's where we signed all the papers for the property. We signed a mortgage for $4,500 and a bond with interest at 5% payable semi-annually. It will be due on Oct. 1st and April 1st. We have to pay a minimum of $300 a year on the principal and we can pay a greater amount in multiples of $100 as long as we notify Mr. Griswold at least a month before the due date of an interest payment. The mortgage is for a ten-year period and hopefully, we may with the Lord's blessing, be able to pay it off earlier.

I received a letter from Mr. Walker that the case that Mr. Austin had brought was scheduled in Warsaw on the 28th so I decided to take the train down and deal with it myself. As you might have guessed, Mr. Austin must have decided that he didn't have a leg to stand on and therefore he never showed up in court. The Squire tossed out the case and declared that all court expenses were to be paid by Mr. Austin. It still cost me 80 cents for the train ride, 50 cents for dinner, 10 cents for candy (for my sweet tooth) and cigars, I had to pay the lawyer $5.00. I hope it costs Austin more than that.

We are stacking up on groceries and since things have settled down some I sat down and wrote out a check to Harry for the $300 he had loaned us. I still have to pay him some interest, but knowing Harry, he will most likely refuse the interest. What a kind brother he is. I have also found a hired hand to help me with trimming the orchard and help me get ready to plant some early crops. Mr. Deyor seems like a great fellow and a good worker and we agreed on $1.00 per day for his help. I also took out insurance on the farm for $3630 divided as follows, $1,000 on the house, $500 on furniture, $400 on the barn, $50 on the corn crib, $300 on the contents of the barn, $250 on the tool wagon shed, $200 on tools, $100 on the wagon and harness, $250 on the hog house, $80 on two cows and $500 on the horses. The total cost comes to $37.88 per year. The cows and horses are now better insured than I am and that should say something about my planning ahead?

Here on the last Sunday in March 1910 we all went to the Palmyra Presbyterian Church and heard a fine sermon by Reverend McKenzie. He preached on "Because I live you shall have life also." It was very inspiring and I trust we will become more involved in the Church as time goes on. I think we are going to like it here.

We are slowly getting settled and I am spending a great deal of my time plowing, dragging and sowing seeds for what I hope will be a fine crop of oats, potatoes and whatever else I am going to plant. I am hiring Frank Deyor on a regular basis and he is trimming the trees in the orchard that were badly in need of it. I don't believe they have been trimmed in several years and will most likely yield a much more productive crop when they are brought into a better condition. If one is a good steward of the land and the trees, they in turn will reward us with a bountiful harvest. Just like children and family, if they are nurtured, loved and cared for, they in turn will reward us beyond our wildest dreams. Abe Haak also brought by 54 raspberry plants which

Robert and I are planting and looking forward to many a fine raspberry topping on the ice-cream that Mazie is so fond of making. I have planted, so far, 16 bushels of oats on the 7-½ acres on the north side.

We have received several letters from folks in Perry including the TeWinkels and Mazie, the children and I have sent them cards and letters. I even sent a check to Mrs. Edgerly for half of the milk sales we had made while still there. The creamery sent me a check for $12.11 so I sent her a letter and enclosed a check for $6.06, which is her share of the proceeds. We have also heard from Lucy and Will and they plan on visiting us sometime this month. We are looking forward to it. Nevins has also stopped by and spent part of a day with us as he was going this way on business and decided to check on his old friends. He even helped me do some of the farm work while he was here, being the great fellow that he is. It must have been that he brought us some good luck since the day he was here, the Purcell cow gave birth to a fine heifer calf that will add to our stock.

We decided to drive the children to school in the buggy the first day that they attended in Palmyra and introduce them and ourselves to Professor Bullocks. He seems like a nice fellow and I hear he is a competent teacher. I am sure the children will love it there and make friends quickly. After this first day they will be hiking the distance with their shoe leather and be better off for it. It is great exercise for them and keeps them in good shape to be hiking rather than being given a ride every day. I bought the buggy we are using from Martin Pierce for $8.00 and even though it isn't the finest buggy in town it certainly is functional and will serve our needs just fine. I thought I got a good price for our wheels and enjoyed haggling with him over the price. As usual, after the fact, I wondered if I paid too much but he also wondered if he let it go too cheaply so I guess it was all fair in the end. After dropping the children off, Mazie and I did a little grocery shopping and it cost me $1.21 for the groceries. We had to buy a little extra as Mazie's mother; Mrs. McGregor, is coming from Bellaire to pay us a visit. Mazie is looking forward to her coming and I am sure she will be a big help to her. She and Mazie can spend a little time out of my earshot talking about me, as I am sure they will do. I just hope Mazie doesn't tell her about my expertise in real estate transactions as shown in the Lake Street house deal in Perry. It would just give Mrs. McGregor another reason to probably say to Mazie, "I always wondered why you married that man." Seriously I am sure she loves me as one of her own as I love her.

Here it is the day I am to take the trolley to Rochester to meet Mazie's mom and the twins are feeling under the weather. I drove them to Dr Darling's, he checked them out and said they should be keep warm and get plenty of rest as they both had bad chest colds and congestion. He charged me $1.00, which I didn't think was too bad for having examined both of the girls. Being twins, they seem to get the same things at the same time. He also gave me a prescription, which we stopped off at Brigg's Drug Store and filled it for 75 cents. We took the girls home, got them comfortable and in bed for rest. I did make it to Rochester on time in the trolley, met Mrs. McGregor and we came back to Palmyra on the train. I think it will be great to have her here for a few days to help Mazie, especially since the twins are not feeling well. Dr. Darling even weighed the twins and Dorothy weighs 56 pounds and Margaret weighs 54 ½ pounds.

My conviction that Dr. Darling certainly did not overcharge me was confirmed when he came to the house to pay the girls a visit, not just the day after he examined them but the next day and the day after that. He did not charge us any extra, said they were on the mend and would soon be up and into mischief again. Even Reverend McKenzie stopped by to look in on them. This sure is a nice friendly community that Mazie and her mother picked for us. They did well.

We are becoming more active here in April 1910 with the Presbyterian Church and we all are trying to make church when we are healthy. Rev. McKenzie preached a fine sermon for those gathered to hear him: "Lord I will follow Thee where-so-ever Thou goest." On that Sunday, I put 13 cents in the collection plate until we decide what to pledge in addition to trying to give a little extra each Sunday. I even contacted Mr. Riggs and rented a shed from the church that faces Church Street, probably named that since there are the four churches, one on each corner. The shed will cost us $5.00 per year but will be great in the bad weather to house old Kit, Maude or Jack, whoever takes us into town. After this service, Mr. and Mrs. Haak, Mr. and Mrs. Langdon and Mr. and Mrs.

Brown all came to visit in the evening, welcoming us further into the community and especially into the church. Will and Lucy even came up and went to church with us one Sunday that he had a substitute minister standing in for him. I told Will after the service that the reverend couldn't hold a candle to the sermons that Will gave, but I don't think he was totally convinced. They both do a fine job.

We decided to pledge $2.00 per month and in addition 75 cents for the mission board. The 75 cents will be allocated to 33% foreign mission, 33% home mission, 5% college board, 5% Sabbath School, 5% church erection, 5% ministerial relief, 5% education, 5% freedmen, 1% temperance and 3% Bible cause. I think I agree with them all but I am not sure about the temperance part. However, I won't bring it up, as I know what I would end up getting from Mazie if I raise the issue. Robert and I even attended a social evening put on by the choir and I put 35 cents in the collection plate. We had a nice time, met a lot of fine folks and maybe we might even decide to join the choir. Some of that singing I do in the barn might finally pay off. We finished out the month with Mazie ordering a few things to make all our lives a bit easier on the farm from Sibley, Lindsey and Curr Co. for a grand total of $14. 77.

I'm never sure about what the weathermen say, but as a farmer, I sure know that May is the wettest month of the year. In between the rain showers, Frank Deyor and I are still trimming the orchard trees, burning the brush and plowing the fields to try to get all the oats, corn and potatoes planted. Jack and Maude have sure been busy and with the wet conditions it has been particularly hard on them, but this is the life of a good workhorse. They certainly don't seem to complain any and they most likely know it wouldn't do them any good anyway. I even loaned them out to Frank for a couple of days so he could get some of his garden ready for planting. Speaking of the garden, I am planting Golden Bantam corn, beets, parsnips, carrots, salsify and many other delicious foods that will adorn our table later on in the year and into the cold winter months. Mr. Haak and I even helped each other with the corn drill and managed to get all of his and all of ours in. It is great to have neighbors and friends that will pitch in and help. I can well remember the great friends in Perry that not only we helped but in turn were helped by them. That is the way things should be.

Mazie has been feeling somewhat under the weather and may have picked up the illness from the twins. I had Dr. Chase come out and check her and he prescribed some cough medicine and some rest. I went into town and picked up the medicine at Briggs' Drug Store for 25 cents. I sure hope that helps because I don't think she will be getting to much rest with baby Howard demanding her time. It is a great help that Mrs. McGregor is still here helping her out with the housework and the children and that should lead to her quick recovery. I sure hope that is all that is wrong with her. I also picked up cough medicine for the twins while I was there. This should be the last they will need, as they seem to be getting much better every day. Dr. Chase also gave Mazie a tonic and that should help her. I try and take my tonic on a regular basis from the secret stock in the barn of that homemade wine and it sure seems to do the trick in keeping me healthy. That tonic, however, I am afraid Mazie would frown upon. We shall keep that a little secret between just you and I. The good Reverend McKenzie also stopped to call and see how Mazie and the twins were progressing. He is a fine fellow and always welcome in our humble home.

I have signed a telephone contract with Mr. Green and we are in hopes that sometime soon the lines may be brought out this far from town so we will be able to get a telephone. I think if all the farmers out this side of Palmyra sign up, we may have a better chance of getting the line soon. In the meantime, it is life as usual with my installing hundreds of fence posts and stringing barbwire around the fields for the cows and calves. I borrowed a barbwire stretcher from H. O. Young and Sons after they sold me 108# of wire and Frank and I cut the posts from some of the trimmed limbs around the property. That is hard, but necessary work to put in fence posts. Fortunately the ground is soft from all the rain so it makes digging all the holes easier.

I took the Purcell cow over to J. H. Walton's registered Holstein bull for hopefully a successful get together. His bull is full-blooded and I am sure will produce some fine calves. Along with this, we have set about 7 hens on several dozen eggs that Mr. Haak has given us and hopefully they will all hatch out into a full flock of chickens to add to our numbers. Even the old red sow had 13 piglets but sadly she mashed two of them. Hopefully the rest will grow up healthy. Haak has already put his bid in for 2 of them and I said he could have them, when they are ready, for $5.00 each, a special price for my friend. Mr. Haak loaned me his lawn mower in exchange for the deal on the piglets as mine is broken down and I had to send to Philadelphia for a part for it. It was either borrow Abe's or buy a goat as Mazie was on my case over the way the lawn had grown with all the rain and said I was to get myself in gear and get it taken care of one way or another. I wasn't going to argue with her, especially since her mother is still here, and I sure don't want to confront both of them.

Mrs. McGregor thought that Robert's bed was sort of rundown so she was kind enough to order him a new one from Sears and Roebuck and I went over to the South Shore railway station, picked it up, and brought it home in the buggy. It is a fine bed and it was so thoughtful of Mazie's mother that I take back everything I ever said about her, as if any of it was negative. Robert was so rested up a few days after sleeping in the new bed that he decided to take a little trip and he rode his wheel bike all the way to Canandaigua and back. It was great exercise for him and fortunately he didn't take any tumbles off it.

The bed has come in handy, as we have had some company here as the month draws to a close. The TeWinkels came over from Perry and paid us a nice visit, and Willard Nevins came over, had supper with us and spent the night. It is so great to see old friends and family. That is what life is all about and we should hold on tight to friends and especially family as life goes by all too fast and then we wonder why we didn't nurture this friendship or that family relationship. Hold on to what is dear.

We have been regular at church this month having attended on the 1st when Mazie, Robert and I were welcomed into the Palmyra Western Presbyterian Church membership by letter of transfer from the Perry Presbyterian Church. On May 8th we heard the Reverend Landon preach, we paid our $2.00 pledge for the month and put 9 cents in the plate besides. Reverend McMerty from Sodus also preached this month while Reverend McKenzie was not available and he gave a fine sermon on the 27th verse of the 107th Psalm, "they reel and stagger like drunkards and are at their wit's end." I don't think he was referring to me but I am sure the next time I take a little sip of the devil's brew in the barn I will most likely think of his sermon.

I have had to shell out $13.00 for tuition for Robert, Dorothy, Margaret and Marion's schooling at the Palmyra Classical Union School. This covers the 4th term from April 11 to June 17th. It seems like a lot of money but education is so important that Mazie and I are happy to pay this each term. The children all seem to be doing well in school and progressing so nicely that it certainly makes us proud. I have even decided to further my education by joining the Grange and I took the 1st and 2nd degree steps to becoming a full-fledged member. This is not bad for a 43-year-old (June 15, 1910) fellow. I frankly don't feel any older than I did at 20, must be all that hard work and worry that keeps me young. I am sure it is the hard work but my concern is the worry and the depression that takes hold of me sometimes that is certainly not adding to my potential longevity. I fortunately have been so busy of late that my old adversary has been held at bay.

Mr. Deyor has been working everyday except the Sabbath of course, which is always kept free in our household as the Lord ordered for rest, meditation and family time. We have been planting beans, cultivating, harvesting some hay and just about any other task that a farmer is faced with constantly. We have even had to draw quite a few loads of manure out to the fields but that is just a normal part of farm life. Jack and Maude have worked so hard that I had to take them to W. R. Phillips, the blacksmith, and have him put new shoes on them. It cost me 95 cents but they should be good for another 1000 miles. After all this hard work and new shoes, Maude even took the time to have a colt, which turned out to be a horse colt.

Have I mentioned in the past that Mazie's mother was staying with us and that Mazie's brother, Howard, also has taken the train up from New York City? Also the TeWinkels have come over from Perry to spend a little time here. Now you may ask why all the company and help for Mazie. As busy as we have been, moving and getting this farm up and running, I may have forgotten to mention that Mazie is expecting and that is why all the activity. I hope that Mazie doesn't find out that I failed to mention this as I may be sleeping in the barn with the animals if she knew. I even went into town and had my hair cut at Mr. DeNoise's barbershop for 25 cents and also had to go to Briggs's Drug Store to get some Rexall Pile Ointment for 25 cents. Being the gentleman that I am, I will not mention what that is used for; suffice it to say that it comes in handy. While I was there I spent another 24 cents and bought twelve 2-cent stamps so that we could send some letters to tell all our family and friends when the blessed event happens. I also was so happy that we now have a telephone that I even stopped by the telephone office and thankfully paid the $1.25 for this month's bill. It is so comforting to have the telephone available in case we need the doctor, or we need just to talk with someone like Reverend McKenzie for encouragement.

This has been a busy month as far as church activities are concerned with our making church each Sunday in June. We went both in the forenoon and again in the evening for Sunday School. On the 12th we went to the children's program for Children's Day. Dorothy, Margaret and Marion all participated, did a fine job and made us proud. I even paid Henry Runterman the 75 cents for the Presbyterian Hymnal that we will now have in our pew. I am not sure why since I don't think I can carry a tune in a hand basket but I sure am loud and Mazie and the children all love to sing the old favorites each Sunday. There are no better hymns than those that were written by our forefathers and are the old favorites that the church has thrived on for centuries. We went one of the other Sunday evenings and listened to Mr. Frink's lecture on the great "Mountains of the South" and watched his stereoscopic show on them. It was an exciting time for us all.

The blessed event is upon us and here on the 22nd of the month Mazie gave birth to not one but two fine healthy babies, one is a girl and one is a boy. We are naming them Helen and Harry, and Mazie and both of the twins are doing fine. Dr. Chase and Mrs. Chapman are here with them and of course Mazie's mother is giving orders and making sure that everyone steps to the same tune. That woman is indispensable when it comes to situations like that. She just told me to get out from underfoot, that I had already caused enough problems when I got Mazie pregnant. Can you imagine a mother-in-law saying such a thing to a son-in-law?

We have had a lot of company from our newfound friends here in Palmyra and Reverend McKenzie and we all bowed our heads in prayer for the health of Mazie, Helen and Harry. You may recall that our first little Helen passed away at a very young age in 1903 and caused us all to have such a depressing time. It even contributed to my nervous breakdown and disappearance for awhile a number of years ago. In honor and memory of that sweet innocent child, we have named this gift from God Helen and pray for her and her brother's health and long productive lives.

It was not possible to keep Mrs. Chapman on any longer to help Mazie with the twins and baby Howard, so I paid her the $30.00 that we owed her for the 2 weeks she has been here and we bid her farewell. She was a wonderful worker and a great help and comfort to Mazie in this very busy time. She had other family commitments so it was not possible for her to remain. I did go over to Walworth and tried to hire a Dutch girl over there that I had heard was looking for this type of work but I had no success. I will need to keep looking. In the meantime Mazie's mother and Robert, Dorothy, Margaret and Marion will need to pitch in and help all they can. Mr. Chapman is still helping out on the farm along with Frank Deyor and we have been very busy. We have been, with Robert's help, drawing hay, cultivating, planting and all those other many tasks necessary to keep a working farm going. Frank took Maude over to Farmington for me to pay a visit, hopefully successful, to R. D. Buckley's Perchern Stallion. I also had to buy a box of Hesse's Healing Powder for rubbing on Maude's leg where she cut it quite badly a few days ago. That healing powder sure is working wonders, as it already seems to be clearing up. Even Lady Edgerly came through this month and had 15 little piglets, but unfortunately lost 2 of them. Hopefully the other 13 will survive, grow and bring us some must needed cash. Mrs. Edgerly is still present in our lives.

We have had a lot of company this month of July with Lucy coming over from Perry to visit and see the new twins. Hans, Virginia and their girls also honored us with a visit and the girls just found little Helen and Harry the cutest little babies. They spent the day holding them and fussing over them. I also received a nice letter from Ma and she mentioned that she was not feeling too well and I am worried about her. She is now 77 years old and life has not been easy for her since she and my father Robert lost most everything in the Civil War. As hard as they worked, they never did get fully back on their feet. It has been particularly hard on her since the passing of my father in 1902. I will be praying for her continued good health and happiness. Hans and family invited Robert to spend a few days with them but since I needed him here for some farm work that had been building up we decided that he would have to delay the visit and go in a few days. He can ride his bicycle over to spend a few days with them as it is only about 15 miles, and for a young strong lad, that is just a short jaunt.

HELEN TYLER
c. 1915

Helen Watterson Tyler
C.1927

Helen and Howard
on farm house steps
C. 1914

You can't imagine our surprise on the day that Robert was due back that up pulled Hans and Robert in Mr. Beman's automobile as they brought him home with his bike tied on the back of his 1908 Haynes. That automobile must have cost him plenty and I doubt if I will ever be able to afford one. I'm not sure if they will ever be as efficient as horsepower or certainly as dependable. It may be just one of those passing fads that takes its place along the roadside of abandoned ideas as the years pass. I know that I will certainly stick with the good old horsepower and I think it frankly would have been better for Robert to have ridden his bike home from Canandaigua than have not had to expend any energy or get any exercise riding home in that contraption. Can you guess that I might be a little jealous seeing someone else owning such a vehicle?

I'll give you a perfect example of the worth of that automobile as compared to horsepower. I needed some timbers to build up along the North ridge to keep it from eroding. The New York Central Railroad runs just north of our farm and I contacted them as there were a lot of old used railroad ties laying along there. They said I could have them if I could get them over the fence and move them to the farm. Mr. Chapman and I spent half a day throwing 62 railroad ties over the fence and then loaded them in the wagon and Jack and Kit pulled them home. I daresay that auto could not have pulled three of them let alone all 62 of them in one trip. It just goes to show the value of the horse over the car.

Mazie made me get my shoes repaired, as I can't afford new ones at this time. She said she wouldn't go to church with me anymore if I didn't take them to the cobbler. I took them up to Johnson and Rogers and had to pay the exorbitant price of 90 cents to get them fixed. They look good however and should last me another 10 years. I wore them proudly to church on the 17th with Mazie, Dorothy, Margaret and Marion. Robert stayed home and took care of the little ones along with Mazie's mom. In the evening Robert and I and the girls went to a Sunday school service in the village park while Mazie stayed at home. We also had a Sunday school picnic at Grinnell's Glen the next day that I took the 4 oldest children to. It cost me 60 cents for us all to ride on the trolley but it was well worth it as the children had a wonderful time with all their friends. I have started to teach Sunday school and I am teaching the Baracca Class. It is a challenge but I am enjoying it very much. Rev. Baker from Wolcott preached in church this Sunday when all of us attended except for Mazie's mother and the newborn twins Helen and Harry. In the evening we all went to the Village Park and heard the Reverend Landon preach. Church in the morning, Sunday school in the afternoon and a revival meeting in the park in the evening. One could say that is a full day of religion. To top it all off, we decided to take Monday off from digging out stumps and picking up rocks and burying them and we all went fishing and had a picnic down at the canal. We didn't really catch our supper. The children did catch a few small fish but of course I took the prize with a 15-inch bass. I just couldn't let the children outdo me. I was even called upon to lead a prayer meeting in the Presbyterian Church one Sunday here in August of 1910 and if I do say so myself I did a fine job. All this religion fortunately keeps my old depression at bay. Of course digging out stumps and picking up rocks and burying them might also contribute to my old crisis being kept in its place.

William and Lucy TeWinkel came over from Perry and are spending some time with us. Will helped me throw another 109 used railroad ties over the New York Central Tracks' fence. He also helped me load them up and deliver a few to Pat McGuire, and the rest we took up to the farm. He is a strong worker and a great help. It is unusual to have a minister in the family that is willing to roll up his sleeves and get into it but Will is one of a kind. After our hard days work, we hitched up old Kit and took the ladies for a nice ride around the countryside. I thought I might point out all the places where Joseph Smith had lived and the other important places that have played a roll in the Mormon religion, but Will suggested that with Mazie I might want to keep those thoughts to myself. Seems Mazie has still not made up her mind as to whether the Mormon religion should be looked upon as equal to our own. I could never see any difference myself as long as one has faith and believes in the Lord and his teachings so I don't care what they call themselves. In my mind we are all equal. I certainly am not casting aspersions on Mazie but she has such strong faith in the Presbyterian way that with anything else she has difficulty accepting it. She is a fine God- loving woman however and I would never question the wisdom or her faith.

Will also is helping me dig out more stumps in the North hill lot which abuts the old Martin Harris farm and that is as I have said very hard, back breaking work. Someday they will most likely have machines to do the work so we can all sit around and get fat and lazy. It doesn't sound too bad but as you might guess, I sure am not in favor of it. Hard work is what keeps us strong both in mind and body.

Robert hooked up Kit and he took the TeWinkel children and the girls over to visit Hans and family in Canandaigua. Will and Lucy are going over in a couple of days and take the children back to Perry and Robert and the girls will be heading back here. It has been great to have the company and a big help to Mazie with little Helen and Harry and of course Baby Howard to all be taken care of. They are all doing well, thank the Lord.

I took Maude up to Macedon as she had a date with Buckley's stallion and we went up to Joe Mumby's farm but Buckley and his stallion never showed. That wasn't all a wasted trip however as I checked out some of Mumby's stock in the hopes of buying a couple more cows to add to the few we have already. Since we are selling some milk, I thought maybe we could make a little more income if we add a few more cows. Our income and outflow has been a little off balance lately, having to buy Robert some new shoes for $1.50 and have new shoes put on the horses for $2.00 plus a few other expenses. I had to borrow $100 from Mrs. McGregor to tide us over until our ship comes in. Whenever that is, only the good Lord knows, but we are working hard and hoping that it will all pay off in the long run. I didn't want to hit up my banker Harry again as he has been so good in the past that I hate to have to keep asking him. Mazie's mom was happy to loan us the money, at least she said she was. I will pay her a little interest on it when we can pay it back. I used a little of the money to buy 500 pounds of coal to get ready for the next heating season from the Sessions Coal Company here in Palmyra.

Speaking of Harry, we have had a pleasant surprise as he and Margaret and one of my other brothers, George has come for a visit. In addition, Mazie's brother Howard is also here as he has a little time off from his teaching duties at Columbia University before the fall term begins. We are, to say the least, a little crowded but it is really wonderful to see so many of the family together. Howard plans on taking his mother Mrs. McGregor into Rochester for a shopping and sightseeing trip here in early September, of 1910. We even decided to all attend church at the same time and there were so many Tyler's and McGregor's that we filled up a couple of pews. We heard a wonderful sermon on the "Value of Family". Now that certainly seemed to be appropriate for our extended family at this time.

Even with all the family visiting and making a fuss over little Howard and the twins Helen and Harry, it is time I got back to reality and back in the fields. Maude and I have been drawing gravel from A. Haak's for our driveway and then the thrasher came and it cost me $12.96 to get the wheat and the oats thrashed. We got 164 bushels of wheat and 256 bushels of oats this time around. I was using Jack and Maude for some of this work but Jack came up lame and so I had to take him back to see the blacksmith, Mr. Phillips, and have him checked out. Seems when he put shoes on both of them in the past week he had driven a nail to close to the "quick" in Jack. For you novices that aren't farmers I will give you a brief explanation of what I am talking about. The hoof of a horse is like a toenail. The outer layer is dead or cornafied with no blood vessels or nerves but the layer just under the hard part is like the tissue under your toenail, full of vessels and nerves and this layer is called the "quick". Mr. Phillips uses a nail with an angled chamfer at the point. When he drives the nail he needs to angle it so it curves out away from the quick or living tissue. He started the nail with the chamfer facing the wrong direction so the nail dipped into the live tissue and caused Jack pain and subsequent infection if it is not taken care of. You should consider this your daily lesson in "treating horses hoofs". Didn't know I was so smart, did you? On top of all this it was interesting that Lady Edgerly has been serviced. I just thought I would throw that in to confuse the reader since I am talking about Lady Edgerly the sow, not Mrs. Edgerly. Mr. Haak's black boar serviced Lady Edgerly and we hope it was successful, as we need some more piglets to grow and sell.

After all this I decided we should all take some time off so Harry, Margaret and all the children and I went fishing down by Mud Creek near the canal. We caught a number of fish and one great big turtle. I suggested to all that we make turtle soup but the children would have nothing to do with it and insisted we let it go. It was a good thing for that turtle that he had the children on his side. We even decided to spend a half-day at the great Palmyra Fair after the fishing trip. You would think I was made of money having to pay 25 cents to get the horse and surrey in plus 30 cents for candy and rides on the merry-go-round for all the children. I guess I am splurging since I just borrowed another $500.00 from the Mutual Benefit Life Insurance Company on one of my policies. I don't think I will tell the children that I am spending some of their inheritance if in fact there is anything there when I go to my reward. In all seriousness, I hope to be able to pay it back and restore the policy in good time. I was so impressed with the great Palmyra Fair that I bought a share of stock in it from H. G. Chapman for $12.00. We stockholders not only own the fair but the ground it sits on. I hope it is a good investment.

It is time to say our sad farewells to some of the family as Harry and Margaret and George and Mrs. McGregor left for Bellaire on the 4:24 train. We will all miss them greatly, especially Mazie since they were such a grand help with the babies, but Mazie is a strong woman and with Dorothy, Margaret and Robert's help she will manage just fine. The day after they left we received a double baby carriage from the TeWinkels for the babies. It will be fun to proudly push our beautiful twins up and down the road. I am sure that the other children will enjoy taking them for strolls as much or more than Mazie and I.

With such a busy month, I have been neglecting some other necessities and finally got up to Briggs's Drug Store and bought some liniment for 25 cents for Jack's sore foot. I also got some much needed pile ointment for myself. As I have said, what I use that for will go unmentioned. I also got a bottle of Dr. Kitchel's Spavin cure, which claims it cures everything from arthritis to the gout. Hopefully it will cure what I need the pile ointment for.

This has been a great month with all the company and the children's continued health and happiness. We have truly enjoyed each other's company in fishing, going to the fair and just sitting around and talking family business. I have been on a fairly even keel this month as far as depression is concerned. I only became a little over tired for a couple of days and became a little down. Interestingly enough I found myself the next few days more upbeat and enthusiastic about things than before the down cycle. I guess the lesson from that is that when you feel depressed, stay busy and just give it a little time and your spirits will be lifted.

We are back to reality here in Oct. of 1910 with it starting out as a very windy day. I told myself that it was just too windy to work on the farm so I picked up the trusted shotgun and decided to go hunting for a change. A man cannot live by work alone, or something of the sort I convinced myself of. I had some luck and even in the high wind I managed to knock down a pheasant, which will make a fine Saturday evening meal for all the hungry mouths. I feel just like early man who went out and hunted for the food for the wife and family and brought it home successfully for Mazie to cook. I'm not too sure she was happy with it but it tasted good and I think everyone enjoyed it. I thought a little about going hunting again on Sunday but Mazie would have none of it and we went to church and Sunday school and enjoyed rally day in Sunday school. When we got home I got up on the barn roof and replaced some shingles that had been blown off in yesterday's high winds.

Farm work never has a season when it ends and Mr. Deyor and Mr. Flynn and I worked on cutting corn, husking it and planting more wheat. I paid them each $1.63 a day for their work and decided that wasn't quite enough so I dug deep and gave them each a raise to $1.75 a day. I am the last of the big spenders or so one would think. I also decided to pay them by the bushel for husking the corn and decided that 5 cents per bushel was a fair price. They both can husk about 30 bushels a day so that will keep my pockets empty. A good thing is that we are selling some of the crops and milk along the way. I did manage to take 1710 lbs. of fallen apples to Clifford's evaporator and they paid me 60 cents per 100 pounds. This was the total crop from the orchard this year, and it means I will need to do some major work on the orchard if we are to realize any gain from it. We are storing bushels of potatoes, beets, corn and many other vegetables in the basement for our use this winter. They should hold us well as we need them for our large and growing family.

Here it is the 12th of Oct. and the children are off from school for Columbus Day. They can help me around the farm and help Mazie with the twins and Howard. I decided since I had all this help to take a couple hours and go hunting again and this time

T. H. and Harry Chapman went along. I can't say we are the Daniel Boones of the Palmyra area as we came home empty handed but had a good time anyway. It is great to do something now and then besides work.

I wrote Hans a letter here in mid Oct. and asked him if he could see his way clear to loan us $200.00 as I have a lot of unpaid bills and also want to buy some yearlings and a couple of cows. I hope to pay Peter Toumoise $2.50 for the wheat drill and W. R Phillips $1.50 for fixing the horse rake recently. I also owe N. M. Barnhart $8.60 and G. A. Tuttle $3.30. On top of all this, the telephone bill is due to Wayne Telephone Co. for $2.50 for the past two months and as usual I have a bill at Briggs's Drug Store for 50 cents to cover. If Hans can come through I can pay all of these and have some left over for the yearlings and cow purchases. I also have to get some goiter medicine from Briggs's for that pesky goiter that I have. The medicine seems to control it so it is well worth the 35 cents it cost me once a month. Briggs will let me put it on my tab until Hans comes through. I even had to buy a book of stamps, which cost the exorbitant price of 2 cents each so I could send the note to Hans making the request. Nothing is cheap nowadays.

I took Marion to Dr. Chase for a vaccine but unfortunately he was all out of it and we will have to come back later on. Marion seems to be somewhat susceptible to illnesses that the other children do not seem to catch so I try to get her vaccine whenever possible to keep my young beauty healthy. While I was there I decided to ask Dr. Chase about my goiter figuring I already was paying for a doctor visit so I might just as well get two for the price of one. He gave me some salve and also told me to give up coffee and tobacco. These two I would consider as two of the few pleasures a farmer has in life. I told him I would think about it and I most likely will over a cup of coffee and a pipe full of tobacco. So much for following the doctor's advice.

Well, old Hans couldn't come through with the money I had asked to borrow so I contacted my old trusty banker Harry and as usual he came through. It is always nice to have someone in the family with enough money to loan to other family members at a reasonable interest. The banks constantly seem to want to rip us off with their high interest rates so aren't I nice in always giving

A JOURNEY THROUGH LIFE

Harry our banking business. With this new founded money, Mazie bought 10 rolls of wallpaper and 2 rolls of border and she hired Miss Deyor to paper the living room for us. With some of the rest of the money, I bought 7 one-year-old yearlings and 2 cows from N. D. Perry and Harry Chapman helped me drive them home. Harry even let me graze them on some property he owns next to the railroad at Gooney's Crossings. I have often wondered where the name, "Gooney's Crossing" came from for the railroad crossing where this road crosses the New York Central Railroad just beyond the old Martin Harris farm. I have yet to name the yearlings but the girls helped me with the names for the cows and we decided to call them Spot and Dunkle. We sure come up with some original names for our animals. Since we had a little money left over, I ordered some coal and it cost me $4.00 per ton. This should help keep us all warm for the upcoming winter.

As we finished out this Oct. of 1910, what more fitting way than to all go to church and hear the Rev. McKenzie preach. His subject of the morning was "we all fade as a leaf." What an interesting thought here in October as we see the leaves dropping from the trees, realizing that our time on this earth is also limited and we should make the most of it while we can.

We are getting some fairly heavy snow and it is cold here in November. We will be using the coal we bought pretty fast if this is any indication of the winter that is just around the corner. I have had to do more work on the shed and the barn to house the cows I recently bought and also those that I still want to buy. I went to the hardware and bought 5 pounds of number 16 nails for the shed to build the stalls. I will have to consider bringing them in from the fields pretty soon if this weather keeps up. Between this work and bringing bushels and bushels of vegetables into the cellar for our winter use I have been very busy. I did find time, at Mazie's insistence, to take the Reverend McKenzie 5 bushels of potatoes and some parsnips, carrots, cabbage and even some pumpkins to help them through the winter. The good Lord knows that he is not paid all that much and so we all try and pitch in and help them, as we are able. The Reverend tends to his flock and like a good Sheppard, his flock tends to watch over him also.

You know things are pretty tight when you have to borrow money from your children. I am selling some milk and a lot of vegetables and even sold 16 roosters to Mr. Perry for 10 cents a pound, but even that doesn't bring in the money we need to purchase our stock. Robert has been very industrious from all his hard work and has quite a bit of money in the Perry Bank and so he agreed to loan me $150.00 so we could buy 5 heifers and hopefully that will do it for this fall. We found 5 fine heifers and had to pay $120.00 for them so there was $30.00 left over. Since we had agreed on the full $150.00, Robert said I could keep it and use it for whatever the family wants. I told him I would pay him back as soon as I could with some interest, most likely more than he is getting at the bank in Perry. I now owe Harry $200 and Robert $150 and I am sure that with the Lord's help and a lot of hard work the time will arrive soon when we are able to cover these loans. Robert was cheerful about loaning it and said he trusted the "Bank of Ben" more than a commercial bank anyway. Let us hope his faith is not misplaced.

I did my civic duty here on the 8th of November and went into town and cast my vote in the local, state and national elections. President William Howard Taft has urged everyone to get out and vote and I certainly want to fulfill my civic responsibility. Mazie of course could not go with me, as women are not allowed to vote. That certainly seems like an archaic rule as most women I know are sure more savvy then men and it is about time that we give them the right to vote along with the men who have done a pretty good job already of screwing up the world many times over. I have a feeling the ladies would do a lot better job of things and hopefully the domineering male leadership in this country will see the light soon. I did vote the straight Republican ticket and I hope I am not disappointed in the efforts that my candidates put forth to solve some of the country's problems. Unfortunately, many of the candidates are more interested in feathering their own nests and insuring their future prosperity than they are in doing the peoples' business.

I'm doing some give and take with the neighbors this month and Mr. Chapman asked me if I would board his Jersey Heifer for the winter. We owed each other some favors so this helps square accounts and I am happy to do it for them. What is another mouth to feed during the long, cold winter months? It will keep me busy and my mind occupied. Speaking of keeping my mind occupied, I helped Abe Haak butcher a couple of hogs and he is sharing some of the ham with us, which should make for a fine meal.

I did find plenty of uses for the extra $30.00 that Robert had loaned me. I paid Dr. Chase for some pills he had given me and I also got my hair cut for 25 cents. What an expensive price to get one's ears lowered a few times a year. I also had to get some Rexall Pile Ointment for 25 cents and I bought some trinkets for 30 cents for Marion's birthday. The school tax also came due for the year and it was the outlandish sum of $6.35 for District No. 5. I paid it reluctantly, trying to keep in mind the fine education that the children are getting, and when you think of it that way, I guess it is a real bargain.

We spent a very quiet Thanksgiving here on the 24th, went to the Baptist Church and heard the Reverend Mek preach. We later went to a chicken and oyster dinner at the Presbyterian Church and spent the rest of the day being thankful for all God's blessings on us.

I finished out the month going to a Grange meeting and listening to F. E. Gott teach three sessions at the farmers' institute. It was a very instructive meeting and I think all of those in attendance came away with many new ideas on farming and some revised ideas on some of the methods we employ all the time. Like any other business, a farmer must grow with the times and become more efficient or he will most likely fail over the long haul.

I planned on drawing as many beans as I could to the West Shore Railroad after Abe and I have spent days cleaning his and ours and getting them ready to ship out. It worked out great that we helped each other and with Robert's help we cleaned tons of beans. It is extremely cold here in Dec. with the temperature at 4 degrees below zero but weather cannot hold up our farm duties especially during this season when we need the money to pay down some debt's and also for some Christmas presents for Mazie and the children. I was planning on using Jack and Maude to haul the beans but Jack had fallen recently so I had to have he and Maude re-shoed at W. R. Phillip's blacksmith shop and make sure they had some solid shoes for this winter weather. It took Abe, Robert, Landon and Jones to get him on his feet again. I sure hope nothing is seriously wrong with him as he has been a great horse and he and I have traveled many a path together. Mr. Phillips charged me $1.60 in full for the 8 shoes and assured me that all the nails went in properly this time so neither horse would come up lame. When Abe and I went to the stable to get Jack and Maude we found Jack down again and he would not get up. With just the two of us it wasn't possible to get him to his feet so we hooked up Maude and one of Abe's horses and trekked off to the West Shore to deliver the beans. We had a timetable to meet, we finally finished the job and I was paid $316 for my part of the total.

This money certainly comes in handy as I paid Robert some of what I owed him and gave Dorothy and Margaret each 44 cents to spend as they wish. The rest of the money I then turned over to Mazie. Women may not yet have the right to vote but they sure have the right to rule in their own home, as I have found out many times over. Believe me I am not complaining only stating a fact of life. I might sum it up by saying that if the woman of the family isn't happy, ain't nobody in the family happy, so it pays to keep her contented. Mazie decided it was time to go to Rochester on a shopping trip so they took the early morning train here on the 8th to do some Christmas shopping for us all and to see all the decorations that are there in the spirit of the holidays. I sure hope they see fit to get the head of the household; at least Mazie lets me think I am, a little something for the holiday.

I have tried to make church each Sunday this month as my time is not quite so occupied with the farming this time of year. Last Sunday Rev. McKenzie preached on "swearing" and I noticed Mazie look out of the corner of her eye at me a couple times during the sermon. I guess on a couple of occasions I have been known to slip and utter a swear word but I try to catch myself and ask forgiveness when it does happen. I think a word or two might have crossed my lips when I have been trying to get Jack up as he seems to want to spend more and more time on the ground instead on his four feet. Other than that he seems fine and after our Herculean efforts each time he seems fit as a fiddle. Maybe he is just getting tired of work and deciding his time may be coming so he wants to relax in the days he has left.

Mazie, I and the family are going to the church fair at the Grange Hall here in mid- December so I killed and dressed two chickens to take to be shared and we were pleasantly surprised when Lucy TeWinkel showed up from Perry for a couple of days and was able to go with us. All had a fine time, even the time when we listened to the Reverend McGarrah talk about the church finances. Seems there never is enough money to do all those things that the local church would like to do and of course the hierarchy of the church is always looking for more from the various members of the churches that make up the Presbyterian Church of the USA. Churches are no different than any other organization and they cannot survive on faith alone, although sometimes I wonder how many layers of hierarchy we need but then again they never asked my opinion on anything but the local church.

Robert and the twins and I went out today and bought a Christmas tree and it cost us 25 cents. In Perry, as I recall, we had some on the farm and were able to cut our own but here in Palmyra we were not so fortunate and had to shell out the money for one. I will say that the children are excited and think it is the best tree ever. It will be the first Christmas for twins no. 2, Helen and Harry and we are buying a few trinkets to make their first Christmas a memorable one. They are such darling children and with everyone's help Mazie has managed well over these past few months since they were born. They are growing stronger by the day and a pleasure to hold and cuddle. The older children helped us get the packages of presents ready for sending to Bellaire and also to Hans and his family in Canandaigua. I shipped them out and the one to Bellaire weighed 5 pounds and cost me 55 cents to send and the box to Canandaigua weighed 3 pounds and cost me 25 cents to send. The children can't wait for the boxes of gifts to arrive from both Bellaire and from Hans and family as they always are very generous and there are great surprises in their Christmas boxes.

We decided to have the family celebration of Christmas on the 26th since Christmas this year falls on Sunday and we wanted to spend as much time at church with family and friends as possible. Sunday is the Lord's Day and we thought it appropriate to spend this day in thanking the Lord for the blessings He has bestowed upon us and celebrate with a fine meal and gifts tomorrow. The children were up, it seems before dawn, and as a farmer and his wife would love to sleep in a little when they can, the children didn't allow that to happen today. They received many fine gifts and Mazie received two nightgowns and each of the twin's number 1 received two pairs of cotton socks and blankets, and little Howard, and Helen and Harry also received blankets. Everyone was very happy with the fine celebration and the excellent meal that Mazie prepared for all. It was a fine day.

Chapter 5

1911

(Roald Amundsen beats Robert F. Scott to the South Pole)

It's cold enough here in Palmyra, New York in January of 1911 without even thinking about the hardship and cold temperatures that Amundsen and Scott are going to endure on their race to the South Pole. It will be interesting to see which team sets foot at the South Pole first. Why anyone would want to suffer such agony just to say they were the first there is beyond me. It is cold enough right here in Upstate New York without venturing to the coldest place on earth where the temperatures can reach 125 degrees below zero or colder. I guess it is man's unquenchable thirst to discover the unknown that leads them into such a wilderness. I suppose some day mankind will even try to walk on the moon, however I would guess that is beyond even the most fantastic dreamers imagination and beyond the realm of possibilities.

I need not worry about such worldly things since I have enough to worry about right here. Hans has written about possibly looking at some farms in the Palmyra area and he and the family came over from Canandaigua. We all attended church and then he, I and his son rode over with Fred Guile to look over the Chapman farm and the Downing farm. Mr. Guile expects the Downing Farm to be sold soon as he has someone else interested in it. It would certainly be great if Hans and the family did buy around here so we would be closer and able to spend more time family to family.

Benjamin and Mazie on the farm
To left: silo and barn

Ben with Kit, Maude & Jack

I guess you could say that all good things come to an end. Old Jack cannot and will not get up so I had to shoot him and since a farmer needs everything he can to help him survive, I skinned him and then buried the remains in the garden. Old Jack and I have been down many a road together but as he has gotten old and sick, I could not bear to see him suffer so I put him out of his misery. I took the hide to the Crosby Frisian Fur Company in Rochester to have it tanned and they will make it into a robe for us. It cost 12½ cents per square foot for the tanning and $6.00 for the best lining that they had. Only the best for old Jack. They said it would take about 6 weeks to finish it. I took the trolley into Rochester and it cost me 85 cents for the ride and 10 cents for a meal. I am now left with just Kit and Maude so Levi Haak Sr. drove me over to the Dayton's to look at a mare called Lopsy that they have for sale. The name would sure fit in with the rest of our livestock and you would have thought the twins named her. I offered Mr. Dayton $75.00 but he wanted $100.00 so we couldn't come to an agreement. I will have to keep looking.

The weather is so bad here in January that I have been driving the children to school and also driving us all in to the Methodist Union Service and the service at the Dutch Reform church. We try to go to as many of the diverse churches in Palmyra as we can although we always go back to the Presbyterian Church and certainly Mazie would have it no other way.

It seems like I could call this the month of the slaughter since I had to shoot Jack I also killed the big black hog and borrowed Tom Hannigan's hog hook and gamble stick and paid him 50 cents for their use. The hog weighed out at 301 pounds and when the meat is cured and ready for us I am going to give some to the reverend and also sell some of the meat for some extra income. I certainly need it as the property taxes are due on our 81 acres and the home and they come to the exorbitant amount of $31.83. They charged $20.10 for the land, $10.41 for the highway tax and a collector's fee of 32 cents. Our dog even cost us $1.00 tax added on. What is this world coming to? I have to wonder what our politicians find to spend all this money on. I also sold two pigs, which weighed in at 119 and 138 pounds and received $25.70 for them. The timing was good as the white sow had 15 piglets and only one of them was born dead so we have 14 to raise for sale later on. On top of all this, Abe Haak called me and asked me to come right over as he had a heifer that was choking to death on a potato that had been lodged in its throat. Unfortunately we could not save it and my trusted shotgun had to be put to use again. I certainly hope that is the end of killing for this month; it is almost enough to get even a good farmer down.

I have been active in the Grange Hall meetings this month and I took the 3rd and 4th degrees recently and it went well. They also had an open meeting at the Grange called "The Old Folks

Day" and even though I don't consider Mazie and I old folks yet, we attended and had a great time. It sure beats drawing out the first of the manure this season into the bean lot. I consider myself lucky as I stepped outside for a brief time during the get-together and happened to find a quarter that someone must have dropped. I am going to buy Mazie 3 papers of safety pins with my ill-gotten gain. I would have returned it but I believe if I had gone back in and announced "I just found a quarter on the ground outside, whom does it belong to?" many hands would have gone up.

This month has not ended on a high note as Dorothy and Margaret have bad colds, then little Helen got it and Mazie had to stay up several nights straight with her. Even Lucy came over from Perry to help as Mazie was getting totally exhausted caring for her. Dr. Perry has been here and checked her over and says he thinks it is just a bad cold and she needs plenty of fluids and rest. Dorothy and Margaret are feeling better so hopefully Helen will also very soon. It is always a worry especially with the young babies in the house and it is still hard to forget the tragic death of our beautiful first little Helen.

As the month draws to a close Helen is feeling better as Dr. Perry prescribed some medicine that seemed to help. Baby Harry is now coming down with it and we will most likely be up with him many a night as we have been with Helen. We are hoping and praying he will bounce back as quickly as baby Helen. Lucy has had to go home so I drove her in the surrey to the trolley station and she told us that if we needed her she would come back, but of course she has her own family to take care of.

February has blown in with very stormy weather but has also brought health to all of us with Helen and baby Harry completely over whatever it was they had. Thank heavens for Dr. Perry and the medicines that he has prescribed to bring them back to full health. With all the illness, and Mazie not being able to get much sleep, I have been trying to find someone to work for her and help her out with the twins and little Howard. Mrs. Martin can help on occasion but is not available full time. I was hoping to hire Carrie Sexton but she only was able to work a few days and found other employment. I will have to keep looking as Mazie continues to remind me that she needs someone.

This has been an active month at the Grange. I spoke at a recent meeting on the kind of Grange I envisioned that would uplift a community. I believe this is very important to a farming community like Palmyra, as it is the center of the farm family's community life. Marion, Robert and Dorothy and Margaret and I all attended a Grange social and I read to the children from Uncle Ramus and Dorothy read from a book called, "When father carries the duck." Margaret read from a book called "Jimmie Brown's Sisters Wedding." The children all seemed to have a great time and between the book readings and the fine foods that all had brought to share, the Grange certainly lived up to its goal of being an uplifting experience. I even was the Chaplin at a recent Grange meeting so February has been filled with experiences at this fine organization for farmers and their families. And last but not least, I have to blow my own horn and tell you that I even gave a talk on the "modern tillage of corn" to the assembled multitudes one day. Not bad for a recent shopkeeper from Perry that everyone laughed at when I decided to become a farmer. It just goes to show that if you follow your dreams and work hard at them you will succeed and you will be the one with the last laugh. So much for patting myself on the back, if I am not careful I will get a big head over all this attention.

It has been so snowy and storming here in Feb. of 1911 that I have given the children a ride to school more than once. The mile walk to school is good for them but even I took pity a couple of days and hooked up old Maude to the surrey and took them in. Old Maude didn't know what to make of it as she usually was hooked up with Jack at her side and these days she is in the harness alone. She performed however, magnificently as the great horse that she is. Speaking of school, we are very proud of Dorothy as she received the award for excellence in making Valentine cards for this Valentines Day. The reward was a full $1.00, which I am sure she will find many uses for. Since we just had a new wall telephone installed, Mazie had to crank up the telephone and call Lucy in Perry and tell her of Dorothy's achievements. A wall telephone, what will they think of next? With all these modern conveniences one has to wonder what we will do with all the time that is freed up using these inventions that are designed to make peoples' lives easier. I would dare say that there might not be too much more to invent since we now have telephones and some lucky folks even have cars.

We have been busy this month with the church and I have been very active in the Baracca Class having met with other members at the reverend's house to discuss the business aspects of the organization. The Baracca class is an international organization of Bible classes for men and the word comes from the Hebrew word, Berachah, meaning "blessing". We also had a Baracca banquet and I was asked to speak on the non-church goals of our men's organization. Other than this involvement we have all tried to attend church with Mazie and Robert, going in the evenings and myself, the girls and Robert going on Sunday mornings. We have all taken turns taking care of little Howard and twins no. 2, Helen and Harry in the times when the others attended church.

This has been a busy month on the farm with Abe and I each drawing almost 4000 pounds of wheat to the New York Central Railway Station. It is scheduled to be shipped to the Barnhart Brothers and my share will net me $56.70. I also am trying to fatten up 4 of my best steers so they will be ready for butchering in late March. For the pigs, I had to take bushels of oat, corn and barley to the mill and have it ground up so that it could be used to feed them. Their appetites seem to be bottomless. Mr. Chapman took his heifer home also as he now has room to board it for the rest of the winter and paid me $5.00 for its keep while it was here. Duffy and Van Norman took their sow's home also since they had been here for about 2 weeks for servicing by my boar. They paid me 80 cents each for the keep and 75 cents for the service of the boar. With all this newfound wealth, I bought a shaggy looking bull from A. Cornelius and hopefully with some care, it will come along and add greatly to our livestock. I will have to ask the girls to name it and when they see it they will most likely want to name it Slim or Skinny or something like that since it is so undernourished. I only paid $12 for it so I think, in the long run, it will be a bargain.

As the month draws to a close I have paid my life insurance premium for the year with Aetna Life Insurance Co. It cost me $40.97 but it is a good investment with such a large and growing family to protect. This has been a very stormy and snowy month and as it ends I am still looking for some permanent help for Mazie. She is reminding me almost every day about the need. Mazie is such a strong woman that she manages while I continue to look. Hopefully soon, someone will turn up that would like the work and also fit in well with the family, and especially with Mazie.

March of 1911 has brought more snow and very cold weather. I had to buy more nut coal from B. Anderson and had to shell out $5.61 for it. If this weather lasts much longer I will be going through this very quickly. We need to keep the house warm for the children especially since there are so many illnesses going around and with the young babies and little Howard they are especially vulnerable to these viruses. Robert went into town for us with the surrey and stopped at Briggs Drug Store and picked up a bottle of cough syrup for the babies for 20 cents. Hopefully that will clear up their lingering coughs. Mrs. Martin is still helping Mazie out, as her time allows, but she is not available every day so it is hard on Mazie to keep up with all the demands of the children and the household. I am still making a valiant effort to find someone on a permanent basis. They say that if March comes in like a lamb it will go out like a lion and this year I hope the opposite is true as it is coming in like a lion and continuing its prowl.

We have been very active in church, as the support from the reverend and all the other church members during the recent illness of the young ones has been so greatly appreciated. It is this kind of community support that makes small town living so rewarding. I was elected as the vice-president of the Baracca class for the next six months for the church and I will certainly strive to do my best in my new duties. I am honored that the other men in the class and the Reverend McKenzie have such faith in my abilities and my great faith in the church to bestow this honor upon me. We even have had a banquet at the Baptist Church for the combined Baracca classes from all the churches and I held forth for a brief time during the festivities. I managed to keep my remarks short as in my opinion few people remember anything in a speech that is longer than about 5 minutes. I have often thought to remind some of the long-winded ministers of that fact but I have managed to keep my mouth shut. I, of course, am excluding

Reverend McKenzie from this evaluation. If I ever uttered this thought out loud to Mazie I am sure she would take great issue with my appraisal as she hangs on almost every word from the mouths of most of the ministers.

I finally separated the pigs from the sow and the boar serviced Lady Edgerly. That may sound a little crude but I think the reader of my diaries will understand what I mean by this. I have also fattened up the four steers that I separated out and it paid off as Mr. Brownell made me a good offer and I sold them to him for $145.00. I also sold another heifer and bought a 15-year-old mare for $80 to replace Jack. We all got together and the twins, Dorothy and Margaret, decided we would name him Logan. It seems fitting with the other names we have given our animals. I will be happy if Logan turns out to be even half as good as old Jack was. He is certainly missed. Mr. Newman also offered me $23 dollars for the largest red sow but my price was $25 and knowing the great negotiator that I am, we could not come to an agreement. An example was the days of trying to sell our home in Perry. You would think I would have learned my lesson from that experience. I am sure that he and I could have compromised at $24 but in my infinite wisdom I thought he would meet my price so as it ended up that he walked away from the deal entirely. Maybe I should, and a lot of other folks, learn that a little compromise is a good thing in life. I felt a little down about the deal so I killed and dressed a hog that weighed 163 pounds and shared the meat with Abe Haak, Mrs. McKenzie and also with Fred Dryer. I hope the reader does not get the wrong impression that when I am down I take it out on the poor creatures that I have in my keep. Rest assured this hog was already in the plan several weeks ago to become meat for our family and some of our neighbors. Since I have to pay $300 as our first mortgage payment on the farm, plus $112.50 as the interest to date, I need all the money I can get my hands on and so I sold the Purcell cow and her new bull calf to Mr. Hemming for $55.00. Hopefully with this money and other funds I can scrape together we will be able to meet this first payment on our $4500.00 mortgage.

As you might have guessed by now, I did have to write to the "Bank of Harry" and ask if I could borrow $300 so we could fill the shortfall that we have on the money needed. Hopefully old

Harry will be able to come through as usual. While I am waiting to hear from Harry I did go out and buy a field spray pump from H.O. Young and Sons for $16.00 as I am hoping the orchard will be much more productive this coming season. It certainly does not measure up in any way to the orchard we enjoyed on Mrs. Edgerly's farm in Perry. That orchard, as I recall, produced so much fruit that I thought picking it would never end. If I am successful and work hard I think this orchard that we now own will be as productive as that one was. Hard work will make all the difference.

As this month winds down, I am afraid we are seeing some more illness in the family. Mazie took Margaret to Dr. Chase and she had a temperature of 103 degrees and seems right sick. Dr. Chase has given her some medicine and recommended that she drink lots of orange juice to help her get over this bug. As it turns out, the orange juice has helped Margaret but now Mazie, Robert and Howard are all sick. I am fortunately feeling fine and it is a good thing as I have gone into town on several occasions to buy more orange juice for all of them. It is wonderful to have kind and considerate neighbors in situations like this as Mrs. Haak and her mother-in-law are both here helping out, as Mazie just is not strong enough to take care of little Howard and the twins no. 2 in her present condition. We received a telegram from Mrs. McGregor that she is on her way back here to also help out. There is a lot of sickness around here in late March of 1911 and Dr. Chase is running from one family to another trying to keep everyone healthy and cure those that are not feeling well. He is truly a gift from God with his compassion and skill as he takes care of his flock.

Well, the month ended on a mixed note as I did hear from the Bank of Harry. He sent me a check for $200 and said that was all he could spare at the present time. Maybe it is and maybe he is trying to slowly wean me off the need to go to him so often for money. A farmer's income is so unstable and seasonable that I really need his help and I hope he doesn't cut me off completely. He is such a wonderful brother as is my entire family. As I have often said, family is so important in good times and bad.

April is certainly a time of renewal for a farmer and the land. We have been very busy getting the fields ready to plant and also working on the orchard in the hopes that it will be productive. Fred Deyor and I have been hauling manure out to the south hill lot and delivering hay that I have sold to Mr. Spires, Tom Hannigan and also to Mr. Albright. I am getting $12 a ton for the hay and the money will help meet our other expenses. I am buying the seed to plant the oats, I have hitched up Logan with Maude and they work very well together getting the fields plowed and ready for planting. I have also spent several days digging up and drawing stones from the oat field and if you have never done that for a full 8 to 10 hours a day you don't realize what good hard work does for one's body. I had to almost drag myself back to the house in the evening after doing this all day. Fred and I also trimmed the orchard to finish it up and we sprayed it with Robert's help with a mixture of lime and sulfur. As I mentioned, I am determined to have this become one of the most productive orchards in the Palmyra area. Mr. Kelly also trimmed in the orchard and I paid him the 20 cents per hour I had offered him in the beginning. His total time was 41 and ¾ hours so I paid him $8.35. He did a fine job so it was well worth the 20 cents per hour I had to pay him.

Logan has come up lame after all this early spring hard work in weather that is less than perfect for outside plowing and planting so I took him to Dr. Earl, the vetenarain but he was no longer practicing so we went on down to Mr. Phillip's blacksmith shop and he trimmed some of the front hoof back in the hopes that was what was bothering him. Robert took his red heifer Cherry over to Walton's to pay a visit to Walton's Holstein Bull and hopefully their meeting will be successful. We have also been fortunate to sell some more sows this month for $25 each and that also will help our cash needs.

With this new found money I decided to settle up with F. Deyor for his work through <u>April 1st</u> as follows:

5 days work at $1.63 per day =	$8.15
102 bushels of corn he husked at 5 cents per bushel =	$5.10
32 hours at .163 cents per hour =	$5.22
Sub-total =	$18.47

A JOURNEY THROUGH LIFE

<u>Contra account</u>
10 bushels of wheat sold to Fred for .90 cents each = $9.00
Loan of team to help Fred move = $1.50
Sub-total = $10.50
Balance = $8.27

I paid Fred by check for the $8.27 I owed him to settle up for his work until April 1st. He reviewed the accounting and agreed that it was fair and proper so we closed this part of his contract for his work for me up to the date mentioned.

With all the sickness in the family, Robert has been holding the fort in church for us some of the Sundays in this month. Reverend McKenzie did call to see if I would be willing to serve as an elder if the congregation elects me to the position, I of course agreed and will try and do the best job possible if the congregation puts their faith in me as the reverend has. Dr. Chase has been here so much this month that I think we should give him room and board. He said he is just overwhelmed with all the sickness around and hoping and praying he has the skills and the medicines necessary to bring everyone that is sick in the community back to better health. It has to be a tremendous responsibility for him to take care of so many people here in Palmyra and especially the children who he is wonderful with. It is certainly a blessing that he comes to the house, I cannot comprehend if that practice ever stopped and doctors refused to make house calls 24 hours a day, seven days a week. Mrs. McKenzie sent a basket of fruit and other edibles for all of us to enjoy and she put a lot of oranges in the basket in the hopes of keeping us healthy. Robert also went into Briggs Drug Store and bought some Spirits of Camphor and some Plaster Clay to see if that would help. It seems that the doctor has a limited arsenal of medicines to help particularly those in the community that have become quite ill. Here in the middle of April Mazie is again sick and bedridden and also several of the children. Dr. Chase even had to lance a swollen spot on Mazie's face that was infected. Mrs. Chapman, thank the Lord, is here helping out until we get through this rough spot in our journey through life.

It seems that everyone is finally getting back to health and all of a sudden, as the month draws to a close little Harry has become very ill. We were up all night with him on Thursday night the 27th and I finally drove in to get Dr. Chase about 2 A.M. as Harry was having so much trouble breathing. Dr. Chase stayed with us and tended to Harry until 5 AM and then told us that he felt he needed council from another doctor on this case and he would bring Dr. Smith around to check on little Harry sometime today after he got a couple hours of rest. He not only has been up some of the nights with Harry but also with some other children in the community and you can see where it is taking its toll on him. Dr. Smith and Dr. Perry showed up with Dr. Chase around noon and they said that Harry has a case of Pleural Pneumonia and is very sick. We are all saying prayers for his full recovery.

"April 28- 1911: Dear little Baby Harry died last night about 10:30. He got worse suddenly and I went for Dr. Chase but the little fellow died before I got to the doctors home. He was 10 months and 5 days old. I telephoned Will TeWinkel at Perry and the telephone co. charged me 50 cents for the message. Lucy got here from Perry in the P.M. I went to the village and arranged with Mr. C.G. Crandall about the funeral. He charged me $12.00 for the casket and his services and $8.00 for 2 hacks. I went to the cemetery and bought the east half of lot no 635 for $23.00. I gave Mr. Clark the superintendent a check for $25.00, $2.00 of this pays for digging the grave. I then called Hans in Canandaigua to tell him about poor little Harry's passing and the telephone company charged me 10 cents for this call."

"Hans came over from Canandaigua early and left on the 6:22 PM trolley. Lucy started for Perry at 2:20 P.M. We had services at the house, conducted by Reverend McKenzie, at 10 AM. Mr. And Mrs. Langdon, Mr. And Mrs. Levi Haak, Mr. And Mrs. Abe Haak, Mr. And Mrs. Albright, Mrs. Cator, Mr. T.H. Chapman, Mrs. Cornelius, Mrs. Corlett, Mrs. Taber, Ruth Taber, Thelma Jones and Raymond Albright were here. We got to the cemetery just about 11 A.M. and were back home by 12 noon. I paid Mr. Crandall $20.00 in full."

I pray that doctors in the future will have more knowledge and more medicines to treat those amongst us that fall ill, especially the little ones. I cannot imagine anything more devastating to a parent than to lose a child, Mazie and I have now lost two with little Helen having passed away and now little Harry. We have been surrounded by a nurturing and loving immediate family and extended family and hopefully that will help us all get through this terrible time in our lives. Only the Lord knows why this happened and it is not our place to question it. I only hope that the 1st little Helen and Harry are now united in Heaven under the watchful eye of our Lord and Savior. With Mazie's help and the Reverend McKenzie's plus all the support of our neighbors I hope to get through this period without falling into the deep despair that I have known in the past. The good reverend insisted I come to church here on the 30th of April and be sworn in as an elder and he also has asked me to teach the Baracca class for the next 4 Sundays as he will be away. I believe he is trying to keep me busy and my mind occupied so that I do not go astray. With the help of the one true love in my life and the strongest woman I have ever known, Mazie, I should hopefully be able to get through this period of grief.

As May rolled around we see much better weather. I had to buy a new lawn mower and went to H. O. Young and Sons, bought one for $3.50 and have been keeping busy mowing the lawn plus planting the garden with radishes, beets, beans, peas, cauliflower, cabbage, tomatoes, carrots and, last but not least, corn. Mazie has encouraged me as well as Reverend McKenzie to keep very busy and keep my mind occupied. Charles Langdon, Fred and I have been spraying the orchard about every week and have gone through about seven 50 gal. barrels of mixed spray. It is long and tiring work as one of us has to pump the sprayer constantly to keep the pressure up. We have also planted rows of potatoes and many acres of corn. I borrowed two corn planters from my neighbor and I am going to pay him $1.20 a day each for there use. Hopefully we can finish the corn planting in a couple of days if the weather cooperates. Fred and A Cornelius are working almost full time for me now that the weather has decided it is the farmer's time to plant his fields.

We are all trying to make church each Sunday and on the 7th we all went with Mrs. McGregor taking care of Howard and baby Dilly, as I have decided to nickname little Helen. I taught the Baracca class after church. The Reverend Adams from the seminary preached this morning while Pastor McKenzie is away.

The author, Bill Parsons, had this marker installed
in memory of Harry in 2006

Mazie seems to be handling the passing of little baby Harry as well as can be expected and she and her mother and Robert went into Rochester to do a little shopping to keep her mind occupied. It is wonderful to have Mrs. McGregor here to help out during these times. She is a rock for all of us. Mazie is also attending missionary meetings at the Huxley's, which she enjoys very much. Without the faith that woman spreads amongst us I don't think any of us would have the courage to carry on! Mazie gets that great faith from her mother and father and shares it with all of us. In fact Mazie, Robert and her mother made two trips to Rochester this month with the second trip being one to interview Agnes Henry about coming to work for Mazie. I sincerely hope that works out for her. In addition to all this, Mrs. McGregor bought some new wallpaper for the living room and Mrs. Dwyer is papering for us. It is beginning to look great.

We had an interesting Baracca class on the evening of the 16th when the topic of discussion was the Barge Canal. Since we live about a half-mile from it and it runs almost through the village there were a lot of stories told about everyone's connection to it. I was also supposed to teach the Baracca class in church on the 21st but the Reverend Reed who was the supply minister that Sunday must have never gotten the word from Reverend McKenzie and he wanted to teach it himself. Most likely he didn't think anyone could do it as well as he could. I guess I was a little upset about not being called upon to oversee the class, however I was careful not to show it in front of the good reverend.

Harry sent us a nice letter and in it he sent us a check for $100 to help us with all the expenses we have had of late. We also had a telephone call from Hans, from Lucy TeWinkel, and my brother George sent a nice letter to inquire as to how we were getting along. I have called or written all of them back and expressed our appreciation for their concern. Family as I have often said is so important all the time but especially in times of crisis and it has proven itself again. Mrs. McGregor, Mazie and I signed the deed together and we sent it off to Mazie's brother, Howard, and hopefully that may help some with the expenses that keep piling up. I wonder sometimes if Mrs. McGregor may secretly wonder whom her wonderful daughter married, if I am ever going to be able to handle our expenses myself and keep our heads above water. I may not be a wealthy man but I am truly devoted to Mazie and I doubt even a millionaire could be more devoted or loving than this poor but hard-working farmer that I am.

It has also been a busy month with the farm animals and I have finally turned the three steers, two cows and the bull out to pasture. We have all been working hard to get the fence holes dug, the posts in and the fence drawn up so we can now let them be free to roam the several acres that are set aside for them for grazing. Fred had been bringing his sows to my boar and I charge him 75 cents for each servicing. I also set the red hen on 14 brown eggs for Marion so she could start her own little egg business and take care of the chicks when they hatch. Hopefully she will be able to sell brown eggs, which many people prefer over the white ones and they think they are better for them. Logan, Kit and I have been drawing tons of manure out to the bean lot and that certainly helps keep the sinuses open which is good for me. I always seem to have sinus trouble and trouble breathing clearly. Mazie says at night my snoring is beyond belief. I also have acquired another horse, which we named Brownie. I took Maude, Brownie and Kit to Contant's stallion for a rendezvous and it will cost me $10 each for the stallion's service if all three are serviced, or $10 each if only two are and if only one is, then it costs $12. We finished out the month with the red sow having 7 piglets. They were all born alive and hopefully will grow fast and fatten up for selling or butchering.

This has been a busy month as all spring months are for a farmer and his family. Between the family, friends, church and work we have managed to slowly learn to live with the reality of little Harry's passing. I, and I am sure Mazie and the entire family, even if we all lived to be 200 years old will never forget the first little Helen and little Harry and that is the way things should be. They remain alive in our minds and our thoughts and we were blessed to have these sweet children if only for a short time.

The Good Lord, I guess, wanted to help keep our minds occupied here at the end of May. We had a lightning storm and it was a particularly violent one. During it, lighting struck our main chimney and destroyed it. After a couple of days, and when I stopped shaking over the tremendous noise that it made when it struck, I did manage to call our insurance agent, Mr. Bramium, and he came right out, looked the situation over and told me to go

A JOURNEY THROUGH LIFE

ahead, have it repaired and send him the bill. Sometimes I guess it is good to have the insurance we carry. It could have been much worse as we were worried about fire from the lighting strike but we were fortunate that nothing like that occurred. I doubt if I would have been strong enough to handle this if we had a fire, with all the other tragedies going on lately. There is just so much a person can take at one time.

We have had a lot of company here in June of 1911 with Mazie's brother Howard arriving from New York City and his job as a professor at Columbia University. I picked him and his luggage up at the New York Central Railroad depot. Also Mrs. McGregor is fortunately still with us, Hans called and Mom and my sister, Norton, are at Canandaigua having come up from Manassas. I am looking forward to seeing her, Norton and Hans soon. We also had a visit this month from Mr. and Mrs. Nevin's from Perry and it was great to see old friends from our previous life in that fine community. Mazie, her brother and Mrs. McGregor also all went to the Saturday entertainment day at the church and they said it was a fine day there. I would have gone but A. Cornelius and I have been putting up fencing, dragging the corn and bean lot and it is keeping us fully occupied. Fred Deyor is not feeling well, has not been able to work very much of late and I am afraid at his age his working days may well be over. I guess it best that I do not take him out and shoot him, as I did old Jack, even though his working days may be numbered. I hope we never come to that sad fact that when people become less than useful, society will decide that they are a burden and do away with them. Only the Lord knows when someone's time has come and that decision is the Lord's to make, not mankinds. Fred has been a great worker and a friend, I hope he recovers from his recent illness and can come back to help me in the near future.

I took old Maude over to Marion to meet with Mr. Content's stallion and it seemed that they hit it off so hopefully Maude will have a fold in the future. Kit's front feet have been giving trouble so I got a bottle of "Save the Horse" from Binghamton, applied the first application to them and I hope that it helps. Maude, Kit, Brownie and Logan have all been working their tails off with all the dragging and plowing, etc. that we have had to do this spring. Hopefully they will all stay healthy along with the family and myself. This is not the time of a year for a farmer to become ill and not be able to work, as the work never ends. I took "Blind Eye" and "Palmyra" over to Walton's Holstein bull to be serviced and hopefully that worked out all right. I would guess the reader could figure out who named those two cows. Blind Eye, of course, was fairly easy for the twins to name since she is blind in one eye and the girls thought Palmyra was a fitting name for at least one of our cows since that is where we live now. Even Lady Edgerly has cooperated, had twelve little piglets and they all were born alive so I hope we can fatten them up for future meals or sale.

A. Cornelius and I with Robert's help have been digging many a fence posthole and stringing wire around the corn lot. There are so many deer in the area and of course the livestock would love to get into the corn so we have had to buy and put up hundreds of feet of fencing. It is a good investment however and should increase the harvest of the crop. I paid A.C. for his work to date at 16.3 cents per hour and since he had 104 hours I wrote him a check for $16.95. Can you believe the exorbitant hourly wage of 16.3 cents per hour, what is this world coming to? In my spare time, as if I had any, I have been planting more things in the garden, or I should call it Mazie's garden, and I bought 10 cents worth of beans, 10 cents worth of pea seeds, 5 cents worth of corn and onion seeds. Hopefully it will all grow and it better or it and I will hear from Mazie about it. We have also sowed 14 bushels of beans in the south lot and they should do very well there as it is well drained in that area.

With all the expenses, you might have guessed it, that I had to hit Mrs. McGregor up for a loan of $50 and also Harry had sent $200 as another loan that will come in handy. The good old "Bank of Harry" comes through again. It may be in competition with the "Bank of McGregor" soon if I find myself borrowing from Mazie's mom much more. It is always good to have two banks competing with one another over my business, I have always said since then maybe I will get a better rate from one or both of them. I should only hope. I don't know what I would do if I couldn't go to family when I need to get my head above water again. Thankfully they always seem to be there for us, I sincerely appreciate it and love them for their support.

Thomas Jones and Sons are fixing the chimney and the plaster that was knocked loose in the lighting storm and it will be nice to get that done. Mazie has been on my case to hire someone to do it and since the insurance is covering the cost I should have gotten around to hiring them sooner rather than later. With being so busy and so much on my mind I just kept putting it off and am just now getting to it.

Today, June 15th, 1911 is a very special day for me. I turned 44 today and we all had a little celebration and the children gave me some little gifts and even a few things that they had made themselves. The gifts that they had made are so much more precious than anything that is bought in a store. We topped it off with a fine meal and a great birthday cake that Mazie and the twins baked. It was a fine day, I am feeling great and the old nemesis, depression seems to be a thing of the past. I can't figure that out but I certainly am not going to dwell on it too much, as if I did, it might come back to haunt me and I am not welcoming that back into my life. Keep busy and your mind occupied and it will not haunt you is what I have believed all along. I am now trying to follow Doctor "Ben's" advice.

Reverend McKenzie is back in the pulpit and we are attending church on a regular basis. It was children's day on the 11th and we decided to have little Helen baptized that day with her full name Helen Watterson Tyler. Watterson is Mazie's mother's maiden name and Mrs. McGregor was so pleased that we decided to give little Helen that middle name. Even Hans, Norton and Ma went to church with us when they came over from Canandaigua; we also had some other visitors from Canandaigua that went with us. I have also been attending the Session meetings since I am now a member of that group and find them quite interesting. Certainly there are some diverse opinions from all the members of Session and sometimes I have to bite my tongue to keep from saying something that I shouldn't say. Reverend McKenzie seems to have a great knack of gracefully handling each of us, as well as our opinions, so camaraderie seems to be enjoyed by all as we continue to do the Lord's work.

Here at the end of the month Mrs. McGregor, Howard and Hans are all headed either home or to Perry to visit the TeWinkels. It will be quiet around here for a while since they have all left but we will soon fall back into our routine of being a farm family. Robert decided to ride his bike over to Canandaigua for a few days to visit his cousins. The twins and Marion have gone to a Grange social so it seems it is fairly easy to get back into the swing of things. All in all, this month has been a full and a good one for the Tyler's of Palmyra, especially after the tragedy of the past months.

July started off with much anticipation for the arrival of a new davenport that we bought from Sears, Roebuck and Co. and it was shipped out, we hooked up Maude and Kit and went to the New York Central Station to pick it up. We had been looking forward to getting it for some time. Like a lot of other things that can go wrong in life, this one was no exception and the davenport arrived broken. We signed some papers with the stationmaster and it will be returned to Sears and hopefully the next one they ship will be intact. In the meantime we will continue to enjoy the old davenport with the few broken springs and worn upholstery. It will be tough to part with the old one anyway as I have spent many an hour resting on this old friend after long days of work in the fields. As a consolation prize I decided to take the entire family, with the exception of little Howard and Little Helen, to the park in the evening to watch the moving pictures. Ma watched the youngsters for us and Norton also came along. Maybe something will come of moving pictures. The more I see of them the more I think that there may be a future for them. I used to think they would never amount to anything but they are getting better and if they can ever figure out a way to actually hear what the actors and actresses are saying it would be fascinating, to say the least. I doubt if anyone will ever be able to put sound with them so we will continue to hear old George play his piano in the park to accompany the motion picture. Old George does a fine job of playing tunes to fit the scenes of the movies.

Church has been a regular part of all our lives here in July of 1911. I have been teaching Sunday school classes and Mazie, the twins and Robert have attended a couple of picnics that have been sponsored by the church. We all went to Grinnells' Glen for a church picnic on the 12th and had a great time in this beautiful spot. Doctor Ostrader preached one Sunday and his topic was, "At the top of the column was lily work." I have to admit that I didn't know what he meant by that any more after the sermon than before the sermon, but I didn't dare show my ignorance of the Bible to Mazie, to Mom or to Norton after church as they all seemed to know what it was about, or maybe they were just putting on that they understood it. Maybe it was one of those sermons where the minister wants you to leave church scratching your head in the hopes that you will come back next Sunday to hopefully have your eyes opened on what he was talking about.

A. Cornelius has been working almost daily with me and I also have hired Isaac McKee and Jacob Cornelius to help out as we are cutting hay, drawing it into the barn and also cutting wheat and taking care of it. When we can't cut and draw these because of the weather we are drawing manure out to the fields on a regular basis. I have turned the cattle and the colt out into the hay lot we have finished cutting. We have drawn in 15 loads of wheat so far and I have lost track of how many loads of hay we have drawn in with Maude Kit, Brownie and Logan. I think they are all sick of working so hard but this time of year the work never stops. The children are even helping and they are picking up apples that the high winds of late have knocked off the trees in the orchard. The orchard is producing nicely and all our hard work in cleaning it up and spraying, etc. is beginning to pay off. The high winds may have done some damage but the children and I have picked up over 2500 pounds of fallen apples. We loaded them up and took them to Abe Forshay's and he paid me $6.30 for them. I gave each of the children 20 cents for their help and I would have been hard pressed to get it done without them. They are all hard workers as children must be on a farm. We have been blessed, or maybe it is just Mazie's authority in the background, but all of the children are always willing to pitch in and they are all great workers. Mazie is a great motivator in her own quiet way, as I have found out many times over.

Robert's Uncle Howard from Columbia University called and asked Robert if he would dig up or pick up about 10 dozen night crawlers, ship them down to him and he would pay him for them and his work. Robert and I have been digging them up in the garden, picking them up in the yard after dark and we have enough to ship them off. Howard didn't say what he wanted them for. He is an anthropology professor at Columbia so maybe he plans on dissecting them and trying to figure out their origin, but I would suspect he may just be planning a little fishing trip and he knows that Upstate New York night crawlers are far superior for catching fish than those downstate worms. Those city worms just never could measure up to the quality of upstate worms. After all this work and all the extra ones we collected, I decided that we should all, with Mazie's blessing; take a day off from hard work. We went to the Macedon locks on the Erie Canal and spent the day fishing. We caught several nice bullheads, a couple of nice bass and one large turtle, which we let go. We had a great fish dinner that evening from our labors. After all the fishing and the fish dinner Ma and Norton decided their stay had been long enough so they are going to take the trolley back to Canandaigua tomorrow and stay with Hans and family a few more days and then head back south. It has been great having them here visiting and we pray for their safe journey home.

We decided to take a day and go over to Canandaigua to visit with Hans, his family and see Ma and Norton once more before they head back. I guess we had not seen enough of them in all the days they were here with us or we just needed an excuse here in Aug. to take a day off from the grind. Mazie, Marion and I left around 8:55 A.M. and drove over arriving there at 11:A.M. Not bad for a horse and carriage. If we were wealthy enough to have a car we could have made it sooner but it wouldn't have been such an enjoyable trip. We spent a couple of hours they're visiting, then we left for home at 2:20 P.M. and arrived back at 5:00 P.M. Mrs. Martin stayed with the children and cleaned house for Mazie while we were gone so it was a double vacation for Mazie. If we were well off I would spend most of my time traveling, but alas it is not to be so. Since we do not get to go that much, we enjoy even more the few days during the year when we get to take a day off and just spend it with our family or our extended family. Who could ask for anything more?

A. Cornelius has been putting in a lot of hours helping as our hired hand and I don't know if it is I or if it is just the strain of all the work, but we did have words recently and he has left my employment. He became upset over the way I was trying to tell him to drive the horses when he was dragging the fields and said he had enough so I paid him off the $15.16 that I owed him and bid him a fond farewell. Since Fred Deyor had gotten sick and

Cornelius has gotten mad and quit, it seems I will have to put in even longer hours in the future to keep up with things around here. Some days when I work from dawn to dusk and beyond I also want to tell myself that I might quit, but unfortunately it just doesn't work that way. When you are a farmer, the hard work and long hours are always there and if you cannot find someone to help, then it is up to you to get the job done, and get it done I will. I find myself spreading lime on the alfalfa fields and plowing with Kit and Maude. I had to do most of it by hand as the drill wouldn't keep up with the horses and me. I also did one of my favorite jobs, as it was time to clean out the privy vault. I did this late in the evening when the outside air was cool and fresh. I wonder if there will ever be "inside" plumbing so this job will not have to be done. It is hard to believe anything could replace the outhouse! After working the horses so hard, Maude and Brownie needed new shoes so I took them down to Phillip's Blacksmith Shop and it cost me $1.70. I also picked and sent several baskets of plums to Mrs. McKenzie, Mrs. Albright and to Mrs. A. Haak. To top off all the hard work, I helped the big black sow give birth to 5 piglets and then the next day the big white sow gave birth to 6 more. All of them were fortunately born alive.

Aug. 5th is Robert's birthday and I paid him the $1.00 that I owed him for his help; I also gave him another 50 cents for his birthday gift. Mazie baked a great meal and a fine cake and we all enjoyed the celebration. In the evening we all went up to the park and watched the moving pictures and Robert said that was a fine ending to his birthday. In fact we are enjoying the free movies in the park so much that Mazie has informed the family that we will be going about twice a week this month. I wasn't sure these movies would ever catch on but by the looks of the crowds that are at the park and our enjoyment of them there may be a future in motion pictures after all. Mazie even made me get a haircut which cost me 25 cents before I could attend again as she said I looked pretty wild with my long hair but when you don't have any hired help and have to do everything yourself there isn't much time left for things such as haircuts.

The TeWinkels came over from Perry to spend some time with all of us. They brought Robert over some new pants and two new vests for his birthday gifts and he was most appreciative. Will preached at the Sunday Service and it was a fine sermon. It is very gracious of the Reverend McKenzie to step down from his pulpit for a visiting minister. It seemed like old times in Perry at the Presbyterian Church there with Will preaching and our combined families taking up an entire pew. Will even preached in the evening prayer session and his topic was "Lo, Here Is My Signature" from the book of Job. Will also accompanied me to the session meeting that was held here in August and we all had a fine discussion comparing the Perry church and the Palmyra Church. I think both congregations are very fortunate to have such fine leaders in their ministers.

I paid off Thomas Jones and Son for fixing the chimney that was damaged from the lightning strike and the bill was $9.54. Mr. Bramium, representing our insurance carrier, gave me a check for $11.52. It was for the $9.54 for the Jones, 23 cents for wallpaper, 75 cents for putting the wallpaper on and $1.00 for my cleanup and fixing the roof. I certainly thought that was fair and we were happy to have insurance in this case. Sometimes it comes in handy even for the small losses and you hope you never have a large loss.

As this month wound down I went to a Baracca reunion picnic at Port Gibson where we played ball and had a fine picnic supper. It was great to see some of the old class members that have not been active of late or have moved from Palmyra. I am also cutting wood for our winter's supply and if you have ever had to cut wood with a hand saw and then split it with a wedge and mallet you sure feel those muscles ache in the evening after a full day of this. I was hoping to get Will TeWinkel to help me but when he saw the pile of wood, I think they decided it was time to return to Perry. I am of course only kidding as Will often pitched in at the farm in Perry and helped me with the farm work. Will and Lucy and family missed the most exciting part of the month when I happened to be out in the fields, heard a noise overhead, looked up, and lo and behold it was a flying machine. I had heard about a fellow named Atwood that was planning on flying his machine from Chicago to New York City and I was fortunate to catch sight of it on its journey. It is the first flying machine I have ever seen. As I believe I mentioned once before, I certainly don't think there is any future in flying machines for people and as I

A JOURNEY THROUGH LIFE

said, if we were meant to fly, the good Lord would have given us wings. Maybe I should be careful in what I say however as I didn't think there was any future in moving pictures either, but as I mentioned, we are going to them about twice a week.

As Sept. rolls around I have found it necessary to write to Mr. Drewey and Co. to see if I have enough cash value in my life insurance policy no. 195243 to borrow the $152.76 to pay the annual premium. Things are pretty tough when I have to borrow from the policy to pay the premium but it would only lower the entire life insurance payment by that amount if anything happened to me, which I think Mazie and family could handle. I sure don't expect anything to happen to me and I plan on slogging down this road of life for many a year to come.

Things are looking up, as it is that time of the year when the harvests start to take place and one can use all the help he can get. Fred Deyor is feeling better and has decided to come back to work if even on a limited basis. We hired Walter Shade and his thrasher to thrash the oats and wheat. Fred and I are working with him and his equipment to get the job done. We finished with 140 bushels of oats and 241 bushels of wheat and it cost me $13.14 for the thrasher and the work. Fred and I are also helping A. Haak with the thrashing he has to get done on his farm as he has helped me many a time with the tasks around our Maple Avenue farm. I also sold three loads of wheat to Levis. It weighed in at 12,195 pounds and they paid me $159.98 for it. We are also cutting the corn and picking apples off the ground as we had some high winds here in Sept. of 1911. We picked up 2300 lbs. of dropped apples and received 50 cents a hundred pound for them for a total of $11.50. Mazie took some of this money and went to town to buy shoes for Robert, the twins and Marion. She even decided to buy her poor old husband a pair of nice shoes so I would be able to dress in my Sunday best when going to the Session meetings and to church. The Palmyra Fair is also on this month and Mazie has taken the children. I have also worked in an afternoon to take them. They sure love the fair and I think they would spend 24 hours a day there if we allowed them to. Mrs. Stewart Tyler, Virginia, Edmonia and Kate have also gone with us. They came over from Canandaigua and have spent a few days with us here this month. We even all went to the movies at the opera house, as it is

154

getting a little chilly to sit outside in the park and watch a movie. In fact, on the 14th of the month it was so cold that we had a heavy frost, the first of the season. It seems too early to be getting this kind of cool weather. It's like it was just yesterday that the weather broke and it was spring. Where did the summer go?

We have to have some of the wheat ground into flour so Robert took about 700 pounds up to Yellow Mills to have it ground and it cost us $2.25. Robert was also going to help Fred and I drag and drill for planting more wheat but Logan stepped on the roller tongue and broke it so Robert had to take it to the blacksmith to get it fixed. I think Logan was sick of dragging and rolling and decided he wanted some time off so he decided to break the tongue so he wouldn't have to work so hard for a few hours. Sometimes I think the horses are smarter in their own way than us folks.

This has been a hit and miss church month for me as I have attended a Session meeting and also gone to church a couple of Sundays, but here in the middle of the month I have such a bad toothache that I had to stay home. Mazie said since I wasn't going to church that I could cook supper as she didn't think I was bad enough for me to be laid up. Dr. Mazie speaks and the rest of us jump. I hope the ache will go away on its own, as I certainly don't want to go to the "painless" dentist any more.

We have had heavy rain here at the end of this month so I have driven the children to school a couple of days. I can't get much work done outside so I bought some new linoleum for the dining room floor and spent a half a day installing that. We also took all the children to the Opera House to see a movie to celebrate the fact that my tooth cleared up on its own and I didn't have to shell out good money to the dentist. Secretly, I didn't really mind the money as much as the thought of his drilling in the tooth.

As the month comes to a close, I have been elected Clerk of the Session, which I consider a great honor and will take the responsibility very seriously. Mazie said she is beginning to get some cabin fever and since she does not have the outlets that I have, such as Session, she thinks it is time that she prepares to take a trip out to Bellaire and visit her mother and the family. She has contacted my sister Carrie in Virginia to see if she would be willing to come up to Palmyra and take care of the household and the family while she is gone. She told Carrie she would send her

A JOURNEY THROUGH LIFE

$15.00 for her trip expenses if she were willing and able to come, which I suspect she will be.

I think I have been here and done this before. October has to be called the month of the "APPLE" as it seems that is all Fred Deyor, I, Robert and also a new man I hired J.E. Kelly have been doing is picking apples. I guess I have to be careful what I wish for as I remember saying with hard work and the devotion to the fruit trees we should be able to get a bountiful harvest of apples from our orchard. Bountiful is not the word for it as we have been picking apples morning, noon and night and also in our sleep. I am paying 5 cents per bushel to all the help except of course myself. My wages will be in whatever we can sell them for. Several parties have looked them over. F. L. Blackford of Blackford and Bodman Co. of Adams Basin, New York has come by and would like to buy them all for 60 cents a bushel but I told him we would be looking for other buyers and taking bids on them. Mr. Rousche offered me a good price but he wanted all the cider apples picked out of each bushel and discarded, as he didn't want to deal with them. With over 1500 bushels, I don't think we are ready to go through each one and sort them out at this time. After about 7 days of picking, Mr. Kelly quit so I settled up with him for the 83 bushels he had picked and paid him the $4.15 that he was owed. He didn't seem to be a great apple picker anyway so maybe he and I are both better off. Here in the middle of the month I did send the following letter to Blackford & Bodman. "Messrs. Blackford and Bodman, Company, Adams Basin, New York. Gentleman: Your Mr. Blackford called at my orchard the 10th instant and said he would like to buy my apples. I am now ready to sell, but would prefer to sell them to be delivered in crates, as our local buyers will take them that way. I am ready for a bid from you if you can buy them as suggested. Yours, Benjamin C. Tyler." We will see what comes of that.

In the meantime I have decided to give the good Reverend a bushel for he and his family and the only pay I ever expect from those is maybe a good word with the Man upstairs when it is my time. I have sold all of the windfall apples to Vanderwater for 60 cents a 100 pounds and he has paid me $23.22 for them. It looks like the remainder of over 1500 bushels will be going to E.C. Reeves as he has offered 62 ½ cents per bushel of 50 pounds each.

This should bring in a tidy sum and much needed funds. We can now switch from apples to the bean crop and concentrate on them. The only casualty of the apple picking was Fred as he got upset over my asking him one day to pick up fallen apples rather than sort the picked ones. I guess he thought that in the pecking order of apple pickers there was more status in working with picked ones than fallen ones. Hopefully, after he gets over being upset, he will be back to work to help me with the bean crop. I think his recent illness is still giving him some problems and he most likely needed some time off. I wish I could take some time off but alas it is not to be.

Harry Nevins from Perry stopped by and paid us a visit. Will and Lucy also stopped by on their way to a seminar in Auburn that Will is attending. It was good to see all of them. It was great that they stopped when they did as Mazie, Howard and little Helen are leaving on the 5:23 P.M. train for Bellaire and she would have missed them if they were a day later. Carrie could not break away to come up and watch over the household and the children that remain home but my sister, Norton, is coming up from Virginia and she will be in charge of the household. The children can't wait to see her as she always has a good time with them. The only problem is when we attend church, Norton has to go to the Episcopal Church, while we all attend the Presbyterian Church. It is not a logistics problem however as they are across from each other with all the four main denomination churches in Palmyra being on the four corners of the main intersection.

As the month winds down I have had several letters from Mazie, and I have written her several in return. She and the children are enjoying their stay with the family in Bellaire and it sounds from her letters like the vacation is doing her a world of good and recharging her battery. Maybe next year I will be able to get away myself for a little while, but then again who would do the farm work if I was not here to take care of it.

I have been active in church having led the prayer meeting on a couple of occasions this month as the reverend has been unavailable. I also attended the funeral and the cemetery service for the little Granger child who recently passed away after being sick for a brief period. I feel so sorry for the Grangers as I know from bitter experience the tragedy of losing a child and it seems to happen all too often as the little ones are so vulnerable to all the diseases that are going around all the time. Marion has even been under the weather a bit this month and I have purchased a bottle of castor oil for 10 cents from Briggs's Drug Store. I hope this makes her feel better and gets her back on her feet soon. My church activities ended here as October of 1911 draws to a close with a special service at the church where we all listened to the Reverend Mr. Boothby who is a member of the anti saloon league and spoke on the evils of the nectar of the grapes. It made me think twice about that little nip I may partake of on occasion although I will say I am not a frequenter of the saloons. If I ever even thought about it I would most likely take my last breaths, as Mazie would see to it that it never happened a second time.

November of 1911 has continued to be the period of the anti-saloon league and the temperance meetings. We all attended church on the 5th and then I went to a meeting at the Opera House in the evening and listened to several speeches on the evils of drinking put on by the Union Temperance Group. Things are heating up on this issue since there is a proposition on the ballot this month on the issue of whether Palmyra will be a dry or wet town. Mazie insisted that we pledge to the anti-saloon league so we pledged as follows:

Benjamin C. Tyler-	pledge for one year $4.00
Robert B. Tyler -	pledge for one year $0.60
Dorothy Tyler-	pledge for one year $0.60
Margaret Tyler-	pledge for one year $0.60
Marion Tyler-	pledge for one year <u>$0.60</u>
	Total pledge- $6.40

I have yet to figure out why Mazie didn't pledge but I am smart enough not to question her about it, as she was the one who insisted that the rest of us pledge for the cause as she calls it. It almost makes a fellow want to sneak out to the barn for a little swig of the nectar of the grapes. After all these meetings and posturing over the issue, Palmyra voted on the 7th to go wet. I noted to Mazie that I thought that was a terrible decision and it most likely is a good thing that votes are not made public as Mazie sort of looked at me after we both voted with that questioning look in her eye about which way I might have voted. She need not worry as I mentioned before I am not inclined, at least at this point in my life, to be a frequenter of saloons. We will have to see where this leads the fine little town of Palmyra here in 1911. I am sure the issue will not go away as there are such strong feelings on both sides.

Mazie, Howard and little Helen did have a great time in Bellaire and arrived back home just in time to get in on the temperance issue. We even had the opportunity to go to a meeting at the opera house to listen to a Dr. Tower talk on the developments and uses of new medicines. Maybe the days of Dr. Kitchel's Spavin Cure-all for everything from a canker sore to cancer is on its way out and the scientific community is actually on the threshold of developing new medicines that will help people fight some of the terrible ailments that are the curse of mankind and especially the vulnerable children that are so helpless. We can only hope with the Lord's help and guidance that new and effective medicines are on the horizon to help fight these terrible unseen killers afflicting mankind. I recently paid Dr. Chase in full the $7.50 that I owed him for his recent professional services to the family. He is a wonderful doctor but like my fear of the dentist, the less we see of him the better. It is wonderful however to know that he and his skill and wisdom are they're for us when we need him.

I hired Mr. Sperry, Mr. Doyle and also Mrs. E. H. Jones and Mrs. Cash Jones to pick up more of the fallen apples. I am paying them 15 cents per hour for their work. I have been delivering many wagonloads of apples to the warehouses over the past several weeks and the money they are paying us has certainly come in handy. Mr. Doyle did not work very long as he was offered a job at the Garlock Packing Co. Fred Deyor and I have settled accounts and time will only tell if he comes back to work at some time in the future. My best guess is that after awhile he will come around and ask to be rehired, and of course since he is such a good worker I will rehire him. His account was settled as follows:

Oct. 18 to Oct. 30, 77 ½ hours work @ .163 cents per hour = $12.63

For picking 500 bushels of apples @ 5 cents per bushel = $25.00

Paid by check from First National Bank of Palmyra total = $37.63

Norton has decided to pay a visit to Hans and family in Canandaigua since Mazie is back home, I took her over on the 18th and bid her a fine time on her visit there and a safe trip home to Virginia. It was wonderful to have her here, and the children all loved her devotion and guidance, even though she attended the Episcopal Church, which of course we will not hold against her. Well, at least I won't but I am not sure about Mazie. Mrs. Martin is helping Mazie, as her time allows, a couple of days a month and it seems to fit in well with Mazie's schedule. She is not bugging me quite as much to find her a full-time helper. Maybe the trip to Bellaire recharged her batteries, as I thought it might.

Tom Hannigan helped me do the thrashing and we got 187 bushels of beans from the 10 and ½ acres that we had planted them on. I also repaid the favor and helped him and Mr. Haak do some of there's. I am loading up on coal from the Sexton Coal Company and also filling the cellar with apples, cabbage, carrots potatoes, turnips, and whatever else I think we may need for the long cold winter that lies ahead. Since I have delivered the last of the apples, 1018 bushels that were sold to E.C. Reeves, and have received the payment for them I sent Harry a check for $153.35 on account. One hundred of it is to go to Harry against the most recent loan that the Bank Of Harry lent me and $50 is for Mrs. McGregor on the loan she gave us and the other $3.35 is to repay Mrs. McGregor for the money she loaned Mazie when she was there on her recent visit. She did not want it back but a debt is a debt and I thought it best to pay her, as I may need to go to *Bank of McGregor* for a loan again sometime.

Harry Nevins came by and wanted to do a little pheasant hunting. He didn't have to ask me twice since it sounded so good to be doing something besides working for a change. I borrowed

A. Haak's shotgun as Harry didn't bring his with him and we had a great few hours out hunting and bagged us a couple large pheasants. Mazie decided she would dress them and Harry joined the family for a wonderful pheasant supper. We great hunters certainly know how to provide for our families.

This month has not ended on a great note, as little Helen has been quite sick. Dr. Chase has been here almost every day on this last week of the month and I and Mazie have spent many a long night up walking the child and trying to help her feel better. Dr. Chase said she has a form of bronchitis and is having trouble breathing and he and Mazie and I have sworn, with the Lord's help we will not lose this innocent child to another disease. Dr. Chase had me get some antiflogistine from Briggs's Drug Store to hopefully help her breathing. It cost me 75 cents but I would have been willing to pay with my soul if only to make her better. I cannot stand the thought of losing another child.

After about a week of almost constant attention from Dr. Chase, Mazie and I, it seems almost like Dr. Chase was living here. He has told us that little Helen seems to be on the mend. We are all thanking the Lord for Dr. Chase's skill and the Lord's sparing this wonderful child. To celebrate, I attended a joint meeting of the session and church trustees where we discussed a Duplex Envelope System of raising more money for the church. It seems the church, just like any family or any other organization, is always short of money and looking for more ways to raise the needed funds. Hopefully this system will prove rewarding. The month ended with Robert attending a union Thanksgiving service at the Holland Church on Canandaigua Street. Mazie and I did not make it as we are still trying to catch up on our rest from being up with Helen almost 24 hours per day for almost a week. I did find time however to deliver 2 bushels of apples to the Reverend McKenzie and his wife plus some turnips, cabbage and pumpkins. I also gave some to Anne Jackson and F. Orloff as he is sick and in need. I also took some to Hud Langdon as pay for his aid in helping us with the thrashing. This was the least I could do in God's name for his blessings of sparing little Helen and it left me with a wonderful feeling that I could be of some help even if it was small compared to the great need out there.

A JOURNEY THROUGH LIFE

If you have ever spent part of a month without water you know that it is not a pleasant experience. Our well has stopped furnishing us water and I have called Mr. Wilber who is an expert in repairing and determining why people are having trouble with their wells. He looked the situation over and said that it needs to be dug deeper before we can have a dependable supply of water again. He is willing to do the work here in December even though it will surely be colder than "a well diggers ass" as the expression goes. We have little choice and it is great that he is willing to dig it deeper this time of year. He will be charging us 30 cents an hour for his work. I believe for this kind of work it is a very reasonable price. In the meantime I have had to water the stock at the spring up in the bean field and Mazie and the children have been carrying water from the neighbors well to help us, as we need it. Along with all this, little Helen who recently recovered from a bout of illness is again not feeling well. Dr. Chase said we need to get fresh water back for the family's needs and so along with Mazie feeling under the weather, it is a trying time.

I have been cutting wood from the orchard to keep the house warm so none of the rest of us falls ill. It is wonderful that the orchard provides such an abundant crop of apples and also when the trees are trimmed it also provides many cords of wood for the stoves. Dr. Smith stopped out at Dr. Chase's request to tend to little Helen and to Mazie and he told me to get my butt to town and buy a thermometer so at least we could keep track of their temperatures. Mazie and I always used the back of the hand method of seeing if anyone of us were running a fever but Dr. Smith said that was old fashioned and a thermometer was needed. I went into town and bought one from Briggs's Drug Store and had it charged. Seems that they both are running a little fever but I could have told him that with the back of my hand on their foreheads. I am not going to argue with him, however, as he and Dr. Chase are great doctors and with the Lord's help both Mazie and little Helen will soon be better.

I ordered from the J. R. Henderson Company in Rochester fifteen pieces of well pipe that were 24 inches long and they are to be shipped to the West Shore Railroad Terminal as soon as they get my check. Mr. Wilber says we will have to dig it at least down to 30 feet to have a steady supply. After his working on it for about 3 cold days and my hauling the dirt away that he has dug out, the side caved in and we had to cut some timbers and reinforce it. On the fourth day he did manage to get it to 30 feet and the new pipe installed, and I put the pump on it so we are back in business. You never know how much you miss the things you take for granted like water until it is no longer available. It cost me $20.00 in total for Mr. Wilber's work but it was well worth it. Hopefully with our own supply of fresh water from deep in the bowels of the earth and a steady supply of firewood furnished from our productive orchard, Mazie and Helen will recover soon and the rest of us will stay healthy. I did go up to the village and picked up a bottle of Walpole's Cod Liver Oil for Mazie and I am sure it will help her if she can stand the smell of it.

I have also spent part of this December visiting congregation members and trying to convince them to raise their pledges so that the church can move ahead under our new system of budgeting our yearly needs. Most of the parishioners have been very receptive and I believe a personal visit is much more effective in raising the much needed money than it is sending out an impersonal note to everyone asking them to support this new plan.

We have received gift boxes from the TeWinkels and from Hans and family in Canandaigua and we have also sent ours on to them. Harry also has sent some things for the children and Mrs. McGregor as always has been more than generous. The children received many a fine gift on Christmas day and Mazie who is feeling fit again, along with little Helen, prepared an excellent Christmas meal for us all. The month was finished off with a Christmas entertainment affair at the Grange Hall on the 27th that we all attended and enjoyed very much.

Chapter 6

1912

*The "unsinkable" Titanic sinks in the North Atlantic
with a loss of 1522 souls*

This month the taxes are due on our farm and therefore I have butchered several pigs and the big red sow with A. Haak's help. After cutting them up, I sold the meat and the seven hogs weighed in at 593 lbs. and fetched us 8 cents a pound for a total of $47.44. The old red sow weighed in at 333 lbs. and we got 6 ½ cents a pound for that meat for a total of $21.45. This money will come in handy for paying the taxes. I thought I might be a little depressed over these high taxes but it never materialized. I had to butcher the hogs anyway, not to get over the anticipated depression, but to get the money to cover the taxes. As I have often mentioned, a farmer lives from day to day and it is hard to save any money over the course of the year so when it is needed, it is time to sell off some crops or livestock. The taxes on our home and 81 acres came to: land tax $31.87, highway tax $10.40 and dog tax $1.00. I'm not sure the dog is worth it but the children would have me sleeping in the barn with the cows if I ever got rid of old Nuppy. Yes, the girls named the dog as you might have guessed from the name. I also had to pay a tax collector's fee of 44 cents, which seems to me to be a little bit much under the circumstances of having to pay such high taxes in the first place. The tax rate was $7.86 per $1000 of assessment on the land and $2.57 for $1000 of highway assessment. I am not sure if I would call this dirt path a highway but whatever makes tax collectors and town officials happy, I guess I will go along with.

After all that expenditure, we went to church and contributed:

Self = 15 cents general fund and 15 cents for benevolence
Mazie = 15 cents general fund and 15 cents for benevolence
(Robert paid his own) Robert = 5 cents for general fund and 5 cents for benevolence
Dorothy = same as Robert except we paid it for her
Margaret = same
Marion = 2 cents general fund and 2 cents for benevolence.

We also gave 8 cents for the Sunday School and I gave $1.00 to the Deacons' fund for help that is needed locally.

It has been very cold here in January of 1912 and I have had to buy a lot of nut coal. I also have spent many an hour cutting and dragging firewood from the orchard and the swamp. It is amazing how much wood we burn when you keep the fires going 24 hours a day, seven days a week. Fortunately with 81 acres, and quite a few of them treed, we have an unlimited supply of firewood. Maude and Brownie have had to have new shoes to get around in the snow and cold and would you believe it but old Kit went to join his buddy Jack in harness in that great horse heaven or wherever good horses go when they die. Of course I didn't want to waste anything, being a farmer, so I skinned old Kit and sold the hide to D. Perry for $2.50. Kit, like Jack, did an admiral job and they are both missed. I didn't need another robe so I decided to sell the hide from Kit rather than have it tanned and made into a robe as I did with Jack.

There has been a lot more activity this month with the livestock. The black cow, old Blackie as the girls call it, had a bull calf and the sow had 4 piglets. Two of the piglets were born dead and I have promised the other two to VendeBrooke for all the help he has given me in the past. As soon as they are ready I will deliver them to him. Cherry, another cow the girls named, also had a heifer calf so we have butchered some of the stock this month, lost some to old age and hard work and also added new stock to the farm. So it is with a farm family.

A JOURNEY THROUGH LIFE

I have been attending the Grange meetings and I paid my yearly dues of $1.20 to cover 1912. Also, the entire family went to a Grange Social, and I even participated by reading the story "How We Hunted the Mouse." It seems the children loved it and if I do say so myself, I did an outstanding job. Robert also attended and was very moved and impressed by the Passion Play movie at the opera house and that finished out a good month for the Tyler's of Palmyra.

It is cold, icy, and lots of snow here in Feb. We have had so much snow that I have had to drive the children to school in the sled, and even Maude had trouble getting through it. Normally I think it is great that the children have to walk the mile plus to school and of course that distance home, even in the cold and snowy weather, but this month has been even enough to melt this old fellow's heart and take them in the surrey. I have driven Mazie and Robert in to town to see the Merchant of Venice at the Opera House and also drove Mazie in to her Women's Church Picnic group at Mrs. Beach's house. It seems to me it is an odd time of the year to have a picnic but I knew better than to question it in Mazie's presence. What the ladies choose to do is their business and I know better than to question them.

I am selling some of the steers and F. D. Stoddard offered me $30.00 each for three of them, but being the shrewd businessman that I am, I held out for $35.00 each. I ended up selling them to some fellow from Walworth for $95.00 for the total so I did make $5.00 more than what Mr. Stoddard had offered. It is better in my pocket than someone else's. I also have rented out the service of the large boar to several of the neighbors and they are paying me 75 cents for each time they bring their sows by. The cows have had 3 calves this month and I sold one of them already. With all this new found money I even made a deposit in the First National Bank of Palmyra for $100.00 which will come in handy in the near future for we will need to buy seed and maybe more livestock and of course there are always the family expenses, the taxes and mortgage to worry about. As you have gathered from my life story so far I am certainly not one to worry about anything. Now if you believe that I have some 6 legged cows to sell you.

It seems we are burning wood faster than I can cut it and also of course the coal that we are buying as we need it. I have been cutting wood in the swamp for the stoves and it has become such backbreaking work that I hired J. Vandebrook to cut wood for us and offered to pay him 15 cents per hour and give him his supper. This should give me a break to start hauling out the manure to the fields and the garden and drawing in the shocks of corn in fodder. This is a particularly hard job with the cold, snow and ice of February.

I took an ad out in the local paper, the <u>Wayne County Journal</u>, for the sale of the new milk cows and also put a sign on the tree out front to see if we could sell them. The paper charged me 15 cents to run the ad and the tree didn't charge me at all. The tree is most likely the better deal as someone will most likely see it there and decide to buy them. I must admit however that the local paper gets a little more coverage that the Oak tree. We even subscribed to the <u>Journal</u> as they were having a promotion, and if you bought one of them new fangled vacuum cleaners for $4.50, you were given the <u>Wayne County Journal</u> for one year. The vacuum cleaner I think weighs about 90 pounds so I am not sure Mazie, being a slight but strong woman, will be to happy using it. As it turned out she hired Mrs. Martin to clean house for her and I saw Mrs. Martin struggling with it. It most likely may not get much use but at least we got the paper for a year.

It has been a busy month with the Presbyterian Church with our making the services every Sunday, as well as prayer meetings, session meetings and Baracca Class meetings. We contributed each Sunday our 42 cents for the current expenses, 42 cents for benevolence and 13 cents for Sunday School. Robert also contributes 5 cents to each of the above causes. We heard the Rev. Schovel of Newark lecture one Sunday on James Chalmer's missionary work to New Guinea and the Fiji Islands. That was a fascinating lecture and I certainly give Mr. Chambers a great deal of credit to be willing to go to the far ends of the earth to spread the Presbyterian gospel. I even heard Mr. DeNine of Rochester speak one evening on the men's religious movement in the church, which is founded in the Baracca Class. We finished out the month taking a freshly dressed chicken to the church chicken pie supper and it cost me 90 cents for the entire family to attend. A good time was had by all.

A JOURNEY THROUGH LIFE

This time of year I find the time to make all sorts of Grange meetings. At one this month, we each spoke a short piece about our homes that we grew up in. I spoke of my childhood at Ben Lomond in Manassas, Virginia and had many a fine memory to relate. It brought back days that I can no longer revisit as time marches on. The older one gets, it seems the faster the march is also. We are also making the movies about twice a week here in March and enjoying them greatly. I do think there is a great future for motion pictures. One evening, however, Mazie announced that she was taking the children to the movies at the Opera House and I was to stay home and use the new vacuum cleaner and clean the carpet in the sitting room. Not being one to argue with Mazie, I did as I was told and had that carpet spotless when they returned home. I was envious when they were all talking about the movie they had seen, "Rivals," but I will have to wait until next time it seems. Mazie said that if I was foolish enough to buy that monstrosity of a vacuum then I darn well better learn how to operate it. Maybe it will break down one of these days and maybe I will help it along, especially if I have to use it too many more times. I think I would rather cut wood all day than push that 90-pound behemoth around.

I have started to trim the trees in the orchard now that the weather is breaking and also have tended to the 6 calves that have been born into our livestock this month. Also, Mrs. Edgerly had 10 piglets, but unfortunately 5 of them were born dead. I think Mrs. Edgerly's days of reproduction are coming to a close. Even old Blind Eye had a calf to make it a full half dozen new ones for the month of March. I also was hoping to sell 3 shotes to Mr. Conant from the Mormon hill farm but he came and looked at them but decided not to buy them. For those of you who are not familiar with this term it means young pigs in this case. I did however sell them to Pete the Polander for $17.50. I wonder where Pete came from originally with a name like that? To round out our money needs I sacked up and delivered 9,489 pounds of beans to Bennet and Mason and was paid $296.53 for them. They paid $2.00 per 64 pounds of beans, which is a good price for this time of year. We needed the money as I had to pay the telephone bill of $1.25 and of course the mortgage and interest to date has come due on the farm. It is $300 for the mortgage and $105 for the interest to date that we had to pay to Mr. Griswold. The balance on our 10-year mortgage stands at $3900. Mrs. McGregor and Mazie's brother Howard also sent us each a check for $25 that I am to use to buy a riding plow. They want to help protect their interest and also they realize I am not getting any younger and need to have a plow that I can ride on rather than walk behind.

Church has been a little hit and miss this month, particularly due to the school having been closed for some time due to an outbreak of scarlet fever in the village. Robert has been ill and we have been worried about him but Dr. Chase seems to think his is just a sore throat. He prescribed some gargle medicine for him, which we pray will help. Dr. Chase and the other doctors have been overwhelmed by the outbreak and we are all praying the illness will burn itself out. People, including us, have been reluctant to go to any gatherings here in March any more than necessary.

We did attend church near the end of the month, as it seems the illness is fortunately on the wane and we contributed our normal weekly amount plus we gave an extra $1.00 for the Chinese Famine Fund. Their need is greater than ours at this time and we are more than willing to do what we can to help. Robert is also feeling much better so we wanted to go to church to thank the Lord for his recovery and pray for the recovery of all those others who have been afflicted. I also rented a shed on the east side of Church Street for the year from Mr. Mitchell for $2.00 and we get to use it on Sundays when we attend church and he gets to use it the rest of the days of the week.

Unfortunately here in April of 1912, the scarlet fever epidemic in the village is still spreading and therefore we are keeping the children out of school for a while in the hopes that the less congregating that people do, the less the disease will spread. Hopefully, Dr. Chase and the other doctors will soon be able to eradicate this scourge from our community. We are all praying extra long for the illness to be eliminated so we can all return to our normal lives without the fear of this unseen menace afflicting any of us, particularly the children. Maybe it is a blessing as the weather here in April has been very cold and snowy and according to the doctor, the cold weather they hope will shorten the illnesses duration in the area. It is difficult to get any plowing, dragging or planting done with the cold, ice and snow but I would rather the weather work to help the good doctors out than to help out us old farmers in this instance.

I did go to Rochester and order the 12 bushels of Barley seed from the Dailey Co. to be delivered shortly. It cost me $1.00 for the trolley fare, 15 cents for lunch and I spent 30 cents in the 5 and 10-cent store, and then I bought a newspaper for 1 cent to read on the way home on the trolley. The very next day, Lucy TeWinkel came over and she and Mazie decided they would take a trip into Rochester and do a little shopping so I gave Mazie a $1.00 and they must have had a great time as they were laughing and carrying on about their trip when they got home. I was smart enough not to ask them all the details and I was just happy they had a good time. Mazie needed a little time off with all the illness to contend with, and now little Helen is feeling under the weather and Robert went up to the drug store and got her some medicine for 30 cents and had it charged. Dr. Chase says it is not the scarlet fever and just another much less harmless bug so we are all relieved at that.

We have had some extra expenses this month with the $13.00 school tuition bill coming due for the 3rd quarter and the seed to buy for the spring planting. I wrote to Collen Ford and Sons to see if I could borrow $100 on another of my life insurance policies (No. 481761) against some of the cash value that has been built up in it. This money should help see us through planting time unless we experience some unforeseen expenses that we have not figured on, which is usually the case. I also sold 2 red sows to Benj. Harbour of Macedon Center for $10.00 and also sold Perry's calf, Blind Eye's and Lame Back's calf for $24.57. This money will all come in very handy. I also decided to sell Spot to Ed Farrell and he paid me $45.00 for this full-grown heifer.

I have been spending a great part of the month drawing manure out to the fields. Finally, the weather has broken some and I was able to do some dragging, and after picking up the barley seed at the New York Central Railroad, I have managed to plant several acres of barley. It cost me 46 cents for the freight for the barley seed, which I thought, was a little steep, but alas prices keep going up all the time except it seems for the farmers' produce. Now that the ground has finally thawed some, I decided it was time to bury what was left of old Kit so with Logan's help we managed to dig a big hole out in the orchard and laid old Kit's remains to rest. I frankly think it was about time I buried Kit as from the smell of things I think I waited a little to long. It is a good thing it has been cold here of late.

The church has had its annual meeting, things went well and we seem to be on the track of growth and prosperity as the pews are filling up more and more each Sunday morning and evening. Mazie, the family and I try our best to attend each Sunday morning to thank the Lord for all our blessings and also to attend the prayer services on Thursday nights and the Sunday service in the evenings. We gave a little extra, 50 cents, for the Easter Benevolence fund. We have also heard Reverend Johnson of Clyde lecture on Jacob Chamberlain and his missionary work in India. It is fascinating that the devotion of the Presbyterian missionaries and their work around the world to try and bring the Presbyterian message to everyone everywhere. We even made an extra donation of 50 cents for this month for the Easter music, which is so moving and wonderful to listen to. The church has a wonderful choir and a wonderful organ to bring the religious music to the congregation at the services. We even had a special meeting of the session to revise the membership rolls since we are growing so much. The only depressing thing connected with the church, at least for me, was Reverend McKenzie's sermon at which he preached on the sacrifice and honored the G. A. R. For one whose father fought for and was captured and imprisoned by the G. A. R., Grand Army of the Republic, I was not into absorbing too much praise for the Union. I realize that we are all one country and great sacrifice was given by men on both sides of the battlefield during the Civil War but when your parents are so caught up in the cause of the south back in the 1860's, and your father fought, was imprisoned and threatened with execution by the Union Army I guess it brought back memories that I would rather suppress. I certainly don't hold any grudge with the good reverend and if we lived in the great South I am sure I would hear the ministers preach on the G. A. S. or the Grand Army of the South as my parents used to refer to them.

**BEN LOMOND MANOR HOUSE
BEN'S BOYHOOD HOME
MANASSAS, VIRGINIA**

I finally got around to buying that riding plow that Mrs. McGregor and Mazie's brother Howard had each contributed $25 to. I bought one at H. O. Young's and if I pay for it by July 1st it will cost me $45.00, and if I pay for it between July 1st. and Nov. 1st it will cost me $47.50. You most likely wonder what I did with the $50 that they gave us for it but rest assured that was spent on something else long ago. Please don't let them know this however. I can't believe I waited this long to buy the riding plow as the weather here in May of 1912 has finally cooperated and I hooked up Maude, Logan and Brownie and off we went to the fields to plow. I felt a little sorry for them for a few minutes, having to lug not only the plow through the fields, but my butt as well but I never want to go back to walking behind a plow again. These new fangled gadgets sure are worth the money and I will promptly write Mrs. McGregor and Howard to thank them. I think we plowed twice the acreage in the same time as before when I would walk behind the horses. I asked Maude, Brownie and Logan if they minded the extra weight and they didn't indicate it was a problem, so from now on, this is the way it will be done. I may even get fat and lazy with this new fangled invention. I was brought back to earth when I started to load and spread manure the next day and realized that farmers have yet to have a machine that will do this wonderful sinus clearing task for them. Maybe some day. I also have drilled and planted several acres of oats and I have used 10 bushels of seed so far. In the middle of this operation I broke the planting drill and had to take it to W. R. Phillips and he and I managed to fix it up good as new. He is a master mechanic when it comes to fixing things, not just a good blacksmith and friend.

I have been feeling somewhat under the weather with a swollen jaw and have had to treat it with iodine. Also Dorothy has been on the family sick list of late but is feeling slowly better. I wonder if my feeling under the weather is from all the spraying of the orchard we have been doing. Mr. Abe. Deslgn, Jr. has been helping me spray and we have spent several days and applied many gallons of a mixture of lime-sulfate and arsenate of lead. Sometimes when the wind is blowing it back on us and we are breathing this mixture, I wonder just how healthy it is for us. Maybe since it kills the bugs that will attack the apples, it also kills the bugs that might attack us. I never mention it to anyone and especially to Mazie but I have a feeling it doesn't do any of us a bit of good to breathe this in. So it is with a farmer's life and his families, you do everything you can to protect and provide for them but I am sure some of the things we handle and have to deal with are not the best for us.

Maude had a black mare colt at 8 P.M. on the 7th of the month. She had been serviced on June 11th, 1911. I have decided to have Brownie serviced and took her to the Percheron Stallion where it will cost $10 if it is successful. I am guaranteed a healthy colt or I get my money back so you can't beat that arrangement. As soon as Maude is back on her feet, I think I will have her serviced again as she has had a fine colt. The bull also serviced Old Blind Eye so this could be called the month of the "servicing."

I bought Dilly a new pair of shoes, which cost 50 cents, and with them on we all attended the moving pictures at the Opera House. I don't think Dilly got much from the movie, but particularly the ladies in the audience fussed over her. Marion is also practicing to be in a play at the Opera House later this month for a May Day performance. We are all looking forward to her performance. She is now 9 years old, a beautiful young lady, and if I say so myself, an aspiring actress. Maybe someday she will be a child star, if so she hopefully will not forget her humble mother and father and her humble upbringing.

To finish out the month of May, I bought 7 bushels of seed potatoes from P. Conant of the Mormon Hill farm and I planted Mazie's garden. We have just about every imaginable vegetable to provide the family with a great variety and see us through the long months that lay ahead. As I believe I have mentioned before, I am not quite sure why Mazie calls it her garden when I do almost all the work but I sure am smart enough not to challenge her on it. When she says it is time to plant her garden, I just ask her what she wants planted and I do the work. She says that hard work never hurt anyone, especially me.

There is a time to sow and a time to reap or something like that as the Good Book says. This time of year is certainly the time to sow as I have plowed, dragged, and planted corn, beans, potatoes and every other crop you can think of. Since school is going to get out for the summer recess soon here in June, Robert will be able to help me as I do not have any other help at the present time. With so much work to be done, his willing hands will certainly come in handy. He is now 15 years old, very strong and always willing to pull his share of the load when he is not in school. Several times he has hooked up Maude and Logan and headed out to the fields to drag and help plant and as the case may be with some heavy rains lately, replant. It is easier on the pocketbook not to be paying hired hands but then again it leaves that much more work for Robert and myself. I do give Robert some money when I can for all his help but he never asks me for any.

I was a little down lately, most likely since I am working from before dawn to almost dark and in some cases after dark. When I do get to give it up for the day and go in and spend some time with Mazie and the family, I sit down in my favorite chair looking forward to some conversation and within a few minutes I am dead to the world and Mazie wakes me up about 11 to go to bed. A farmer's life is sure not an easy one but then again I am my own boss, set my own hours and am the master of my destiny wherever that may lead us.

Here in mid June when all the work and struggle to make ends meet is getting me down, I look up the road and here comes a Model T Ford and low and behold it is Hans, Virginia and the children driving over from Canandaigua to show us their new car. To say the least I am a little jealous and wonder what Hans is doing right in the farming business and what I am doing wrong. I certainly couldn't work any harder, maybe smarter, but I have yet to figure that out. Hans told me he paid $750 for this shiny black Ford and he is sure proud of it as I am sure I would also be if I was fortunate enough to be able to own one of these beauties. I guess old Maude, Logan and Brownie are my Model T, for the time being anyway. Enough of my being jealous of my younger brother who of course is also a farmer but somewhat more successful than I it seems. If I weren't so darn proud I would ask him his secret to success. Maybe in a few years I can also own one of these beautiful cars.

I decided to sell the Cornelius Bull, Cherry and Big Line Back to B. F. Harbor for $72.50 and the money as usual will come in handy. I am also selling cream to the dairy and that is bringing us in a regular $5 to $10 a week depending on the output of the cows. Hans and the family all decided to go up to the village and go to the movies so we hitched up old Maude and off we went with little Dilly and I driving the rest of the family in and following Hans and his family in their car. I thought it might be a good idea to have Maude take us in just in case that Model T got stuck in the mud I could pull it out for them. That would show them who has the more dependable model. Alas, it didn't happen so Dilly and I came on home while the rest of the family enjoyed the movies.

Mazie's brother Howard is coming to stay for a while. Mazie and Robert went into Rochester on the trolley and met him at Sibley, Lindsey and Curr Company. They took the trolley and it cost me 80 cents out of pocket for their round trip. Howard arrived in time for the children's day program at church and we all went, watched the twins and Marion as they were part of the program and they did a fine job. Marion is becoming quite the accomplished actress. On top of this, Reverend McKenzie gave a talk in the evening to the Palmyra School graduating class of 1912.

As the weather has gotten so much better we have gone to a Sunday School picnic at Grinnell Park and enjoyed it very much. Also it is nice that the evening church services can now again be held in the village park as the weather cooperates.

We were all saddened to see Howard head off for New York City and his job at Columbia University but we were thrilled that Robert accompanied him on the return trip and is going to spend a couple of weeks staying with him and enjoying the sights and sounds of the big city of New York. Robert has indicated that he always wanted to see New York City and Howard was gracious enough to invite him to go back with him and spend part of his summer vacation on what for him will be a fascinating adventure. We will miss having Robert around but look forward to hearing all the stories he will have when he returns in a couple of weeks.

While Robert is away, we had a lot of company with Mrs. McGregor, Harry, Margaret, George and Eleanor all coming to visit and spend some time here in Palmyra. It will mean a lot more mouths to feed, but Mazie will love to spend some time with her mom and her siblings and just maybe I can get a little work out of Harry. We all attended church and listened to the Reverend Schorville from Lyons preach on the virtue of helping each other out as we travel our journey through life. I think Harry took it to heart as the very next day he was out in the fields helping me draw in the hay and we even spent a half a day cutting and splitting wood. It sure was nice to have the extra hands and the muscle, especially in the woodcutting and splitting department. I secretly am hoping they stay around for a while as I have buckwheat to plant and lots more hay to draw in. Mr. Langdon has been helping me some with the hay as I have been returning the favor and helping him but it will give me a leg up to also have Harry help me. I will have to be careful not to work him too hard however or he might decide to move up their day of departure from what they originally planned.

It certainly hasn't been all work and no play as Mazie decided to hook up old Maude and drive them all over to Canandaigua to see Hans and the family. I am sure after that 15-mile trip behind old Maude that when they saw Han's new car they wished I had one that they could also drive. Maude is dependable however and they can rest assured they will get there and back in one piece without any breakdowns with her. When they came back they said they had so much fun visiting with the Canandaigua Tyler's that they didn't want the day to end so they all went to the picture show in the village. Mazie informed me that I was to stay home and take care of little Dilly, which of course I did not argue about. Little Dilly and I had a great time anyway, just the two of us for a little while. On top of all this, Mazie and her mother took a day and went into the city to spend the day shopping. Mazie informed me that the laundry was piling up, as she was so busy with her family that I was told to take it to Mrs. Smith to get it washed, and I promptly did. I thought it best to take it there right away as I think Mazie was thinking of telling me to get my butt in gear and do it myself while she was off shopping.

Robert arrived home from New York City on Sunday the 21[st,] wide eyed with stories about big city life. We all blessed his safe return, went to church and also went to the evening service in the park. Robert was so fascinated with New York that he informed Mazie and I that someday he will make his mark and work there. It is great to have such ambition at 15 years of age and I hope and pray it comes true for him. In the meantime, I brought him back to earth with some cultivating behind Maude and Brownie and also sent him into town to buy some much-needed lubricating oil. It cost the exorbitant price of 36 cents for three gallons. I thought that price for 3 gallons was outlandish but we had to have it so we paid the going price. Of course the gasoline they make out of it for those new fangled automobiles has to set the owners like Hans back a pretty penny as that costs all of 14 cents a gallon.

With all this work and excitement over Robert's return and all the company, I decided that I also needed a little break so I organized a fishing trip to the canal for all of us. We spent a great half-day on the canal and we caught 42 fish, which Mazie and the other ladies cleaned and cooked, and we had a wonderful fish dinner for our efforts. In fact they all enjoyed the day so much that they decided they would do it again and I was looking forward to it until Mazie told me that there was work to be done around the farm and that it was time to trim the hedges. As I watched them drive off behind Maude for their day of fishing, I was trimming the hedges and I said a little silent prayer that I had at least enjoyed the one day with everyone and our great fishing trip. I am sure they will never come up with the catch that we all did when I organized the trip, and sure enough when they got home, there was hardly enough for a meal for everyone so I dressed a couple of chickens and proceeded to tell all those gathered around our table my secrets of fishing. That will certainly show them. Of course I am only kidding and just a little jealous.

August of 1912 has been the month of the monsoons and also the month of family visitors. Harry and Margaret, Mrs. McGregor, George and Eleanor all left on the 4:24 P.M. train on the West Shore Railroad for their trip back to Bellaire. We will surely miss them as they were great company and I of course had the extra help in the fields that is always appreciated. A couple days after they all left Will and Lucy and the children came on over from Perry to spend a few days with us so we were not alone long. Mazie loves the company, as do the children and I. It's a good thing we have a big farmhouse to take in all the family. Will is helping me out on the farm in between the rains, which never ceases to end here in August. Hopefully we will soon have a week or two of better weather to dry things out. Usually this time of year things are so dry I am praying for rain, but this year I and other farmers are praying for some dry weather. Things do seem to have a way of balancing out so I guess the Good Lord and Mother Nature seem to know best.

In between helping me out, Will preached in the Presbyterian Church service on the 4th and his sermon was a rousing good one, "Behold I stand at the door and knock." It makes one think of their mortality and just how many more days, weeks or years we may have on this earth and what will be the response from the Lord when we "Stand at the door and knock." In between going to church Robert, Will and I have been cultivating as best we could with all this rain in the cornfields. We have also been cutting oaks on the west side with the binder and I am in hopes that we can start plowing soon in the south lot to prepare it for planting wheat.

Brownie, Maude and Logan are just as upset over the wet weather as I am as it makes it much more difficult for them to pull the plow and binder and whatever other tasks are required of them. I took Brownie and Maude to Mr. Phillip's blacksmith shop and it cost me $1.10 for Brownie and 20 cents to have a shoe replaced on Maude. With all this rain, Will and Robert and I decided to give up trying to work and we all went fishing with the families in the Erie Canal and had pretty good luck. Life is so short I guess one should just take more time to fish a little rather than work 7 days a week. Whatever the reason, we did have a good time and the work will still be there waiting tomorrow. It is also best for my peace of mind to take a little time off now and then.

My respite from all the work was short lived however as I need to remove a number of stumps in the 6 acre lot so I went to Bird Brothers and bought ten caps and fifteen feet of fuse so we could dynamite the stumps out. H. Fox came by and helped me and we did a job on many of the stumps. The horses, Robert and I will drag them down to the swamp when we have a chance. Mr. Fox is much more of an expert in the use of dynamite so I figured it was great to have his help or I might just have blown myself up along with the stumps. Mazie tells me I don't always use the good sense that the Lord gave me but I proved her wrong in this case. Mazie also reminded me that we needed to start thinking about our wood supply for this coming winter even though it is only August. She is always one to look ahead and keep me on my toes. Robert and I decided we could spend a day dragging the stumps to the swamp and also cutting and hauling wood from there so we ended up drawing in two loads of wood which is at least a start. Wouldn't it be nice if we had such a mild winter that two loads would do it but if the past few years are any indication we will most likely need at least about 20 loads.

Hans and Virginia came over with their girls for a visit and the girl's plan on staying a few days. While they were here we all went to hear the Reverend McCann preach and then we all went to the evening service in the park. Along with these services, I am attending the prayer meetings on Thursday evenings and teaching the Baracca Class. The session meetings also require my attendance in the evenings so we are spending considerable time with the church activities. It is time well spent. In fact, on Sunday the 18,[Th] we all went to Sunday school at the Presbyterian Church in the morning, then to the Baptist Church in the afternoon and to a Union meeting at the Methodist Church in the evening. We didn't manage to hit all of Palmyra's churches as we missed the Reform,

Catholic, Episcopalian and the Mormon services but we certainly did our part with the others.

The TeWinkels left on the 26th to head back home after many a tearful goodbye as it is always sad to see the family going their separate ways each time they leave but with the Lord's blessings we will all see each other many more times in the future and have the pleasure of each others' company.

Old faithful Brownie brought Robert, Margaret, Dorothy and Marion home from Canandaigua here on the 2nd of Sept. Old Brownie is much more dependable than one of those Model T Ford cars. At least I will continue to say so as long as I cannot afford one. The children had a great time in Canandaigua but school is about to begin again and so they needed to get home to get ready for another semester of their studies. Robert helped me pick some apples and we took the Reverend McKenzie a bushel and also exchanged a bushel with Phelps for sugar, I also gave Mr. Cann and the Cutones a bushel each.

We all attended church here early in Sept. and partook of Holy Communion and then I attended a session meeting held at the Manse. In the afternoon, even though it is Sunday, I needed to get some more harvesting done, as with all the rain it has been anything but easy to work in the fields. We did cut the alfalfa for the 3rd cutting and then Logan came up lame. I took him to Phillips for a new set of shoes but unfortunately it didn't seem to help and he is still lame. He will bear watching to make sure it doesn't develop into something worse. I hate the thoughts of having to shoot old Logan, as I had to shoot old Jack after the years we worked so closely together.

With all the rain, the cistern has overflowed and the pump has given us trouble so I went into town and bought a new washer for the pump and it cost me 8 cents, which I charged. This is a tough time of the year for a farm family as the crops have yet to be harvested and sold and so money is tighter than usual. I had to hit up the "Bank of Harry" again and he sent me $100 to tide us over until we could sell some of the bounty produced by our hard work. I told Harry I would be able to pay him back soon and Robert and I did draw 3 loads of wheat to D.H. Levis at the New York Central Railroad and they weighed 2715 lbs., 2765 lbs. and 2660 lbs. respectively. They paid us $133.27 for the wheat and I hope part of this will go to repay Harry as I need to keep my banker happy since I am sure I will be going to him again and again most likely for a bail out.

It is thrashing time and most all the farmers get together and help each other as the thrasher becomes available. I helped Fred Herbert and several other neighbors and then they helped me thrash our wheat, oats and barley. I got 176 bushels of wheat and 294 bushels of oats and 98 bushels of barley from our efforts. It seems like you just get through harvesting one crop and it is time to plant another so we are drilling the new wheat and adding about a ton of phosphate to the 25 bushels of winter wheat we are planting. The work sure never slows down for a farm family. Someday maybe with more productive equipment, farming will be a prosperous business with less effort, but for now it is a backbreaking business with little or no profit. The one thing it does give us is good health from hard work and it sure keeps my mind occupied. Therefore the old depression doesn't have any time to come home and roost. We are cutting more wood for the winter and also I paid B. Anderson $10 on account for coal and Robert brought 320 lbs. home to store for this winter.

The only diversions we have had this month are of course our church activities which are numerous and rewarding and Mazie and I also took the children to the Palmyra Fair on a Saturday and a great time was had by all. It is a wonderful experience for the children and I hope it continues to be a yearly event far into the future for Palmyra. The only other diversion from the work on the farm and the daily worry about where we were going to find the money to keep going was that on several occasions I had to hook up old Maude, drive the children the mile plus to school and also pick them up in the afternoon because of all the heavy rain. It is so much healthier for them to walk but in such heavy rain I took pity on them, or I should say that Mazie told me to get my butt in gear and give them a ride. She said even though I walked several miles to school in Virginia in all kinds of conditions that the weather in Upstate New York was much more demanding, that a few days of riding would not hurt the children at all and would most likely keep them healthier than being out in all that rain. Mazie knows best, or at least I always let her think she does. As the month draws to a close here at the end of Sept. we have had our first frost and a taste of what is ahead for us this winter.

Fall is certainly a time of harvest and in the Tyler family of Palmyra it is no exception. I have been cutting and putting up shocks of corn and picking apples until I never want to see another apple. Buckwheat is also being drawn in and I am digging what seems like tons of potatoes and putting them up in the cellar for part of our winter's supply of food. I am doing most of the work myself as at present I cannot afford to hire any help and it is backbreaking work but necessary. Robert is helping me when he is not in school and I am grateful for his assistance. We delivered here in Oct. over 7,000 pounds of apples to Frank Clifford's evaporator and he paid me 40 cents per 100 lbs for them. This is below the price of 60 cents per 100 lbs. we have gotten in the past but since this has been a bumper year for apples, the price, of course, is set by the availability and even though we produce more we are getting paid less. It doesn't quite seem fair but then life isn't always fair, as Mazie and I have found out over the years.

I have been spending every Thursday evening at the prayer meeting and session meetings where the good reverend is tending to his harvesting of souls. On Sundays most of the family has been going to church with the exception of my staying home every other Sunday with little Dilly and making dinner for the rest of the family. Mazie says I need to do this to remind me what cooking is all about and keep my skills in preparing a meal up-to-date. I'm not sure if that is the only reason, but whatever the reason, I enjoy the time with baby Helen. I also enjoy preparing the meal but I hesitate to let Mazie know that I enjoy it or she may have me doing it more often. I have been attending the union services at the Baptist Church on Sunday evenings so I am fulfilling my church obligations on a regular basic.

We have all been a little worried about Mazie here in mid-Oct. as she went to see Dr. Chase and he said she is not at all well. I believe the stress and strain of taking care of all the children, the house and being a farmer's wife is getting to her somewhat. I contacted her mother to see if she could come out from Bellaire, spend some time helping out and Robert is going to pick her up at the station in Rochester if she can come. I think the constant money problems also are taking their toll on her. I did manage to send Harry a check for the $100 he recently loaned us, and low and behold, he sent it right back and said we should keep it as long as we need it. That is the kind of banker to have. Since we have a few extra dollars, I splurged and bought myself some much needed items, a pair of Long Walker shoes for $3.50, and a pair of overalls for 50 cents and a shirt for 50 cents. I also need socks so I bought 3 pair for 25 cents. I decided to charge all of this since I wasn't sure if I should hang onto the $100 or start spending some of it. As it turned out, Mazie started to feel better, she and her mother, who came out immediately, went on a shopping trip to Rochester and she decided to spend some of the money as she figured she might just as well or it would be gone shortly and the opportunity lost. I did spend some to pay off the $10.00 that we owed Dr. W. H. Marks and I also paid $4.00 to Dr. L. H. Smith for his services. Both of these fine fellows are paid in full to date for their services.

As we always do, I and several of the neighbors are pitching in and helping each other do the thrashing. It is always a good feeling when we all get together to make the work lighter for each of us. I sometimes wish that I could have all this help with the apple picking but alas it is I that end up being the main picker, I finally finished up with all of them on Tues. Nov. 19th and tallied up the delivery to Clifford and it came to 1236 bushels of apples at an average weight of 48 lbs. per bushel. That is about 30 tons of apples, and if you don't think that is backbreaking work, try it sometime. To reward myself, I finally went into town and got my ears lowered at Mr. DeVoist's barbershop and it cost me 25 cents. It was long overdue. When I try to complain about all the hard work to Mazie, she just tells me it keeps me fit and to stop complaining. I did draw some dried apples for Clifford's to the siding at the New York Central Railroad for shipping out. I also managed to set aside 18 bushels to take to Wissick's for making into cider. As it turned out, we got 47 gal. from this pressing and it cost me 94 cents to have it done. It will sure taste good on some of those cold winter nights, especially if it is warmed up a bit and maybe on occasion a little of the devil's brew mixed with it might add to the flavor. This I would do in the barn, as Mazie would not approve. In fact she might well divorce me about it if she knew. Of the remaining apples, I gave some to W. R. Phillips for taking such good care of the horses and also to the Reverend McKenzie for taking such good care of our souls. The month was rounded out with my paying the school tax of $6.92 and on a more pleasant note Mazie's brother; Howard has come for a visit. I picked him up at the New York Central Station at 9:25 A.M. on the 27th of November and we are in hopes that he will be able to spend some time with us, grace us with his wisdom and beautiful drawings that he has a gift for. I have also been doing a lot of research, thought about "Modern Day Tillage of the Corn Crop" and offer the following as thoughts on the subject from my research.

"It is possible within a few years to double the acreage production of corn per acre in the United States and to accomplish it without any increase in work or expense. It is not understood from this statement that it is desirable to double the present corn crop, but that it is desirable to produce the same yield on a smaller number of acres and with less labor.

If 60 bushels are raised on 1 acre instead of on 2 acres, the labor of plowing, harrowing, planting, cultivating and harvesting is greatly reduced. The 10 years, previous to 1910, the average production of corn in the U.S. has been 26 bushels per acre. Few farmers would like to admit that their average production of the past 10 years has been as low as 26 bushels per acre. Twice this quantity is a fair crop, 3 times 26 bushels is a good crop and 4 times 26 bushels per acre are frequently produced. Poor corn crops are usually attributed to unfavorable weather conditions, and frequently this is the true cause for there are but few summers during which this crop does not suffer more of less at some stage of its growth. The most that can be done regarding the weather is to take the best possible advantage of the conditions as they exist. But there are other conditions that are responsible for low production, conditions that are directly under the control of the farmer and it is these that make possible the doubling of the average yield per acre within a few years. The lines of improvement that will most easily and quickly double the present production per acre are as follows:

1- Improvement in the quality of seed planted.
2- Improvement in the condition of the soil.
3- Improvement in methods of cultivating.

Improvement in the quality of seed is the sure and inexpensive way of increasing production and is the means that usually receives least attention by corn growers in general. Many farmers who give considerable attention to improving the fertility of their farms and bettering their methods of cultivation take their seed corn from the supply that happens to be in the crib at planting time without considering that their production is largely dependent upon the quality of seed they plant. Careful breeders of productive strains of corn are needed in every community, and growers who do not care to grow a special seed patch and select their seed with care should buy the best seed obtainable. If of the best quality it will be worth $25.00 per bushel more for seed purposes than unselected corn. The opportunity for the improvement of the soil offers a wide and inviting field of effort to the intelligent and progressive farmer. While it is true that proper attention to seed selection and methods of cultivation will greatly increase the average production per acre for all land, now devoted to corn growing, it is equally true that the cultivation of corn will never be found profitable on very poor land. The man who cultivates poor soil and harvests poor crops cannot compete with his neighbor who grows good crops with but little if any greater expenditure of labor or capital. Poor land should be brought into a fertile condition by the growing and plowing under of leguminous crops, the application of manure, etc. In the meantime, some crop that requires less fertility than corn may be grown. It should be remembered that the nature of the corn plant is such that it will not produce grain unless the soil is rich enough to afford a considerable growth of stalk, and that, in general, the richer the soil the heavier will be the yield of grain." Word well written and words for a farmer like I to try and live by.

It is hard to believe we are writing the last chapter of 1912 here in December. It has been an interesting year highlighted by the terrible tragedy of the sinking of the "unsinkable" Titanic ocean liner on April 15th of this year. Such suffering and tragedy is hard to imagine and gives one pause everyday to thank the good Lord for the blessings he has bestowed upon us. May the souls of those 1522 passengers and crew that sank with the vessel rest in peace?

We took a break from our daily toils and went to see "Across the Sierras" at the movies and we all enjoyed it very much. We used some of the money that Mr. Clifford paid me for the apples we had taken to him plus those dried apples that I had taken to the railroad siding for him and helped load into the freight car. He paid me $116.12, the balance he owed me on the total of $240.00. When we arrived home from the movies I found that an old hickory tree had toppled in the yard and taken the telephone wires down with it so I know what my work for tomorrow will be.

The Newark Presbyterian Church is looking for a minister and I had mentioned it to Will a while back, but he wasn't interested, as he wants to stay in Perry where he feels he belongs at present. Our Reverend McKenzie preached in Newark on the 8th while Reverend Macarthur from Philadelphia preached in our church in the evening that day so that the committee of members of the Newark Presbyterian Church could listen to him and see if they wanted to make him an offer to come there. It is a slow process to replace a minister in our faith and I sometimes think an overly burdensome process that results in a lack of continuity in the religious community of the church. The hierarchy, however, doesn't seem to ask my opinion on such things and Mazie is constantly reminding me that I do not run the world even though I think it might be better off if I did. We have had a couple of socials at the church this month and were privileged to have the Maggie Lantern show as part of one social. I also received a letter of resignation, which I promptly turned over to R. M. Smith that Mr. Usshers would not be continuing as the church's choir director effective at the end of this year. Dec. also saw the meeting of the Sunday school group and they elected me to be the Sunday School Superintendent. Unfortunately I had to decline the honor and I told Reverend McKenzie that due to my schedule on the farm I could not guarantee that I would be there each Sunday so he best find someone else. Mazie thought I should have accepted it but she is not the one that would have to be there each and every Sunday. After turning down the Sunday School and the good reverend I felt somewhat guilty so I gave a little extra money to the Baracca class project of buying a Christmas gift for Rev. McKenzie and they ended up giving him a fine mahogany table. It is well deserved.

Tuition has to be paid this month also for the children to attend the Palmyra Schools so I wrote a check for the $9.00 that we owed. It is money certainly well spent as the children are all getting a fine education and are all doing well in school. We are very proud of them. I also settled up with Davis and Company for the $10 I owed them, Barnhart and Jeffrey for $3.40 and also H. O. Young the $14.05 I owed him. After paying off Henry Runterman, that just about clears up our current debts. We also ordered some more coal from Sexton' Coal yard and I finished out my obligations by sending 415 lbs. of apples via the railroad to Bellaire on the same train that Mrs. McGregor returned home on.

Christmas Day dawned bright and cool with a light covering of snow on the ground. The children enjoyed all their gifts and we had a wonderful chicken dinner that we baked in the new Lisk Roaster that Hans had given us for a gift. We all said a prayer for the first little Helen and also for baby Harry who have each gone to be in heaven with our Lord. Someday may we all be reunited with them after our children lead long, productive and happy lives.

Chapter 7

1913

Ford Motor Company introduces the first
movable assembly line for the Model T Ford

Mr. Brown, Mr. Runterman, Mr. Stoddard, Mr. Devoist and I are very busy planning the annual social sponsored by the Baracca-Philathea classes here in Jan. of 1913. I ordered five gallons of ice cream and 10 dozen rolls from the Parsons Bakery. We are expecting a large turnout with all the goodies that are being offered. I also picked up a dozen fried cakes at the bakery to take to the Grange meeting and they cost me 12 cents.

Taxes have come due here in January for 1912, we had to shell out $44.53 for the property tax and also we had to pay $1.00 for the dog tax. I guess the old hound is worth it, as the children seem to enjoy her company. We had enough money left over for a couple of trips to the moving pictures here in January so we considered ourselves lucky.

I am spending a lot of time trimming the old orchard and cutting wood for the stove to keep us warm on these cold winter days. Every time I trim the trees I think of those 30 tons of apples I picked last fall and realize the better job that I do on trimming will produce more fruit and I may well have to pick 40 tons next fall. What else am I here for than to work I guess? I took the small white sow to H. J. Jackson's white boar and it cost me $1.00 to have her serviced. She should have piglets in 112 days and I calculate that should be about April 28. I can't wait for the piglets and the warm weather of April. In the meantime, I butchered four hogs including Lady Edgerly who had been as faithful as the real Lady Edgerly, but alas, every good thing comes to an end. I am making a lot of sausage and even took The Revered McKenzie a pork roast and some spare ribs. We sold two of the butchered hogs to W. T. Brown for $32.00. They weighed 157 and 163 lbs. respectively and he paid me 10 cents per pound. Since the hogs are gone for a while, I didn't need all that space for a hog house so I am converting the hog house to a chicken coop. I also sold Stub Horn to Mr. Brownell for $35.00. The following is an accounting of each of the cows that were serviced in 1912 and their offspring's. You will recognize some of the lovely names that the girls gave them.

Dunkle was serviced March 29 and had a bull calf Jan. 8.
Cherry was serviced April 12 and had a heifer calf Jan. 19.
Big Line Back was serviced April 19 and had a bull calf Feb. 1.
Spot was serviced April 25 and had a heifer calf on Feb. 2.
Stub Horn was serviced May 26 and had a heifer calf on March 10.
Little Line Back was serviced June 13 and had a heifer calf on March 26.
Perry was serviced June 20 and had a heifer calf on March 21.
Blind Eye was serviced on June 22 and had a heifer calf on March 28.
Palmyra was serviced on June 26 and had twins, a bull and heifer on March 25.

As the book of ledgers says, "You can not be diligent unless you keep a record of your business."

The parishioners from the Newark Presbyterian Church have decided they would like to hear Will preach and Will has decided to go for it, so it was set up that he will preach at the Palmyra Presbyterian Church here in early Feb. and they will send a committee from Newark to see if they like him and make him and offer. He would then have to decide if he wished to leave Perry and start savings souls in Newark. Only time will tell. We have also heard Reverend Yergen from Auburn preach this month, and for all I know, maybe he is also in the running for the new preacher position in Newark. Two other highlights for our family and its church life were the big spelling bee that was held at church on Feb. 12th where all had a good time. The other highlight that has made Mazie and I very proud is that Dorothy and Margaret both went before the session on Feb. 27, 1913 and were admitted into church membership on confession of faith in the Lord Jesus Christ. It is a very pleasing moment for the parents.

On Ground Hog Day this month, the ground hog, if he was crazy enough to venture out did see his shadow so I guess that means we are in for six more weeks of tough winter weather. Maybe the ground hog was smarter than the average and stayed in his hole where it was warm and that might mean an early spring. I can only hope. At least the ground is frozen and allows me to draw out ton after ton of manure onto the fields and not get stuck with Maude, Logan and Brownie. I did decide to splurge a little since those three are getting along in years and get almost as tired as sometimes I feel. I bought two new horses and the girls helped me name them, or I should say they named them Pete and Prince and I will take some time to break them into the harness and pulling the surrey and carriage.

Mazie's mother has bought her a new Singer Sewing Machine and I have to go to the New York Central Railroad Station and pick it up, so Mazie asked me to pack up a box of apples to send to her brother Doctor J. H. McGregor at Columbia University in New York City. I may have mentioned that he received his Ph.D. from Columbia in 1899 and has been a member of the zoological staff there since 1897. He was also a member of the Marine Biological Laboratory at Woods Hole, Mass. from 1899 to 1906. We are all very proud of Howard and know that his career is going to take him far and wide across this great planet we all call home. He is extremely interested in prehistoric man and has done extensive work in that field and continues to. I seem to have gotten a little off the track since I was talking about the 33 pounds of apples I am sending him and it cost me 35 cents freight for their being shipped. I did get the new sewing machine home and Mazie is in her glory working at it. It was nice of her mother to send her that as a gift.

DR. JAMES HOWARD MCGREGOR

We have managed to make the movies a couple of times this month in between little Howard being quite sick, Dr. Chase having to come out once in the middle of the night and also call on him each of the next couple days. Fortunately his illness cleared up and we are certainly grateful for that. One of the movies that we saw was Oliver Twist and we all were enthralled by it.

I ended the month by bringing home two suits to try on, one is a blue surge and costs $18.00 and the other is a black one and costs $16. Mazie says it is about time I bought a new suit so I will be trying to decide between the two of them. I have been wearing the same old suit to church and church functions it seems forever and I am sure some of the faithful will not know who it is when I come into church some Sunday with my new duds.

I did end up buying the black suit as I figure it would be a good looking one to lay me to rest in, just in case. I am of course only kidding although I did recently call R. W. Marble to bring me an application to fill out for $1,000 of life insurance with the Mutual Benefit Life Insurance Co. It will cost me $38.55 and they insisted, which is their policy, to have Dr. Smith examine me to make sure I didn't have one foot in the grave and that was why I was applying for the insurance. As it turned out, I only had a loose crown on a tooth, which I promptly went and had Dr. Marks fix for me. Since I bought myself a new suit I thought it only fitting to buy something for someone else in the family so I bought Margaret and Dorothy each a new pair of shoes and they cost me a total of $4.00. They are both very fond of them.

I wore my new suit to the Grange social and we saw the Larking pictures there. I also renewed our fire insurance through the Grange Fire Relief program for the year. Mazie says that no one recognizes me in my new duds and if I walk into church with the new suit she thinks they will ask me to fill out a visitors card since I have been wearing the old one for so many years.

We need to raise some money to pay the interest and the third principal payment of the mortgage so I have sold the black mare colt Twilly for $60.00 to the Beal Brothers. I also sold the latest calf that old Blind Eye had for $9.72. A. Jones wants to buy Prince and offered me $125.00 for him but I am holding out for a while in the hopes of getting $135. I may need to bend a little, however, since the interest payment is $97.50 and we are going to pay $300 to Mr. Griswold as the third payment on the principal. In addition to this, I needed a tooth crowned by Dr. Earle and he and I worked out the payment. He will take some barley from our stock to cover his costs.

Dorothy and Margaret have been publically welcomed into the Palmyra Presbyterian Church as new members by all the faithful. Their new shoes and my new suit were the highlight of the service that Sunday. The month finished out here in March of 1913 with my getting some bids from Mr. Powers and also from Mr. Herbert for repairs to our barn. I also wrote Sears, Roebuck and Company and the Chicago House Wreck Company to have them give me a quote on the lumber we will need for the project. We hate to spend the money, but then again, it is a good investment to keep up the property.

This area has seen some recent flooding and H. Runterman is collecting to help flood victims, so we contributed $1.00 to the cause and also took a pair of used shoes to the Palmyra King's Daughters' building to be given to someone who needs them more than we do. We had hoped to do more but at present, as usual, we are stretched pretty thin.

I prepared my welcoming talk for the get together of the Baracca and the Philathea classes and it is as follows:

" Friends and members of this church, Sunday School and congregation. I welcome you in the name of the stalwart Baracca's and the fair Philathea's Classes and hope that we may spend an enjoyable, profitable and pleasant evening together. We rejoice to see so many gathered here, and to the older ones, we say welcome as your minds turn back to occasions in the past when you have met here for social fellowship, may you live over again in your memory those happy times. May your enjoyment of this occasion be sweet? To the middle aged ones I say welcome to you who are on the firing line of life so to speak and who have its complex, perplexing problems to meet. May you banish these from your thoughts for the time and really enjoy yourselves this evening.

We would say welcome to the youth of the congregation and will enjoy ourselves in your enjoyment. Make the most of these gatherings and may thoughts of this evening linger in your minds as a pleasant memory long after your raven locks have turned gray. To our pastor and to his family we say welcome. His presence and sunny face are always an inspiration to us and may these meetings serve to bring us closer together and may we here receive a foretaste of the joys, pleasures and fellowship of that meeting which is reserved for us in the hereafter. Again, I say welcome to one and all."

That little speech put everyone in the room in the proper frame of mind to enjoy the evening, especially the part about meeting in the hereafter. If I do say so, I outdid myself in eloquence in this presentation. As it turned out with or without my introductory remarks all had a good time, which is what it was all about.

April brings again in life a time of sowing and to the Tyler family of Palmyra it is no different. Robert and I have been plowing, rolling and planting potatoes, alfalfa, barley, timothy and it seems hundreds of other crops. I have enjoyed plowing with the riding plow but it still requires a lot of back-breaking work even with such a modern invention, especially for the horses in the wet weather so far this spring. I even found the time to set out several of Mazie's favorite rose bushes, she certainly loves her roses and makes sure we plant new ones every year to go along with those that survive the harsh winter. I have managed to do all this even though I have a swollen neck and face from some more teeth that need crowning. I finally took the time to see Dr. Earle on the 10th of the month and he finished the work, I paid him $20 on the account and owe him another $50. He wanted cash this time as he said he had all the barley he needed at present. Along with my problems, little Helen got sick and Robert drove into town and brought Dr. Chase out. He tended to her and fortunately it was a minor problem. He gave her some medicine and said it should clear up in a day or two. I even felt so well after my new crowns that we all went to see the play, "Cricket on a Hearth," by the High School students who put it on at the Opera House. Robert played a role in the play and did a fine job as he always does.

We are getting about 40 eggs a day from the chickens and the sow had eight little piglets, two of which unfortunately were born dead. The six seem to be doing fine however and the girls should nurse them on to health in a short time.

We did receive the new fire insurance policy through the Grange and it was for $3600 of coverage broken down as follows:

$1,000 on our home, $300 on our furniture, $75 on our wearing apparel, $50 on the picture books, $20 sewing machine, $20 silverware, $250 on carriage house, $50 on corn house, $200 on hog and hen house, $500 on produce, $200 on harness, tools and wagon and $935 on the livestock. Seems to cover it all I hope.

In between my being so busy and trying also to keep that old enemy, depression at bay, I have tried to figure out which part of the year is the busiest for a farmer. Certainly spring planting and fall harvesting run neck in neck as the busiest. In fact, I am so busy and without any hired help that I had to resign as Clerk of the Session of the Palmyra Western Presbyterian Church. Mazie was not to happy with my decision but the reverend understood that there just were not enough hours in the day to do all that is required of me to attend all the meeting, take the notes, keep the church records and record all activities. It seems the reverend is more understanding than Mazie but she is most likely right, that I should have (found the time). Along with all this, I am in great discomfort as Dr. Chase tells me I have ringworm on my neck, which is caused by a fungus growth. He prescribed some salve for it and I hope it clears up soon.

Maude had a horse colt just 350 days from her being serviced and everything seemed to be fine, but the day after she gave birth, the colt died and I haven't the slightest idea what was wrong as both Maude and the colt seemed fine. I will let poor old Maude rest a few days and I am using Logan and Brownie to help me drag in the North Hill lot, I am going to give Maude about 10 days rest and then take her over to Mr. Cole's' stallion and have her serviced. No rest for the weary is my motto. Along with these problems I did manage to contract with Mr. Powers and his son for the work that is needed on the barn, I am to pay them $310 and I furnish the materials. I wrote the following letter to the Kanneberg Roofing And Ceiling Co. in Ohio for the needed items.

"Please ship promptly by West Shore Railroad, 160 sheets, 26 gauge and 10 feet long for the barn and 60 sheets 26 gauge times seven feet long for the shed. This material is to be the best quality of galvanized corrugated roofing. Also ship 83 feet of ridge roll for the barn, 41 feet of flashing for the shed. I enclose a check for $156.27 as we agreed upon with the discount for cash.

Please refer to your letter of April 23rd and May 2nd. Please be very particular to have the items delivered by West Shore Railroad as it is much nearer to me than the New York Central. Please be particular about this. You agreed to pay the freight. I note that you did not let me know whether this steel was O.H. or Bess, please let me know this as having been a steel man I would like to know.

Yours very truly

Ben C. Tyler, Maple Ave. R.F.D.

P.S. I may be able to get you some business in this section from the farmers. No steel roofs used here yet."

I ended up here in May hiring an Italian fellow to help me spray the orchard but he only latest one day and did not show up again for work. I was fortunate to find Cassius Jones to help me. He is very dependable and shows up bright and early every morning. Now all we have to do is find the money to pay for all these things or of course go back to my friendly banker, Harry for another loan.

Well, as it turned out here in June, I did write Harry and as usual my friendly banker (brother) did come through with a check for $200 to help tide us over until harvest time with all our bills. Family is so important in so many ways. On top of that Robert, took second place in a speaking contest at school and won $4.00, but that of course is his money so I will not look to him for a share of it. Here I am 46 years old and seem to be getting further behind the preverbal eight ball financially every year. It certainly is not for lack of hard work but farming is not what anyone would call a get rich quick business. It is a healthy life and with our loving family, friends and church I think life has been and is being good to us. We all went to the church's children's day service on the 8th and we have been going to church every Sunday and then to the union meetings in the Baptist church on Sunday evenings. The twins and Marion all had parts in the children's day service and of course as any proud father would say, their performance was spectacular.

Hans and the boys are over visiting from Canandaigua and just about the time they arrived we had some bad news that Mr. Shilling had suddenly passed away so Mazie, I and Hans went and paid our respects to Mrs. Shilling and Amy. Mrs. Shilling asked me if I would be a pallbearer on Thurs. and I told her I would be honored to. Such a happening reminds one of how fragile life can be and that we should each enjoy every moment, as we never know when it might be our last. Mazie suggested that I get my ears lowered before the funeral so I took Little Howard and he and I went to the barber and both had our haircut. It cost me 50 cents for the two of us. We are two fine looking gentlemen with our new haircuts. I decided to take all the children fishing since, as I said, one never knows when he might take his last breath so the work can wait. I told Mazie to get the skillet hot and be prepared to clean and cook fish and, of course, you can imagine what she told me. Something like, "you catch um, you cook um."

Mr. Powers and his son have started the barn work and are working most every day here in June of 1913. At the rate they are going they will have the work done in no time if the weather cooperates. I sold the heifer Palmyra to young Mr. Brownell for $42.50 and that along with the income from the eggs, milk and some early produce should help cover some of the bills. Mazie's brother Howard also has come for a visit and he has always been generous, pitching in, buying groceries and a few other things, which help. The month finished out with Brownie having a horse colt and Brownie and the colt are doing fine. I sure hope I don't lose this colt. I am giving Brownie 10 days and then I am going to take her to Mr. Cole's stallion for servicing.

I went to the prayer and session meeting at the manse until 11 PM. and undertook the sad task during the meeting of turning over the books of the Clerk of Session to the Reverend McKenzie. I almost had some second thoughts as I did it, thinking that I was letting the church down somewhat, and my faith, but I did go through with it. As I mentioned before it has become much more difficult to find the time to do justice to the job. If I was still a shopkeeper in Perry and could work on the records during slow times it would be one thing but as a farmer there just aren't any slow times. We are continuing to split our regular church attendance this month between the morning service and the services in the park in the evening.

It has been a busy month for visiting and visitors with Dorothy, Margaret and Marion taking the trolley to Perry to spend time with the TeWinkels. Also Mazie's brother Howard has taken the train back to New York City and his job at Columbia University. Robert even rode his wheel to Canandaigua to visit with Hans and family. When they all returned, much to my chagrin, they were brought back by automobile, Hans driving over from Canandaigua with Kate and Boydon and Mr. Wyckoff driving his Model T Ford over from Perry with the twins and Marion. I of course kept the horses handy as we have had some rain lately and I thought maybe their cars might need towing out of a mud hole in the road, but alas, they did not get stuck. Maybe I am just a little jealous. I needed to get my mind off my jealousy so I decided to splurge and went to the store and bought new underwear for 50 cents, two pair of socks for 30 cents and 10 cents for collar buttons. I charged the 90 cents to Lawrence Brothers. This didn't work too well to end my depression so I decided maybe a fishing trip would help so the next day I took Robert and little Howard and we went to Red Creek and caught some nice fish. Howard is five years old now and he is a natural when it comes to fishing, I think he is going to be a life long, very successful fisherman as he certainly seemed to enjoy himself greatly and caught the biggest fish of the day. That certainly helped as fishing doesn't cost any money and it reminded me of the wonderful things in life that are free. Material things are only fleeting and those that are important, family friends, health, church and even the stars in the skies at night are what make life worth living.

Mr. Powers and his son are coming along great on the barn. I need to get them some siding and some 2 x 4's so I ordered them from Rowley and it came to $206.66 and I took out a note with him, which will be due on Nov. 12 of this year at 6% interest. Hopefully, we can find the money between now and then. I did manage to sell Prince, Maude's 3-year-old colt to Abram DeWolf for $150.00 so that money will be there to help. We finished up the month cutting wheat and Raymond Albright helped me, I paid him 10 cents per hour. Labor is a little cheaper than it used to be so it is easier on the pocketbook.

It is the time for thrashing again and all the neighbors are helping each other out. This is when it really pays to have great neighbors and friends. I worked with T. W. Corletts to help him and several of the other farmers in the area and then they came and helped out with our thrashing. We thrashed 190 bushels of wheat,

306 bushels of oats and 71 bushels of barley. It cost me $17.38 for the thrasher and its use for the days needed and I have taken many pounds of barley, oats and wheat to the Huddle Mill for grinding. It cost me $2.43 to have about 2000 lbs. ground up. Robert has been a great help as he just turned 17 here on Aug. 5th, 1913. Where does the time go? It seems like yesterday when he came into this world. Mazie's brother Howard sent Robert a gold watch for his birthday and Mazie baked him a big birthday cake so we all enjoyed his celebration. The only downside was that Margaret ran a rusty nail into her foot and had to be taken to see Dr. Chase but he treated it and said she would be fine.

William TeWinkel has been preaching here in Palmyra on several Sundays filling in while vacations are being taken. At the end of this month I taught the Baracca class in Sunday School and for want of a minister on the 31st no regular service was held. I was surprised they didn't ask me to preach but after teaching the Baracca class I guess they had all of me they wanted for one day.

We had a pleasant surprise here early in September with Harry Nevins coming by from Perry to pay us a visit. He joined us all in church and we partook of communion together. It is always good to see any of our old friends from Perry. Shortly after Harry left I took Mazie, Howard and Helen to the West Shore Railroad for their 4:39 P.M. train ride to Haymarket, Virginia to visit mom and all my cousins and siblings. They are excited about their trip and mother is excited about seeing them all, especially Howard and little Helen.

Mr. Powers and his son finished the barn and shed and I have bought some paint. Robert and I are trying to get it painted in between the plowing, planting, thrashing and drilling in of the wheat. Robert stepped on a rusty nail also and was laid up a few days and unable to help but Dr. Chase said he was a tough young man and would recover fine, thank the Lord. I think Logan also got a nail in her foot so I took him to Mr. Phillips to be re-shoed as he was acting slightly lame and Mr. Phillips said his front hoof was inflamed so he couldn't shoe him at this time. He will need some rest also, just like Robert is going to rest a few days. It seems like everyone is resting except myself, but that is the way it has to be.

E. C. Reeves and also Mr. Sessions came out and checked the apple crop. I can't wait to pick 30 or more tons of apples again, and they offered me 60 cents a bushel, but I plan on holding out for more and letting them bid against each other. We have had a heavy frost here in mid Sept. and I hope that does not effect the quality of the apples, as we need the income from that crop.

Mazie and the children arrived back home from Haymarket on the 26th. They reported that everyone there was in good health and she and the children thoroughly enjoyed the time there. I ended the month going to a temperance meeting with Mazie in Newark and naturally agreeing with everything that the speakers were shouting about the evils of the devil's brew. I'm not sure it is so evil if it is used in moderation but I sure didn't say that in front of Mazie or any of the speakers there. After that, we decided it was time to take the children to the great Palmyra Fair and so we all enjoyed Sat. the 27th there. All had a good time. It's too bad the fair only comes around once a year as so many people attend and have such a great time with all the produce, animals and displays and also the rides and games of chance.

All I have to say about October is APPLES, APPLES, APPLES. That would just about cover this month except for the fact that I have had some help this year picking them. Will came over from Perry and he, Mazie and I picked for several days. I outpicked them handedly but it was sure great to have the help, as every apple they put in the crates is one less I have to handle. Several parties are looking at them including Mr. Levis but I still have not made a deal with anyone. I did buy 100 apple crates from Young and Sons and paid them 17 cents a crate. I also bought a 22-foot ladder, paid 10 cents a foot for it and I bought a 16 foot one and paid 5 cents a foot for that one. I think I will take a price of $1.50 per 100 lbs. for the apples, which seems to be the best I can get. I am also trying to trade some for sweet potatoes, which I think is going to work out. I have also hired John Denaring and John Cooks to do some picking and agreed to pay them the exorbitant sum of 7 cents per bushel. It's just as well, however, as we may well get over 30 tons this year and I am just not up to the task lately as I have not been feeling all that well. I hope that passes soon and I will be back to my old self.

We ended the month with Robert and I going to a union meeting at the Baptist Church in the evening and staying for the temperance meeting afterwards. I did manage to pledge the same

JOHN W. PARSONS

amount of money as I pledged last year to the anti-saloon league run by Mr. Tower. Frankly it seems to me the money could well be spent on something more worthwhile. However, Mazie would not speak to me for a month if I didn't help this cause at least a little bit.

If an apple a day keeps the doctor away as the saying goes, I shouldn't ever see a doctor again if I live to be 700 years old. Unfortunately I am still not feeling all that well, have an ulcerated tooth, a swollen jaw and Mazie is trying to nurse me back to health. She insisted that I go to Dr. Marks and he lanced my jaw. Hopefully that will help, as I can't afford to be sick especially with all the apples we are doing currently. We are still picking apples, also picking up a lot of them that have fallen and I estimate that we will get about 35 tons of them this year which will sure help pay the bills. I think we will end up making slightly over $1,000 for our crop. If I didn't have so many bills to pay I would consider a down payment on one of those fancy Model T Fords but I guess that will have to live in my dreams only for the time being.

Mazie went to Reverend McKenzie's house for a meeting on missionary work and when she got home she instructed me to go and vote on the referendum to make the area dry as far as consumption of liquor is concerned. I can't understand why our women don't have the right to vote as they sure seem to have more brain power and common sense than most of the men that I know. Some of the fellows have sure made a mess of the world and maybe it is time we give the power to the ladies to see if they can straighten it out. I daresay Mazie was actually voting even if she didn't fill out the ballot as she thoroughly instructed me as to how I was to vote.

With all our new earned money I paid off F. E. Rowley for the lumber for the barn, the $206.66 that I had owed him. I also had to pay him $4.13 which was the interest on the money at 6% for the time that I had the loan. I'm happy my personal banker, Harry, does not charge me interest at the exorbitant rate of 6% on all the loans he has given us or I would be in the poorhouse. As I have often said, it is great to have a family that is willing to help through tough times. With all this money I bought 45 young roosters and set them in the old hen house and Robert took Brownie to Dr. Earl's to have her teeth filed but the doctor said the teeth were fine and gave Robert a bottle of tonic for Brownie which cost us 75 cents and said that should clear up her problem.

As mid-November 1913 rolled around I delivered several bushels of apples to Mrs. Seals across from the Eagle Hotel and also gave the reverend and his wife several bushels. We celebrated Marion's 10th birthday with a party and I gave her 2 bars of soap and a jar of candy. We had a fancy chicken dinner with all the trimmings and Mazie baked a great cake and all had a good time. On Thanksgiving Day Hans and all his family came over from Canandaigua and we had a turkey and oyster dinner with all the fixings. All had a grand time. The only sad part of the day is that we heard Mr. Griswold had died this afternoon so that sort of put a damper on our Thanksgiving celebration. It is sad to see old friends and neighbors passing on to their rewards but that is the way of things. Since the weather is still great for this time of year Robert ended the month riding his wheel to Spencerport to visit friends. I told him to drive carefully and watch out for all the crazy drivers out there and especially the ones with those fancy cars. He is always careful so I am not too concerned that he will make it there and back in fine shape.

December is starting out where November did and I am still not feeling to good as my jaw is swollen again. I seem to have problems fighting off these infections and hopefully with Mazie's nursing and the doctor's help I will soon be fully recovered. Of course, I didn't go to the doctor when Mazie told me to so she wasn't too sympathetic with me and she even went shopping in Rochester with Robert and Howdy as I had given her $10.00 to buy everyone some Christmas gifts. I guess I should listen to her and get my butt over to Doctor Marks and let him have another go around to lancing my jaw if I am ever going to get rid of this infection for good. Mazie also told me to stop thinking about it and worrying about it so much but to get back to work and a routine to speed the recovery. She told me a busy mind is almost as good as the doctor's liniment so I took the three sows to Wm. E. Spire's boar and had them all serviced and it cost me $3.00. They should be due on April 20th if everything worked, as it should. I also went and bought some new bobs for the bobsled and had H. O. Young and Sons install them for me. I am also buying sweet potatoes from a sweet potato farmer in Maryland and having them shipped to me for about a penny and a half a pound plus the shipping costs. I am reselling them to Henry Runterman for his store and to several others that want them for 3 cents a pound and it seems like a good business arrangement to me. I also gave some to the good reverend and his wife so there goes my profit, at least in this life.

It has been a fairly busy month as far as church is concerned with a 25 cent per plate dinner, which we all attended, and then the annual congregational meeting near the end of the month. Other than that I did take a trip to the Geneva Experimental Station to see if I could pick up some pointers on being a better farmer and decided to take a little side trip via Canandaigua and Rochester to and from Geneva to do a little sight seeing. I had a good time and it helped me forget about the jaw discomfort that I am still experiencing. Mazie, the family and I also attended a free Grange dinner and after dinner elections were held, I was elected Chaplin for the coming year. I consider that a great honor and will do my best to uphold the office to the highest standards possible.

The twins Dorothy and Margaret are making some extra money this Christmas season picking hickory nuts and also butternuts and selling them to F. J. Stoddard for $2.00 a bushel. It will give them some spending money for buying some gifts they have been talking about. I also shipped some apples out to Will TeWinkel and his family in Perry via the West Shore Railroad and it cost me 29 cents in freight. I also sent some to my mother Mrs. R. H. Tyler in Haymarket, Virginia and that cost me 83 cents in freight.

I asked Mr. Haak to come by and advise me on trimming out the apple trees and he was kind enough to do so. My hired hand and I are doing the cutting and trimming and since nothing is ever wasted on a farm we are cutting up the trimmed trees and wood and will of course use it to help keep us all warm and healthy this winter. Mr. Haak has had a great deal more experience than I have with this type of thing so his advice was more than welcome along with the knowledge I gained at the Geneva Experimental Station.

The month drew to a close with all of us celebrating the birth of the baby Jesus and exchanging gifts. The children got lots of gifts and I received a pair of gloves, sewing awl, a box of library glue, a cake of soap and a book entitled, Taibill's Teachers Guide" that I will use to help me with my teaching of Sunday School classes and the Baracca class. All had a fine time.

Captain Robert Horner Tyler

Sallie Chinn Tyler
c. 1875

Chapter 8

1914

World War 1 Begins

It has been very cold and stormy as this new year gets underway. I have had to drive the children to school in the surrey on several occasions. It seems about every evening we have had to drive into the prayer meetings also. The world appears to be more and more on edge and Reverend McKenzie is having us all work overtime in our prayer sessions in the hope of continued peace on earth. It seems mankind would rather fight each other than learn to live as Jesus showed us. Maybe someday we will truly find the peace that so many yearn for. I was honored as I was elected an assistant Sunday School Superintendent and I begin my new duties this month. I am looking forward to them. One of the first assignments was to organize the first spelling bee of the year at the Western Presbyterian Church in which all the young church members took place and had a great time.

In between trimming and cutting down some more of the older trees in the orchard I found the time to help put up storm windows at the Grange Hall. I also killed and butchered 3 hogs and they weighed in at 197, 194 and 178 pounds. I am selling a great deal of the pork to various outlets at 11.5 cents a pound and that money will also come in handy especially as the taxes are due for the year. We had to pay John VanHall, Jr., the tax collector, for the house and the 81 acres of land $39.33 and of course $1.00 for the new dog that I recently bought Howdy. To top it all off they also charge a collector's fee of 40 cents. The grand total came to $40.73, which seems outlandish and I often wonder what the town government does with all that money.

We ended the month with a great sleighing party at C. Luppold's and it was attended by just about everyone in Palmyra and vicinity. We all enjoyed the sleigh rides and the hot cider that they served afterwards to warm us up. We were already warm with the friendships we shared with our neighbors and friends. What a wonderful way it was to end January at the start of a new year here in 1914.

It is very cold here in Feb. and you would think that it would kill off all the germs that are around, in fact here early in the month it has been running below zero and even reached a minus 12 degrees the other morning. Even with all this cold weather and my keeping the wood stoves and the coal furnace going full blast we are still seeing some sickness with Robert not feeling well and also little Helen has been quite ill. Dr. Chase is tending to both of them and with his expertise and Mazie's and my loving care I hope they will be back to normal soon. Even Mazie wasn't feeling too well as she had a toothache and so it fell upon Pappy to take care of everyone. I have broad shoulders so I didn't mind and they all, including me, seemed to get a lift from my being the nurse in attendance. Even old Brownie was very sick but fortunately it wasn't anything too serious as Dr. Forsythe gave her some medicine and it seemed to clear up whatever ailed her. Maybe I should have Dr. Forsythe take a look at Robert, Helen and Mazie since he seems to have so much luck with the horses. I am of course only kidding as we have great faith in Dr. Chase and as it turned out after a few days they were all feeling fine again.

Now that everyone is well again we have been social butterflies with a surprise party at the Grangers for E.D. Brown and a sleighing party at Newell Reeves. The only problem with the sleighing party was that it was 13 below zero so you can imagine how we all bundled up under the blankets as we sleighed over hill and dale or over county roads might be more appropriate. In any case we all had a good time and passed the hot cider around more than once. I'm not sure that was all that was being passed around but with Mazie there I sure wasn't about to find out, especially since our recent involvement with the anti-saloon league. We also have been attending the movies and the school students including Robert, the twins and Marion were in a school play that was put on at the opera house. It was a fine performance and we all had a good time.

Mazie and I attended church in the evening of the 22nd of Feb. and we heard a fine talk by a Negro man, J. O. Thomas, and he spoke on the interest of the Tuskegee College. It was an inspirational talk as to the need for all races to be educated and continue to rise above generations past. In addition I have been attending each Thurs. the session and prayer meetings. I also was honored that the 3rd and 4th levels of Grange membership were conferred upon me this month, the 3rd level being charity and sharing, the 4th being husbandmen and matrons. The Grange, "The Order of the Patrons of Husbandry," is a fine organization dedicated to uplifting and educating the farmers of this land in order to make theirs' and their families' lives better and more productive. There are three more degrees possible and hopefully I will be able to achieve those in the future. As part of this education for those of us that are farmers, I recently sold three small sows to H. Kniest for a total of $80. This money will come in handy, as the 4th mortgage payment is due quite soon. I also introduced Lawrence Duffy for possible Grange membership and I hope he finds the Grange as fine an organization as Mazie and I do.

We started out the month of March with very stormy weather, high drifts and cold. In fact it was so bad that even the U. S. mail didn't get through which is unheard of. Robert was the only one to make it to school a couple of the days early on this month as the twins and Marion just couldn't make it. I finally ended up driving them in and picking them up with the bobsled when the road was finally passable. Mazie and I even made it to the movies one night and saw the 3-hour movie, "Quo Vadis" which was brilliant and kept our interest for the entire three hours.

I have had to ask Harry for another loan and it looks like it will work out since he has negotiated the sale of the piece of land that the family owns in Pittsburgh and Harry and I will get $1200 for it. Harry sent me a letter and accounting according to his records of our business arrangements as follows:

1911 - March 29 - loan - $200.00
1911 - May 3 ----- loan - $100.00

A JOURNEY THROUGH LIFE

1911 - Dec. 1 ---- by cash--------------------$100.00
1912 - Sept. 1----- loan - $100.00
1913 - June 20 –tax due- $17.52
1913 – June 28 ----loan - $200.00
1914 – Feb. 26 grading - $138.43
1914 – March Interest - $54.05
                    BALANCE - $710.00

"Now if the price on the lot is $1200.00 this would leave me to send you a check for $490.00, or if the loan of $200 is continued then I would have to send you at this time $690.00, if this arrangement seems fair to you." How can I not say it is fair as Harry is always there for us when we need him? The only thing that is changing is he has decided to charge me 5% on the loans and I guess I can't blame him, as I seem to have to turn to him often. This money will come in handy as we are making the 4th payment on the mortgage to George Tinklepaugh, attorney for R. Griswold, estate of G. Griswold. The payment is for $390.00, $300.00 for the principal and $90.00 for the interest to date. This leaves us a balance on the farm of $3,300. I also had to appear before attorney Tinklepaugh as a witness to the will of J. Parks who passed away on Feb. 27th.

We have had a busy month with church activities having listened to Palsy Geehe from Bulgaria preach one Sunday. I also had to take over the reigns of the Sunday School Superintendent as Mr. Chapman is away and the duties fell upon my sagging shoulders. I too had to speak in Sunday School one Sunday on decision day and how we should think about it. Since this month was so filled with activities we even had a social at the Grange and I was asked to read "Uncle Remis Church Experience" to the assembled audience. The reading seemed to go over well and afterwards I was given several compliments on my fine rendition by some of those in attendance. The McKenzie's and the Hannigan's also have had us to dinner this month and we have repaid them the compliment. We are certainly becoming social butterflies it seems with all this socializing and other activities.

You might think with all this going on that I have neglected the farm work but rest assured I am still hauling lots of manure, cutting lots of wood and even found the time to buy two cows from

VerPlank's auction and I paid $66 for one and $44.50 for the second one. I trust they will be a good investment. We are also producing about 4-dozen eggs a day and I am selling them to several persons including Henry Runterman for his store and we are fetching 28 cents a dozen for them. We are in need of a silo so I finished the month trying to negotiate a good price for one with Mr. Adams of the Craine Silo Company. He wanted $200 for a 12 foot by 24 foot high one and I offered him $175.00, being the great bargainer that I am. He countered that he would sell me the silo for $173.00, which seemed like a good deal and I was patting myself on the back until he told me this did not include the roof. Now what good is a silo without a roof? That deal is off, needless to say.

April has finally rolled around and the weather is getting better and between the rain showers Robert and I are managing to do some plowing, dragging and generally getting ready to plant. I bought some seed from E. C. Reeves and it cost me $16 for one bushel of timothy, a quarter bushel of alsyhe, quarter bushel of alfalfa and three quarters of a bushel of medium. It is good seed and hopefully will grow a great crop. Also Mr. Shanon called on me and I bought some Great Dane Seed Oats from him with the stipulation that if I like the results I can get more later on for the same price. We are also going into the pickle business and I hope it will be profitable for all as Mr. Gassner and Mr. Tuttle called upon me and asked if we would commit at least one acre to growing pickles as they are going to open a pickle factory and they need so many farmers to commit to growing the produce for their factory.

I finally ordered a silo, as we agreed upon the price, it came to $190 for the 12 by 24 triple walled, cypress wood silo. They are to furnish one man to assemble it at a cost of $2.50 per day with our providing him with board and keep. They are to deliver it to the West Shore Railroad siding and we will transport it from there.

The month finished up with our going to the school in the evening for some entertainment provided by the students with Robert, the twins and Marion taking part. They did a fine job. Robert also was chosen by the school to represent Palmyra in a speaking contest in Rochester and we are all very proud of him and we know he will do well. On the 30th of April we had a fine party for Howard, or as I like to call him, Howdy, on his 6th birthday. Mazie baked a great cake for supper and we had it with six candles on it. Everyone had a fine time. It is hard to believe he is already six years old. Where do the years go?

May of 1914 sees the 10th anniversary of Reverend McKenzie as minister of the Palmyra Western Presbyterian Church. We had a reception for him at the church and he also preached a fine sermon the next day on his anniversary and what the 10 years in Palmyra have meant to him. It has also meant a lot to those of us that are parishioners as we have been the beneficiaries of his leadership. This month we also had the installation and ordination of elders for the church.

I have become involved as part of the school board for the Palmyra district and we are having regular meetings to discuss issues facing the Palmyra system. I managed to meet with Mr. Murray and Mr. Durfee at the District 5 School House and we are discussing, amongst other things, if a new school should be built at Murphy's Corners. We will have to decide that very soon as the school enrollment is growing steadily and we as parents and teachers have a grave responsibility to provide a quality education to our children and our neighbor's children.

I picked up the materials for the new silo at the West Shore Railroad siding and brought them out to the farm to await the contractor that is to build it. They look like top quality materials so I am looking forward to seeing the finished product. I have started to dig the foundation as the time and weather allow, in between fixing fences and spraying the orchard. I have also done some early plowing. I needed 15 fence posts for the repairs and bought them for 25 cents each. They are to repair the fence along the north side of the north hill lot. Mr. Scottney is helping me spray the orchard as this is a two-man job, and I am paying him 17 ½ cents per hour and also giving him dinner. It seems like a lot of money but he is a good worker and doesn't eat too much so I guess it is a good deal for me.

We are seeing the fruits of the servicing of Old Blind Eye, Line Back and Perry as they all have had calves this month. Line Back and Blind Eye each had a bull calf and Perry had a heifer calf. I have already agreed to sell them, will deliver them in a few weeks and I will be getting $25.22 for the three of them.

The month ended up with our receiving a box of used clothing from Mazie's mother and family in Bellaire, which we can certainly use. I in fact found some coveralls that I am wearing around the farm and especially in my efforts to plant the corn, which will all, go to the silo this season. I have also finished the spring plowing and I made a commitment for the new pickle factory so I am preparing an acre of ground for planting of our pickle contribution. I have plowed the ground and I am drawing out a total of 17 loads of manure for that acre so I am confident that we will have the biggest and best pickles in Wayne County, bar none.

We all went to the Children's Day service at the church in the evening of the 14th and then the next day was a very special day in the life of Benjamin Chinn Tyler. If you hadn't guessed it yet I am celebrating my 47th birthday today and Mazie has baked an enormous cake, put lots of candle on it and we are also having my favorite, strawberry ice cream, to top off the celebration. I am healthy, have a fine family, church activities and that old nemesis depression seems to be staying in the barn so it is a good day for old Ben on this birthday.

We are participating in many activities connected to the finishing out of another year for the school children. We heard a fine baccalaureate sermon from the Reverend Wright and also had a picnic in Union Park for the graduates. We also had a great time at the Opera House with the annual "Class Night" affairs. Activities were not over for the graduates until the festivities at the Grange to honor all the graduating seniors. After all these activities and honors for the graduates, they will be brought down to earth soon enough knowing that the future is all theirs and they will soon be facing life with a lot of hopes and dreams. I pray for their sakes that they will all come true.

Along with all these school functions I managed to find time to ride, in his automobile no less, to Walworth with Ed Brown, Tom Hannigan, Tom Corbett and Mr. Coveney to see Mr. McMurray about school matters of the board and also the question of approving the construction of a new school at Murphy's Corners. We all agreed it should be done, as it is necessary, and approved its construction. Now all we have to do is find the money for it but I guess that is like any other public project. Let the folks pay for it and spread the pain. Speaking of paying for it this month ended on my sending a letter off to Hans and Harry and hinting that I could sure use a loan from one or the other of them. I hope someone, or both, come through.

July started out with a fishing trip to Red Creek. Mazie's brother has come for a visit and we decided that it would do us all good to take some time off and spend it in a relaxing way like doing a little fishing. I think Howard McGregor enjoyed the time particularly as it is a far cry from his duties as a professor at Columbia University. We even took the time to all go over in the buggy to visit Hans and family in Canandaigua. We left at 7 AM and it took us about 2 hours to get there with Brownie and Maude doing their best speed yet, I think they are producing about two horsepower and certainly are more dependable than those fancy automobiles. Hans told me during our visit that he could loan me a second $50 so that makes a total of $100 from him. I have yet to hear from my usual banker Harry but maybe he and Hans got together and decided it was Hans turn to bail me out. In either case it takes a load off my mind that we have the money to tide us over for a while.

Ed Spickett came to work on the silo as agreed and I worked with him as Harry drove the binder for cutting the wheat. I may not have mentioned that Harry, Margaret, Mrs. McGregor, George and Eleanor have all come for a visit and are pitching in around here to help out. We are a little crowded but everyone is happy and enjoying seeing each other so being crowded is not a problem, especially when it is family. I didn't bring up the letter I had sent to Harry a while ago about a possible loan and I think frankly he was just as happy that I didn't bring it up. He also cultivated and hoed a lot of the corn for me so in a way he is making me a loan even if it isn't in dollars.

I am not feeling all that well as July closes out and I hope it is just a temporary bug that I have crossed paths with. I had to miss some church services not only in the church but also in the park on Sunday evenings as well. I did feel well enough however to figure out what I owed Hans and send him my note for the loan. I figured he loaned us $50 on June 19th and another $50 on July 11 so I dated the note July 1st, approximately halfway between the dates of the two loans and I owe him the $100 plus 6% interest both due and payable on Jan. 1st, 1915. I sent this to Hans and hope he is in agreement with it.

August of 1914 finds everyone healthy including yours truly, thankfully. We are hearing rumblings from across the ocean that a war has started in Europe. Germany has invaded some of her neighboring countries and possibly Great Britain. We all pray that it will be over soon with a minimum loss of life. As I have often said, when will mankind learn that differences between nations and peoples can be worked out peacefully and finally make plow shares out of their swords. Wishful thinking maybe. Speaking of plowshares, I am hoeing corn in the mornings starting at sunup and then lately I have decided to take the children fishing either at the locks on the Erie Canal or at Red Creek in the late afternoons. Seems like a much more desirable way to spend ones days than working in the fields from dawn to dusk.

Mrs. McGregor, Margaret, Harry, George and Eleanor left on the 5 PM train on the West Shore Railroad for their trip to Bellaire here on the 4th. We greatly enjoyed having them with us and hopefully the children and Mazie and I will be able to have more vacations like when family comes, or the children go to live with their aunts and uncles for a few days. We are not wealthy enough to take a real vacation like some city folks that actually travel to all sorts of exotic places but we enjoy ourselves just as much by having family spend time here with us and we spending time at the relatives.

I am a little upset about the lack of progress on erecting the new silo so I wrote the following note to G. F. Adams in Caledonia, NY. "Where is the man to erect silo? Have written twice, answer." I sent it collect. Hopefully that will wake them up and someone will be here to work fulltime on the new silo rather than letting the pieces all sit here and wait to be covered by snow. In the meantime, I am picking cucumbers and sending them via the South Shore RR to McGuire for the pickle factory they started. I sent 408 pounds of small ones and 100 pounds of large ones in my first shipment to them and it looks like we will be getting many more from the acre we planted. Its all that manure I put on the land that produces such great cucumbers. Looks like this might just turn out to be a moneymaker for us. One thing about picking cucumbers that is different than picking apples is that you get to bend over rather than reach up for them. One sort of balances out the other as far as wear and tear on the body is concerned. Even Will TeWinkel is helping Robert and I pick them, as Will has been here to preach on several Sundays and at the park services in the evenings. Rev. McKenzie is tight lipped about his plans but we have noticed he has been absent from the pulpit on a number of Sundays lately and we are wondering where he may be or if he is looking to move to another calling. We are in hopes that is not going to happen as he is a fine preacher and we would sorely miss him and his steadying hand. Only time will tell us, however, so we will need to be patient and just wait to see what transpires.

I hooked up the horses and Mazie and I took the twins, Marion and Helen to Canandaigua to spend some vacation time with Hans and Virginia and we brought Boydon home with us so he could spend some vacation time with us around the farm. They are to stay over there for a week and then we will go and get them and bring them, Virginia and Kate back to spend some time with us. I don't know what I would do without family around. I feel sorry for folks that are not blessed with family, as it has to be very difficult at times being without loves ones. I am sure I would be a basket case, as they say, if I were alone.

The month finished out with the thrasher arriving and we thrashed for a day and a half. I paid J. VerPlank $10.14 for the use of the thrasher and his time. Also I may have failed to mention that the silo installer did show up after my very abrupt last letter to them and he certainly knew his business as he had it fully up in a week and a half. I have gotten some white paint for $1.85 and a gallon of linseed oil for 70 cents to get started as I have time to paint it. It is a fine silo and adds an air of distinction to the Tyler farm on Maple Avenue in Palmyra, New York.

We still haven't been told anything about Reverend McKenzie's plans and I guess that is the way it has to be until something definite is decided upon. I am still hoping that he will not be leaving Palmyra's Western Presbyterian Church but what will be will be. As much as I would like to control things, it just doesn't seem that it ever works out that way. I was called upon to speak at the Methodist Church on the 6th of Sept. and I spoke on evangelism. My talk seemed to go over well as several of those in attendance told me that they received a great deal out of what I said. Hopefully, I was instrumental in moving some minds on the subject.

I picked up a load of sand from the Palmyra Sand Company for the silo and also picked up some more paint for it. Ed Brown, Ed Spichett, J. Blankenburg and Tom Hannigan all pitched in and helped me work to fill the silo now that I have gotten it up, finished and completed except for the little bit more painting that needs to be done on the outside. I tried to pay all those fellows for their help, but alas, none of them would take any pay. If and when they get silos and need to have help filling theirs I sure will be available to help them out. It is so rewarding to see neighbors helping neighbors rather than what is going on in Europe with the World War when nations can't seem to get along with one another. Hopefully this will be the war to end all wars. I can only pray it will be.

Lucy, Gordon and little Joy came over from Perry to spend some time with the Palmyra Tyler's and Mazie and the children are enjoying their company hugely. We all made the fair on the last Saturday of the month and the children enjoyed themselves immensely. I do believe they would live at the fair if they could.

I finished out this month paying G. Tinklepaugh, attorney for R. E. Griswold the $82.50 that we owed on the mortgage of $3,300 at 5% interest for the six months from April 1st to Oct. 1st, 1914. It came to $82.50 and hopefully John, the Italian I hired to pick pickles, will pick enough to cover his costs at 10 cents per bushel and also the cost of the interest payment.

Well here in October we have received some good news and some bad news. The bad news is that the good reverend is taking a calling in Utica, NY and will be leaving at the end of the month, so Palmyra Presbyterian Church is looking for a new leader. Hopefully, the process will be speedy as no organization can survive long without a leader and the church is certainly no exception. This certainly brings back to mind that time when I was still living in Bellaire and our church was without a minister and I was the clerk of the committee to find one. A lot of time can be taken up in such a search. So many of our members lean heavily on the minister for assistance, prayer and guidance that we can ill afford to be without someone for even a short period of time. We are all praying for Reverend McKenzie's success and our success in finding a quick replacement. Whoever is given the call will have large shoes to fill and hopefully will fill them well. The good news is that we tallied up our pickle picks and we shipped 15,101 pounds of small pickles and 37 pounds of large pickles in all. They will fetch us $151. 94 less the dollar for seed so we are going to net $150.94 for our efforts. This money will sure come in handy as we just paid the interest on the mortgage and we are facing apple-picking time and I need to hire some help for that task. A farmer just cashes in one crop and another is ready to work on and requires some outlay of expenditure so it is an every turning circle. O well, this is the life we chose and it so far has been a happy and healthy one even thought we find ourselves short of cash on a regular basis but not short of love.

The children are back in school and going strong. We had a rally day in the main auditorium and then a parade that the entire family went to and we all greatly enjoyed ourselves. Not only the students but the teachers and parents showed a lot of enthusiasm as well. A good education is not just between the teachers and the students, it involves the parents as well and that is what Palmyra schools are all about.

The Reverend Garrett Flikama stopped by to look at our apples and I agreed to sell him 200 barrels of apples to be shipped via the West Shore Railroad by the 23rd of October. They are to be shipped to Muscatine, Iowa. He has agreed to see that I am paid $2.10 per barrel. That will take a lot of apples, as one barrel of apples is over seven thousand cubic inches. I'm not sure what a reverend is doing in the apple business but it is not my place to question it as long as I am getting what I consider to be a fair price for them. I hired J. Hughes, Mr. Henry and Ed Harrington. Ed only picked three bushels and found that job was not to his liking so he quit. Levi Haak is also helping me pick since we are under pressure to get them ready to ship by the 23rd. We ended up picking 937 bushels and that made the 200 barrels we had agreed upon. We shipped them via the West Shore on the 26^{th,} only two days behind schedule, and I wrote the following letter to McKee Brothers in Muscatine about them. "Gentlemen: I have today shipped you in car M.D.T.X 30016, 200 barrels @ $2.10 per barrel = $420.00. You to pay the freight = $90.00. Balance due $330.00 through the 1st National Bank of Palmyra I have made sight draft on you through the State Bank of Muscatine with original B & S attached for $330.00. The B & S is made to my order with instructions to notify you. This is the agreement made with Reverend Garrett Flickama of Palmyra and I am to pay him his commission out of the $330.00. Hoping that everything will come to hand OK and that you will want more of my apples, I am yours very truly, Benjamin C. Tyler." Fortunately the two-day delay in shipping the apples did not seem to be a problem as all the paper work has fallen in place nicely along with the banking. I will soon be calling this the "**TYLER APPLE AND PICKLE FARM**" or something to that nature. Hopefully the road to prosperity goes through the apple orchard and the pickle vines.

The other day I was cleaning out some of the dresser drawers and I came across a memoranda booklet that I had kept in 1894 and thereafter for a few different years when I worked for the Bellaire Nail Works in Bellaire, Ohio and our lives afterwards. An entry on the first page caught my eye: "Sept. 15, 1894, one of the prettiest and the best girls I ever met promised this day to marry me, which we expect to be in two years." I didn't need to read that entry to be reminded of how lucky I have been with a fine, beautiful wife like Mazie and a wonderful family. As I continued to read through it I came across another entry I had made in my courting days, "Thursday, Nov. 29, 1894: Took dinner at the McGregor's and spent the afternoon there and went back in the evening and stayed until 10 P.M. Mazie was looking prettier than I have ever before seen her." The last of these entries in the short time I spent looking at my book was made on Sunday Dec. 2, 1894: "Walked home with Mazie after church. She is the best girl in the world."

Back to reality here in Nov. of 1914. I received a telegram from the McKee Brothers asking that the carload of apples on the South Shore Railroad be diverted to Wilton, Iowa instead of their original destination. I contacted the agent, Reverend Flikama, and he advised me to telegraph them that any such request should go through him. They also asked if I could send them another train car load of apples but I told the reverend that except for the fallen ones I had no more to sell this year.

Reverend McKenzie officially resigned as pastor of the Palmyra Presbyterian Church on Sun. Nov. 1st. We will surely miss his guiding hand. We had a congregational meeting and issued a proclamation stating our support for and recommendation for Reverend McKenzie and I was asked to read aloud the report during the congregational meeting. We also had a farewell reception for him and have formed a pulpit committee to start the task of replacing him. We also met in the church to help get the Christmas presents ready to send to colored children in the south, which we have done for several years. As the month drew on I also helped Rev. McKenzie draw his household goods to the New York Central RR for transport to his next assignment.

We all celebrated Marion's 11th birthday on the Nov. 21st since tomorrow, her actual birthday is Sunday and that day is devoted to church. Marion received some nice gifts and Mazie backed a fine cake for all of us to enjoy as we celebrated this special occasion. The only damper on the party was that I received a letter from Ma telling me that my brother Bailey's wife, Anner had passed away. She was a fine lady and so sad to think of her gone.

We had a fine Thanksgiving dinner and Mazie cooked my favorite, which is roasted chicken and oysters. The month finished out with my cutting a lot of firewood for the winter and also buying a lot of nut coal from the coal yard to hopefully keep us all warm and even more important, healthy.

Dr. Hutton has preached several Sundays here in December while we await the calling of a new minister. I am on the pulpit committee and we have been meeting regularly at F. W. Griffith's to decide what our next steps should be. We even had a brief meeting at Red Men's Hall where there was also entertainment by the Sunday School. It seems this is the month for involvement with doctors, either in the pulpit or medical, as I have had a bad toothache and had to go to Dr. Marks for treatment, I also went to Dr. Chase who gave me some sleeping pills to help me get through this period of agony.

The hired hand and I are cementing the cowshed floor and I have lost count of the number of bags of cement we have bought, mixed and poured. I had to draw water from Mr. Albrights since our well pump has broken down and I needed to draw about 100 gallons for the house and this job. The shed should be a lot easier to clean up and keep clean. Robert would have helped also but he went to Bellaire to spend some time with our relatives and is also going to spend Christmas there. It will not be the same Christmas with Robert away, or for that matter; any family gathering is only complete when all the family is in attendance. The first little Helen and that precious baby Harry who have gone to live with God will be there in our memories.

We have had very heavy snows here as 1914 draws to a close, so heavy that I have had to take the children back and forth to school for a number of days in the bobsled. One might think they would close the school down when we have snow this deep but they keep plugging along and expect the students to get there by whatever means they can. Most likely a good policy since once they started closing for bad weather in Upstate New York they would be open very few days in the winter. It was even so heavy that I had trouble getting to town to buy Mazie and the children some Christmas gifts. I think young Howdy will be particularly surprised and pleased with the number 45-snow sled that we bought him from Barrett's for $1.60. It seems like a lot of money but he is worth every penny of it as are all my children and beautiful wife. I received Tarbells' Teachers Guide, two handkerchiefs, necktie; box of cigars, a check for $5.00, and a good time was had by all on Christ's birthday.

Chapter 9

1915

Germany Sinks the S.S. Lusitania

I am very busy what with the family; farm and helping other members of our church look for a replacement in the church pulpit. Rev. McKenzie left in November and it is now Jan. and the longer we are without continuity of leadership the more at risk the church is. Substitute ministers are helpful but in no way do they provide the stability of a full-time leader. In my opinion the replacement process is taking too long and I would hope in the future that somehow the powers that be in the hierarchy of the Presbyterian Church could find a way to speed this up so that that ever-valuable presence of permanence is kept alive. I have gone to the Newark church this month and listened to the Reverend Boyd McCleary preach at the Park Presbyterian Church and he delivered a fine sermon on Phil. 3:30. We met afterwards at F.W. Griffith's in the evening to discuss our impressions. I have also traveled to Port Byron to hear Rev. Andrews and also to Lyons to hear Rev. McCleary a second time this month. We also had the pleasure of Reverend Crane of Port Byron coming and preaching at our church so the congregation could get a feeling for him.

We all went to a sleighing party at the Reeves and I took 27 folks down in the bobsled and brought 28 back. It seemed like I picked up a straggler on the way. We all had a good time even though the weather is cold. We enjoyed some of the ham from the 7 hogs I recently butchered and smoked. I had sold 536 pounds of the meat to Mr. Brown and he paid me nine and a half cents a pound for it or a total of $50.92. I have also sold D. H. Levis a lot of kidney beans and he settled up with me for $273.84. The money always comes in handy as we have a lot of bills to pay including the taxes and my life insurance policy with Aetna. I sent them a check for $38.63 to cover that policy for the year.

I took a half-bushel of potatoes and a half-bushel of apples to W. J. Brown for the Baracca class social and we are all looking forward to it. I even had to have young Howdy's shoes repaired, as it seems he is so active he has already worn the soles out. It cost me 60 cents to have them repaired. A seven year old can sure go through a lot of shoe leather in a short time. Young Howard even helped me when I took Old Line Back and Blind Eye to Mr. Corletts', Holstein Bull to be serviced. This servicing cost me 50 cents each and to have the young sow serviced it cost me a dollar for Dickson's boar.

The month ended up on a high note and a low note. The high note was that on Jan. 28, 1915 the congregational meeting was held and Reverend McCleary was called unanimously from all those assembled. We also heard a sermon after the meeting from Dr. Hutton and he talked on the Kaiser and his war in Europe and the hopes that the United States would not be pulled into it. I pray also that will not happen as Robert is getting to the age where he could be called into the service if we were to go to war. There should be a rule in life that any politician that goes to war, no matter what the reason, must send his own children first to fight before he sends others. I dare say there would be many less wars. The low note was that I received a letter from the Scott Lumber Company about a bill I owed them and they claimed I was delinquent in my payment. I realize that we are always short of cash but I have always prided myself that we pay our bills on time even if it was with money from the Bank of Harry, or Hans. I wrote the Scott Company the following letter. "Gentlemen: Your letter of the 19th inst. reminding me that my note of $79.46 with interest for three months amounting to $1.19 making total of $80.65 would be due mid February is received and I thank you for all of it except the last part in regard to protest fee. I have never had a note of mine go to protest and never before had a holder of any note of mine even insinuate that there was any likelihood of protest. I enclose you my check for $80.65 in payment of this note and will then make you stop any worry in regard to protest. Please return the note to me. Yours respectively, Ben C. Tyler." Needless to say, I will not be doing business with them in the future. To insinuate that I was late in my payment was not true and infringes on my good name. I was almost depressed enough over this incident that I would have slaughtered a bunch of hogs but I recently did that and seems I haven't any more to do. That last statement is said in jest as I have learned to live with my depression better than ever and sometimes it pays to laugh at oneself rather than let things like this bother you.

February brings word that the Reverend McCleary has accepted our call to the pulpit in Palmyra. We are all very excited about his deciding to come here and look forward to it. We heard this good news at George Mertz's party on the 2nd and it was such a great party that we didn't get home until midnight. For a farmer and his wife, that is a late hour as we are usually up at the crack of dawn or well before, but maybe we will pamper ourselves and stay in bed just a little longer tomorrow. It seems we could call this the month of the party as I took a full load of 5th graders to Port Gibson for a party and I also delivered a large group of ladies to Mrs. Luppold's for a party. I have yet to figure out who talked more, the group of 5th graders or the ladies I took to the party. Please don't even think about mentioning that comment to Mazie or I will be living in the new silo for a few days. I have found as life goes on those kinds of comments are best kept to oneself. In either case the children and the ladies seemed to all have a wonderful time and I was happy to transport them.

Things on the farm have been humming along. I bought three Jersey cows at an auction at the Hopkins place on Johnson Road and paid $46.00 for each of them. They are 8 to 10 years old and the girls will have fun naming them. We brought them home in the bobsled since there is so much snow on the ground at this time. I also sold 50 hens and one duck to Barney Lazerson for 14 cents per pound and he paid me $25.20 in cash. We have also signed a contract with the Brighton Dairy to sell them our milk for all of 1915. On top of these farm activities, I sent Mrs. McGregor and R. Howard Tyler each a bushel of apples and it cost me 44 cents on the West Shore RR for the 230 pounds that went to Bellaire and $1.09 for shipping 246 pounds to New York City.

Property taxes are due, buying cows, investing in the farm all are adding up. We are very fortunate to have a wonderful extended family and Mazie's sister Lucy TeWinkel has agreed to loan us $500 for two years at 5% interest. We sent her our note and agreed we would pay the interest semi-annual along with payments on the principal semi-annually.

We all attended church except Robert who cut his lip playing basketball and we heard Mr. Fred Tower speak from the anti saloon league. I pledged 33 ½ cents per month for all of 1915 to support the effort. Mazie made sure I pledged and I wasn't going to pick any argument with her over this issue, as I know I would have lost that one big time. Reverend McCleary started his calling on Sunday February 14th and spoke and the title of his sermon was "Scarlet Made White." It was an excellent sermon and we had 252 souls out for it. It is great to see so many of the pews filled with folks that it brings a lump to my throat. I think he will continue to have a great following and hopefully even have standing room only. I took him some Baldwin apples and a bushel of potatoes the next day and told him how much we enjoyed his service. It never hurts to butter up the minister a little as maybe he will put in a good word for you when you need it with you no Who. The month ended with our participating in the 41st anniversary celebration of the Grange and a great get together it was.

It is so cold here in March of 1915 that Robert and I have spent several days cutting and hauling wood from the swamp. I also have had to order a lot more coal to try and keep us warm which with this cold is a difficult job. It is a particularly tough time of year for everyone. H. G. Chapman passed away and Mazie and I visited with the family to offer our condolences. Howard and Helen are also under the weather and have not been able to accompany us to church services. Robert has stayed home and taken care of them and the good doctor says it is nothing serious and they should bounce back soon, thank the Lord. In fact they were not even able to go to church on the 12th for the installation service for Reverend McCleary. We are also having a reception at the church for Mr. and Mrs. McCleary and we are looking forward to all making that. The rest of us have been faithful church goers this month, going to services on Sunday morning, Sunday afternoon and prayer meetings in the evening on Thursdays.

I am busy cementing the rest of the cow house floor and bought another cow from W. D. Perry for $55.00. She also had a calf a week ago and the calf is part of the deal. Hopefully the cow will be a good milk'r as we are in hopes of starting to increase our milk sales to the Brighton Place Dairy. I also have bought for $1.50 each and am installing six swing stanchions for the cows. You wouldn't believe that the girls named one of our cows, Blankenberg, and I recently took Blankenberg to Walton's Holstein bull for servicing. We are getting quite a few cows so the girls are busy talking about different names for them. They sure seem to be original in the names they come up with. I had to hire Dr. A. Y. Earli to come and look over the milk cows and give us a certificate that they were all healthy. Therefore we could start selling the milk, although we ran into a problem when Robert went up to the Brighton Dairy and was told that one of the requirements was that we have a milk house so that is our latest project. It seems like nothing is easy anymore but it is all to the good as it assures that the milk we produce and sell is up to the health standards of the state. I ended up selling three of the calves to B. F. Harbrow for $28.29 and that money will come in handy to put towards building the milk house now that the cow shed is complete.

The month was not all work for Mazie and I as she went to a meeting of the Social Ten at Myra Smith's house and we all attended a school play one evening. The name of the play was Romantic Mary and the children did a fine job in the performance. We also had the privilege of picking up Reverend and Mrs. McCleary one evening and we all drove over to the Reeves. We had a fine supper and some wonderful conversation. Mazie and I both believe that the good reverend and his wife are a tremendous asset to Palmyra and especially the faithful of the Western Presbyterian Church.

The month had to end on a low note however as Mazie had some tooth problems, went to the dentist and he had to pull several teeth. Her face is very swollen. When you are a farmer or a farmer's wife with a large loving family you don't get a lot of time to feel down and recuperate. Maybe that is a good thing as we can

JOHN W. PARSONS

start to dwell too much on ourselves and not those others that mean so much to us. At any rate Mazie only had a couple of days to get over the swollen face and jaw and she is back taking care of the family, particularly myself as I require a lot of tender loving care.

I have hired Ed. Spickett to help Robert and I build the milk house and I even went to town and bought two windows for it so it will be a fine milk house. Since it didn't take too long to finish, Robert went back up to Brighton and spoke with the milk inspector and we can begin to ship milk anytime now. We are shipping it to them, usually 2 34-quart cans each day via the trolley. It is a steady income and the money we can sure use. It cost me 30 cents for shipping it each day on the trolley but it is well worth it. In fact we are so short of money with planting season coming upon us, Maude having to go to the vets for a problem with her right foot and the cost of the medicine for her. Mazie decided to contact her brother, Howard McGregor at Columbia University and see if he could give us a loan to buy the clover, alfalfa, timothy and pickles we need to plant to get us through this season. Howard has recently been in Africa since he is teaching zoology, is very interested in prehistoric man and has gone there to further his education on the subject. He fortunately is back from his journeys and agreed to loan us $300 at 4% interest for 3 years. I drew up the note and sent it on to him. It makes me sometimes wonder, should I have been a teacher or maybe stayed in Bellaire. Ohio where Mazie and I met, started our love affair and continued to work in the steel mill there. In balancing everything out however I think we are better off being a farmer and his wife even though the cash flow is sometimes a problem. It is a hard working life for both of us but we are our own bosses (Mazie more than I) and have to answer to no one but God.

It has certainly turned hot here at the end of April and I have been drawing out a lot of manure using Maude and Pete. I was surprised how first rate Pete worked. Maude is still a little lame with her right foot problem but Pete certainly made up for it and pulled more that half his load. In fact he was so good in harness that he and I have been plowing the field of oats for several days. The temperature is about 85 degrees in the shade so it hasn't been easy work but we both are the better off for it. I have also contracted with Mr. McGuire to grow one acre of pickles

A JOURNEY THROUGH LIFE

for his factory and I hope they will be as bountiful and profitable as they were last year. With all the other work, I have not had time to trim the trees in the orchard so I hired Morris Hickey to trim for us and I am paying him $2.00 for a ten-hour workday. I sure wish sometimes that I could limit my workday to ten hours but that doesn't happen very often.

We ended the month by taking supper at the Aldrich's with them and Mr. and Mrs. McCleary and enjoyed the evening very much. We also took the entire family to the picture show and saw "Birth of a Nation" and found it very informative and entertaining. It would be wonderful to hear the words the actors and actresses were saying but I don't think that will ever be possible. I am happy at least that we have "moving" pictures for us all to enjoy.

I came across my memorandum book again the other day that I had kept in my other life in Bellaire. One of the entries was interesting as it was an account of our tax return of 1899. It showed the following entries:

Value of household goods	$125.00
Two watches	$5.00
Jewelry	$3.00
Money in D. L. Bank	$1,165.00
S.Total	$1,298.00
Less amount exempt	$100.00
Total	$1,198.00
Amount added by the Bellaire Board of Equalization for 5 Shares of National Steel Co. At $90.00 per share	$450.00
Grand total	$1,648.00
Payment at $4.75 per $100.00	$78.28

I paid it then in two installments of $39.14 each. It seems like taxes have gone up quite a bit since then but it sure was interesting to look back and see that we had $1165.00 in the bank at the time.

Ben and Jack with Mr. Phillips, blackswmith
Top right, Ben C. 1882
Rev. McCleary and the Whitlocks and Ben

So much for reminiscing, it is time to plant Mazie's garden and she wanted Swiss chard, radishes, beans and corn planted so I plowed up the garden and put the seeds in for her. I am also planting a lot of silo corn and have been paid by the Brighton Dairy $60.66 for the 3,279 pounds of milk we shipped them in April. The money will come in very handy as it always does.

Will TeWinkel stopped by on his way to giving a sermon in Newark. He is still preaching in Perry and it looks like he will stay there for some time to come. We were in hopes that Will would accompany us to the first Philathea Class banquet at church but alas his schedule did not allow for this. Mazie and I went however and had a wonderful time. Even though I have not been feeling very well of late and Dr. Chase has given me some medicine to help correct the problem, we did get to a full day of religion on the 23rd of May. We heard Reverend W. H. Landon from California preach in our church in the morning and he mentioned the latest offensive by the British and French troops in the war in Europe. It seems they are using tanks for the first time ever in a conflict. If only mankind would put as much effort into developing more modern plows, etc. instead of wasting all the monies on fighting each other. I hope it is over soon as I have mentioned Robert would be of the age to be drafted if we get dragged into it and I can't imagine how upset Mazie and I would be over that. Pray that it doesn't happen. Then in the afternoon we went to the Baptist Church and heard the Reverend Sam Small preach on National Prohibition. He and his organization are pushing hard for the prohibition of all alcoholic beverages and I am beginning to think they might just be successful in getting it banned in the near future. In the evening we went to School No. 11 in Farmington and heard Reverend McCleary preach. That certainly finished out a full day of religion.

It is the end of the month and I decided we have had enough work for the Tyler family so I told (asked) Mazie to get the skillet hot and took the entire family fishing in the canal. We had great luck with Howard bringing in the biggest fish and all of us enjoyed not only the fishing but also the great meal Mazie put on for us when we brought our catch home.

We started out June with a dinner party for Reverend and Mrs. McCleary and also invited Mr. and Mrs. Newell, Mr. and

Mrs. Reeves and Mr. and Mrs. Aldrich. All had a fine time and Mazie cooked, as she always does, a wonderful meal. We also all attended the children's day service at the church on the 13th and the twins and Marion took part and did their usual fine performance.

It seems that this time of year could be summed up with a few words, cultivating, dragging, planting and rolling. It seems like that is all I am doing from sun up to sun down. The only other activity is that I have drawn 20 loads of manure to the pickle area and I intend again to produce the best pickle crop in Wayne County if not in all of New York.

I am 48 years old today, the 15th and I am wondering if I am getting ahead at all. I will soon be 50 and it doesn't seem like we are profiting at all from all our efforts. As I have said before, maybe I should have stayed in Bellaire and continued to work for the steel company. At least I am my own boss but I need to tell myself, as long as I am the boss to work smarter and more prosperously. I have even decided to discontinue my story from this date until July 7 since I need to take some time to evaluate where I am at and hopefully not fall into deep depression, it seems that is always just lurking around the corner.

* * * *

My down time is over and I have been working as hard as ever. I sold Walter T. Brown 23 hens at 15 cents a pound and they totaled 182 pounds and it netted us $12.30. I also received the milk check from the Brighton Place Dairy for the 4,782 pounds of milk we had sold them in June and the check was for $61.69. I used a little of the money to help Marion buy 30 eggs from Mr. Albright at 20 cents per dozen and we set the two red hens on them. Marion is anxious for them to hatch and have a little chicken and egg farm of her own. Nothing is easy however because just as I was feeling better, with a little money in my pocket, I got a letter from the Health Bureau in Rochester saying our milk must be cooler. This will mean we will have to buy more ice to keep it cooler and that will eat into the profit more. It is tough to get ahead.

We have a lot of company here in July 1915, Momma, Hans and family, and Winston Carter have all come to spend some time with us, hopefully it will keep my mind occupied. We decided to have a picnic so we all went to Red Creek and had a wonderful time with family and then we all went fishing in the canal. Robert even went to the Seneca River to do some fishing and brought a great catch back, which along with the fish we caught in the canal, we had a fine meal. I even decided to get my ears lowered, went to John Devoist and it cost me 25 cents for the haircut. Mazie said it was about time, particularly with family here. I also went to Lawrence Brothers and bought two work shirts, which I needed badly and they cost 50 cents each and I charged them.

The entire extended family all went to church and then we went to the park service in late afternoon and heard Reverend McCleary preach. His sermon was entitled "Wild Grapes" and I will leave it up to the reader to use his or her imagination as to what it was about.

I must say that I am going to stop again for a while keeping my diary and maybe I can pick it up again in a few weeks if I feel up to it.

*   *   *   *

It is August 10th and a bright sunny day and I am feeling better and so I am going to resume our story of a "Journey Through Life." This day Mamma and Dill went to Canandaigua on the motorbus. I seem to give everyone a nickname these days, even Mazie as I noticed I am calling her Mamma in my writings. Dill of course is the nickname we gave little Helen as I have mentioned in the past. When Mazie came home the next day she brought Aunt Jennie and the boys to spend some time with us. I am sure the children will enjoy having the boys around to play with and explore the large hill just south of our farm. Some of the children spend quite a bit of time up there finding Indian arrowheads and they have quite a collection. We also had the pleasure of Mazie's brother Howard stopping by to spend some time here on his trip out to California. I can only dream of taking such a trip and even in my dreams I most likely was a little short of cash.

I am picking lots of pickles and delivering them to the factory and that should help with our cash flow over the next few months along with the apples that are always staring me in the face. I often wonder how I will be able to pick them all. In years past however I have wondered the same thing and still we brought the harvest in. Some of the days here in August of 1915 are very rainy and gloomy and certainly do nothing to lift my spirits. I feel better in mind and body when I see that the Lord has blessed us with a bright and sunny day. It certainly helps to lift my spirits and I would imagine a lot of other folks as well.

We have been attending church on a regular basis and Mr. and Mrs. McCleary have taken supper with us on several occasions. The good reverend even came out one day and pitched in and helped me draw in the oats from the north field. I wouldn't imagine many ministers would be so kind as to help some of their flock out in the fields. That gesture of help also has lifted my spirits. We have also attended a Grange social this month, a Philathea picnic and even made the motion pictures one evening. We ended the month on a high note as Hans and the boys came over from Canandaigua and we all went fishing in the canal and caught a fine catch which we all enjoyed after Mazie fried them. It was a good way to end the month.

It is hard to imagine that Howard is now 7 years old and is to attend his first party at George Lawrence's. He is very excited about it and will most likely have a wonderful time. Along with that social outing others in the family have been busy gallivanting around. Mazie even went to Rochester with the Reeves in their new automobile. You can just imagine how jealous I am when I see our friends and neighbors driving up in their new cars. Maybe someday, Lord willing. Howard and I did take the motorbus to Canandaigua for a day and had a fine time-sharing conversation and a meal with Hans and family.

It was sort of a sad and a happy occasion here in mid Sept. as Robert left on the 10:24 A.M. New York Central train for Amherst College. He was very excited about going and we of course will miss him greatly as he has been such a fine young man, helping on the farm and even doing the chores for me when I have felt too down to work. After Robert left and we all went home we found he had left some papers that he should have taken so I went

A JOURNEY THROUGH LIFE

to the post office and had to put a 3-cent stamp on the envelope to send them to him. One has to wonder what the government does with all the money it collects in the postal service when they charge such an outlandish price to send one letter through the mail.

I am delivering a lot of pickles to the factory and the twins spent a day picking and they got 275 pounds picked. We packed them up and sent them and they will be the recipients of the money they fetch. Along with their efforts being rewarded, Marion received 75 cents in a school contest for writing the best letter of her class. Mazie and I even attended a talk by Doctor Ostrander and his topic was "women's suffrage." I didn't mention it to Mazie after the meeting but I thought maybe he should have talked on "men's suffrage" as in this family there is only one boss and they sure aren't named Benjamin Chinn Tyler. I do agree that women certainly should be given the right to vote and most likely will do a better job electing representatives of the people than we men do. We also attended a banquet at the Grange Hall that was put on by the men of the Presbyterian Church and I and the other fellows did the entire meal, preparation and cleanup. All had a good time.

It is thrashing time again and everyone is coming together to help everyone else out with the thrashing on their farms. I have worked on about four different farms helping out and those four fellows have returned the favor and helped out when our crop was ready for thrashing. It is so uplifting to see so many people coming together for the good of each other. I also hired Raymond Albright to work for us and I agreed to pay him $2.50 per week and he is to work from 7 AM until 6 PM with an hour break for lunch. He is also required to take his meals at his home. I have guaranteed his job until at least Nov. 1st and hope the arrangement will work out well for both of us. I also hired Maurice Hickey to start trimming the orchard. Brighton Dairy paid us for the milk we shipped in August and the check was for $79.91, which will come in handy to settle up some bills and to pay the help we need to hire at this time of year.

I attended a meeting of the Baracca class recently as I have been neglecting some of the meetings lately and my conscious was bothering me about it. We met at H. D. Runterman's. We also attended a service at the Tabernacle Baptist Church and heard a talk on temperance. Being in another church reminded me of that which I recently read in my memorandum book that I found. When we lived in Bellaire I was a faithful member of the Episcopal Church and I came across the letter that was from my minister dismissing me to the care of the Presbyterian faith. The reason I may have mentioned as Mazie and her family were at the time and still are faithful members of the Presbyterian Church and we agreed prior to our marriage that I would join her faith. The latter was as follows:

Rectory of the Trinity Church, Bellaire, Ohio
November 25, 1898
Dear brother:
The bearer hereof Mr. B. C. Tyler is a communicant of Trinity Church in good standing, and for sufficient reasons desires to unite with your congregation. I part with him with reluctance as I regret to lose so faithful and valuable a member from our numbers; but he feeling that duty constrains him to make your congregation his church home, I dismiss him with my blessing, and commend him to the Christian fellowship of your people and to your pastoral watch and care. Yours for the one Lord, Christ and Master.
John T. Foster.

The move was a fulfilling one and I have never regretted transferring although the Trinity Church played an important part in my life's story when I was in Bellaire. These services reminded us that we are to be charitable and share what we have with others so we donated one bushel of oats, one bushel of wheat and one bushel of Baldwin apples to the Palmyra King's Daughters Library to be used as they see fit to help out others.

I have been busy on the farm, having sold all the dropped apples and those we could shake off the trees, to Frank Clifford for 60 cents per 100 pounds. The money comes in handy as we sent a money order to Robert at college. We hope the $25.00 we sent him will last quite a while, as it will be difficult until all the apples are sold to come up with much more money. He is very frugal so I believe it will last him quite a time. All of the neighbors have gotten together also to help fill all our silos. Again, life has meaning when you see so many come together to help each other.

I hired two young men, Pete and Henry, to help me pick apples and agreed to pay them 7 cents per bushel and they are to pay $5.00 per week for their room and board. The only problem with this arrangement is that Pete worked two days and left and Henry worked three days and left. Don't young people have any conception of work and what it is to put in a full day and see the fruits of your labor at the end of the day? I believe I will stick with older hired help as they generally are much more dependable. For the time being I am picking by myself until I can find the needed help. In between picking I am cutting wood in the swamp for this upcoming winter, which always seems to come around whether we want it or not. Mr. Reeves stopped out and looked over the apple crop that is on the trees and he offered to pay me $1.05 per 100 pounds but I didn't think that was enough so I am going to hold out for more. With the picking and negotiating a price, I have also had to take care of Old Blind Eye as she had a bull calf this month and Baker also had a bull calf. I sold both of them to Mr. Perry for $4.00 and $5.00 respectively.

We were saddened to hear that Mr. Langdon had died here the first part of November. Mazie and I called on the family and I was asked to be a pallbearer for his service, which I graciously accepted. It is sad to see old friends go on but he being a good Christian fellow is I am sure in a better place. God rest his soul. Levi Haak and I were also asked by the family to appraise the personnel property as they are planning on having an auction since a proper time has passed. We were happy to oblige. I also did a good deed by drawing nine bundles of goods to the West Shore Railroad from the Dutch Reform Church parsonage. I was happy to help but Reverend Flikema insisted on my taking a dollar for my help. Things have a way of coming full circle as I helped the reverend out and shortly thereafter Reverend McCleary came out and helped me draw in 4 loads of corn and he partook of supper with us. He absolutely insisted I not pay him for his efforts. He said he was just tending his flock.

Mr. Reeves paid me for the 16,510 pounds of apples that I delivered to him and it came to $173.36 less the $26.94 I had bought from him to spray the orchard. Brighton Dairy also paid us $76.25 for our milk delivery for last month. On top of all this, D. H. Levis paid his bill to us for the wheat I had drawn for him and it came to $103.43. It seems for a time we have some money in our pocket as even the pickle factory paid the $40.00 they owed us. But alas money comes in and also goes out. I paid several stores in the village the money I owed them on account, gave Mazie $10.00 and also sent Robert $25.00. On top of that, I had to pay the telephone bill of $4.46 and the school district tax of $32.06. The last I do not hesitate to pay in the least as a fine education for our children is the hope of tomorrow.

The month ended with a wonderful Thanksgiving dinner with roast pork for the whole family and we also sent a Thanksgiving box to Robert at college. It was not the same without him here for the holiday.

I am feeling a little better here in December but I'm not sure I am completely out of the woods yet. We have spent an enjoyable evening at Reverend and Mrs. McCleary's here in early December and also reciprocated and had them to dinner a couple of times. I need the steady hand and nurturing presence of the good reverend, especially on these long and gloomy days and nights this time of year. I even attended a Baracca class social at the Griffith's and had a fine time.

We received some extra money from the dairy this month so we managed to send Robert another $25.00 part of which he is going to use to buy his ticket home for the Christmas holidays. He is expected to come in on the midnight train on the 21st of this month. We are all anxious to see him and hear about his experiences at college. Mazie and Dorothy went to Rochester on the trolley to do some Christmas shopping and I gave them what money we could spare for their trip. The rest of the extra money we have had I spent buying a cow named Betty at the Langdon's auction. She cost me $68.00, is four years old and is expecting a calf on Feb. 24th. I also had four new shoes put on Maude by Mr. Yoacum. They are a new kind of horseshoe and are called never slip shoes. They sound like something I need. I also made a dollar selling a bushel of potatoes to the old lady who lives next to the trolley station.

My last entry of 1915 in this book of life is Dec. 22, as I still am not feeling all that well and just don't have the energy or the will to keep the diary for a while. Hopefully with the coming of the New Year I will pick it up again.

Chapter 10

1916

*Prohibition Gains Ground as 24 States Vote
Against Alcoholic Beverages*

I am still feeling under the weather here in early January and did not make church on the 2nd. In fact I am feeling so down that it took me all of the forenoon just to do the chores. Robert helped me some but he is leaving tomorrow to go back to Amherst College so I will be without his help for some time. I miss his steady hand and great help but I am happy that he is going on to college to better himself. Maybe whatever life he chooses will be a little easier than that of a farmer. Come to think of it, most paths that one takes down this road of life must be easier than that of a farmer and his wife. But then again, I need not go there, as I will just get myself depressed again. I do believe that Mazie is also feeling the pressure as she is experiencing a problem with her facial nerves, which Dr. Chase says is called neuralgia. He said it comes from the shingles virus, which they think hangs on in the body from early age chicken pox and then rears it's ugly head whenever someone gets stressed. Mazie is as always the rock that I lean on but even she can get stressed and that is what most likely brought this on. I did go to Dr. Chase and he gave me some medicine for her and we are all praying for her speedy recovery. I paid Dr. Chase 3 bushels of potatoes for the medicine and the house call. Even Marion stayed home a couple of days from school to look after her mother until she felt well enough to get out of bed.

As in the past I may have to butcher some hogs to lift my spirit. I am of course only kidding, as this is the time of year when the neighbor and I normally get together and do some butchering and this year is no exception. After we finished and I cut up that which was for us I delivered some to the good reverend and his wife and also took them some popcorn that I had grown and stored for the winter. In addition to butchering some hogs I also sold Old Line Back to Mr. Perry for $50.00 as she is not producing a great deal of milk anymore. Mr. Perry thinks he can get her up to full output again and I hope he does but he is a better man than I am if he can pull that off.

I hired an Italian fellow to help me with the farm work and agreed to pay him 50 cents per day and his dinner. Unfortunately he never showed up for work. I can't understand why some people agree to work and then don't show up or only work a couple of days and quit. Maybe I am too difficult a taskmaster. I did hire Walter Hassler for $2.00 per week and his board and he has agreed to stay on until April 1st when he is committed to another job.

As the month drew to a close, I paid our Grange dues of $1.20 for 1916. We are all grateful also that Mazie is feeling much better; in fact she is feeling so good that she and Dorothy decided to walk the mile to church here on the 23rd of the month for the evening service. It is about 20 degrees out and breezy but they didn't seem to mind the walk even in the dark. I guess when you have the pain of shingles and it finally goes away you would be willing to walk ten miles through heavy snow and cold just knowing the pain has finally left. We ended the month going to a prayer meeting and we said an extra prayer for Margaret who burned her ankle the other day on the living room stove. Dr. Chase said it will heal and he gave her some ointment to put on it and we are to call him if it shows any sign of infection.

It is Mazie's 42nd birthday here on Feb. 1st and we had a fine meal to celebrate it. You are most likely thinking that fine meal was prepared by Mazie but to no ones surprise, not even the good reverend and his wife, the twins and Marion did all the cooking for this joyous occasion.

I never believed that simply cold turbulent weather was the root cause of illness but it sure seems that way, especially here in this stormy month. Dorothy, Howard and Helen are all under the weather and Marion has been nursing them hopefully back to health. I hope she chooses someday to be a nurse as she has a natural ability for it. She even is helping me, as would you believe it, I also have neuralgia. Mazie just got over it and now it has reared its ugly head again with me. I also have the grip which I am sure will hang on a few days as it always does. I just hope the rest of the family doesn't come down with it also. As I have mentioned, with so much stress lately, it is not surprising that we are so ill.

Once I felt better and am able to function again, I went out and bought a new axe for $1.00 and I have been out cutting wood in the swamp. I also had the crosscut saw sharpened and set and that cost me 50 cents. Maybe someday there will be an easier way to chop and cut firewood but as of this date it is all elbow grease.

The month did end on a high note as Abe had a bull calf and also, Betty had a bull calf. I decided we needed a little money so I sold them both for $4.00 each. I expect we will be having some more soon that I will hang on to.

March sure came in like a lion this year. The weather is very snowy, cold and windy. I took the bobsled into town on the 7th and gathered up 14 of the twin's friends and brought them out to the farm for a party they were hosting. They certainly, from the sounds of it, had a great time and I drove them all home and had them home by 11 P.M. I also took Howard and some of his little boy friends for a sleigh ride on one of these very stormy, cold March days. I even had to run Mazie to a missionary meeting at the Methodist Church with the bobsled, as the snow is so deep.

Mazie hired Mrs. Taber to wallpaper the hallway and she did a fine job. On top of that I asked the twins and Marion to name the two calves that Perry One and Perry Two had. They were both heifer calves and the girls came up with some unique names. One they called Saddle and the other one they named Patches. Don't ask me where they get these names but it helps keep them all separated and I am happy to put them in charge of naming the livestock.

As April rolls around we are again reminded how short life is as we are attending the funeral of Mrs. James. DeBrown at the Dutch Reform Church. Sometimes moments of reflection on our lives and just how long the Good Lord will give us on this earth is worthwhile to bring everything into perspective. This is particularly true in this time of annual preparing and seeding and looking forward to new life springing forward from the good earth. Along with our attendance at this solemn service we also attended the annual meeting of the congregation of the Presbyterian Church on the 6th of the month and voted for the election of officers. I unfortunately will not be serving again as particularly this time of year my duties to the farm and family leave me little time for other commitments as important as they may be.

It is plowing and planting time as I mentioned and it is also borrow money from the family time as it usually is this time of year. Mazie's brother Howard agreed to loan us $300.00 and I sent him a note for it due April 1st, 1921 at 4% interest. He also loaned us $77.50 on another note due April 1st, 1918, also at 4% interest. I can remember the good old days when I used to be a lender to the family when I worked the steel mills in Bellaire. All that has changed now and I be a borrower instead of a lender. I have to remember this was my choice with Mazie's approval so this "Journey through Life" was not chosen for me but I chose it with sound mind and body. Well, lets just say sound body as Mazie sometimes likes to remind me that my ancestors often were found to have cousins marrying cousins and that may not lead to what one would call sound minds. We used some of the money to pay G. Tinklepaugh $77.50 which is the interest due on the Griswold mortgage and I also had to pay an extra $1.00 interest for 30 days for being late from April 1st for the principal payment. The current balance due on the farm is $2700. This also reminded me of a memo I came across the other day in the drawer of memories from my past life in Bellaire. It has to do with Mazie and me buying our first house, "On October the 1st 1897 Benjamin and Mazie Tyler bought the house and lot no. 3724 Tallman Ave. from Miss Belle D. Beazel for $2,750 on the following terms. $200 to be paid in cash Oct. 1st. 1897, $500 Oct. 1st, 1898, $500 Oct. 1st, 1899, $500 Oct. 1st. 1900, $500 Oct. 1st. 1901 and $550 Oct. 1st, 1902. Notes have been given for the last five payments bearing interest from Oct. 1897 @ 7%. The interest is to be paid semi-annually, April 1st and Oct. 1st of each year beginning April 1898. Miss Beazel gives Ben. C. Tyler the privilege of paying any and all of the notes at any time after giving her 30 days notice before the time that he may wish to pay them." Wouldn't it be nice to even think about repaying our mortgage now but I don't really think that is going to happen any time soon.

It helped that the cow Blankenberg had a bull calf and I sold him for $4.00 and we also received a check for $54.63 from the Brighton Dairy for the March milk sales of 2,876 lbs. of milk, rated 1.90 at a test level of 3.8. This all came in handy. I also took Old Jersey" to Walton's bull for servicing and that cost me $1.00. With a little money in our pockets we shared some of it with Robert who is currently in Absarokee, Montana on a school project.

The month ended with my hiring Emil Kunz as a hired hand and we agreed on a wage of $20.00 per month, a trial basic, plus his room and board. I sure hope he works out, as it is getting more and more difficult to find good help these days.

The Reverend McCleary has honored us with his presence on at least one evening a week here in May, taken supper with us and led us in prayer for the blessings the Lord has bestowed upon us all. We enjoy his company immensely and hope that he never chooses to stay away very long. We also attended the "Blue" entertainment at church this month and enjoyed it very much.

It has been an interesting month as spring usually is with my signing a contract with the pickle people to set aside another acre of ground to grow pickles on this year. Lots of manure and hard work and we will again be rolling in pickle dough. I have also finally been able to put the cows out to pasture as the ground has firmed up enough so they will have a firm footing. I am even letting them stay out all night also as it makes it easier on them and me. Most likely a good thing as we had terrible high winds here in the early part of May and it took part of the roof off the cow shed and the cows being outside they all came through it unscathed.

The Brighton Dairy came through with their check on time and with the $87.44 I managed to pay off about 7 of our creditors including Mr. Runterman at the grocery store and Mr. Chison who recently put a new top on our surrey for $1.75. You can imagine, for that price, it wasn't a surrey with a fringe on it. I even went to Briggs's Drugstore and bought some gum camphor for all my aches and pains. It cost 10 cents and I charged it, as I didn't want to get carried away with paying too many of our bills all at once.

My brother Robert C. Tyler has agreed to loan us some money to tide us over and he sent a money order for $150.00 and I sent him a note for one year from May 5th 1916 made out to Weith and Tyler and payable at 6% interest. I guess I have just about hit up all my siblings at one time or another, as well as Mazie's, but we always managed to pay them off and hold up our end of the bargain. As with any close family they always come through for us as we would for them.

Emil sure didn't last long as he quit after working only 17 ½ days and I paid him off at 66 2/3rd cents per day less $2.75 he had borrowed from me. I gave him a check for $8.91 and told him I was sorry to see him go. It is almost impossible to find dependable help. A couple of days after Emil left, a tramp stopped by in late afternoon and wanted work and board so I hired William Kerr, but alas, poor William only lasted a day and a half and moved on with my 80 cents wages in his pocket. He will most likely always be a tramp going from door to door and always looking for something but never finding it. It reminded me that when we are feeling down and maybe a little sorry for ourselves it is good to remember that there are always those that are much worse off than we are. I am sure Mr. Kerr would give his right arm to be married to a fine gal like Mazie and have a nice farm and a wonderful loving family.

Here in June of 1916 I have been active on the school board and the school auditing committee and we recently met at the Jeffrey's to go over the books for this past school year. We found everything in order as we expected to. Margaret is beginning to have a sight problem with her eyesight so Mazie took her to Rochester to see the oculist and see if in fact she needs to wear glasses. Since she and Dorothy are twins, I wouldn't be surprised if Dorothy will also need them soon. Whatever the case, we will find the money to get them for them as their studies are so important and without good eyesight they will have a hard time keeping up their fine school records. Mazie and the girls also went to a picnic at the Walker farm on Walker road and had a fine time. I decided with all their activities I would take some time off from the farm work and so Howard and I went fishing in the canal. As usual, Howard caught the biggest with of course some assist from his father.

We are having all sorts of family visiting, along with Howard McGregor coming up from New York City and Robert getting home on the midnight train from Amherst. Hans, Jamie, Virginia and Boydon all came over from Canandaigua to spend some time with us and we all made the children's day service at the church. Howard stayed home as his rheumatism was bothering him some in his back, most likely from all those slow boat rides on his trips to Africa.

Robert, Hans and I have managed to fix the cow house roof that was recently damaged from the high winds and we also spent a lot of time planting potatoes. I had to replant the field to the north of the barn as we have had such heavy rains lately. I do not remember that field becoming flooded like it has here in June since we moved to this farm. We have had so much rain lately, the ground is so saturated the water just has no place to go. That is, of course, the fate of a farmer who is always at the mercy of the weather. The month ended in my buying two nine-week-old pigs for $10.00, selling two cows Hack and Abe to Wm. Brownell for $100 and I also bought two younger cows, one for $55.00 and one for $65. Hopefully the younger cows will be good producers of milk.

Reverend McCleary has been taking dinner with us almost every Sunday and he also has helped me with the planting of some potatoes. He is a good worker as well as a great minister. We are also attending the Sunday evening park services in the village as often as we can. The good reverend will not accept any money for his labors but I am paying Robert for all his help as we have no hired help at the present and I just could not keep up with the work if it wasn't for him. He could go out and get a job but has chosen to stay and help us and wants to save up some money for his return to college in the fall so I agreed to pay him if he stayed, which he willingly did. I have decided to again suspend my diary entries and will pick it up when I feel the urge.

I am getting my act together again and it is August 24th, 1916 so I have again resumed my entries in my book of life. I think one of the things that is bothering me along with everything else I can find to worry about is the war raging in Europe. This country fortunately has not been drawn into it yet but the news headlines continue to talk about the horrors of it and the fact that there are those that feel the United States should help Britain and France in their struggle against Germany. My worry is that Robert is of the age when he could be drafted and be called upon to go to that hellhole where all this terrible fighting is going on. I am not sure I could accept or survive his being called up and the constant worry if he were involved in battle. Only time will tell but I pray we will stay out of the conflict but powers much higher than I will ultimately decide this country's involvement or non-involvement. Thankfully, we had company from our past life in Perry, the Stewarts have been spending some time with us and that has kept my mind off my worries. If anyone ever was looking for someone to worry for them I would be the perfect candidate and I am sure I would work cheap and do a great job being their official worrier.

August is ending with my covering our grocery bill at H. Runterman's of $35.17 which also included a few dollars he has loaned me this past few weeks. I paid it off with the $85. 71 that the Brighton Place Dairy paid us for the July milk. The rest of the end of the month has been taken up with that brand new task of pickle picking, always something to look forward to. Even the good reverend is helping me pick pickles and I think he is finding it easier to stand erect in the pulpit than constantly bending down to pick them. I so appreciate his help as I have often told him. Robert is dragging Mr. Tack's wheat lot with Logan and Pete and in turn Mr. Tack is also helping me pick pickles so every one that he picks and the reverend picks is one less that I have to face. That is a good feeling. I have paid Robert $14.75 to date for his work and he has decided to go to Rochester to look for work as he is unsure if he is going to go back to college this semester what with expenses and the war hanging over everyone's heads. I hope he eventually decides to continue his studies however as education is so important.

The Canandaigua Tyler's children have come to spend some vacation time with us here in early Sept. and our children plan on going over there for a few vacation days when they return. They all enjoy each other's company so much that it is fun to see them interacting together.

We were hoping to take all the children to the Palmyra Fair as they always look forward to it so much but there is Infantile Paralysis in the village and it is too dangerous to expose them to it.

A JOURNEY THROUGH LIFE

They are even going to delay the start of the school year because of it. It scares us even to think about any of the children coming down with it so we are keeping them all close to home. Even Mazie and I are curtailing our outside activities. However I did manage to go with Mr. Whitlock and visit some perspective new members for the Presbyterian Church that lived on Maple Ave. and on Town Line Road. I am always willing to do the Lord's work even if it is with some risk attached as with this current epidemic. Hopefully we will get an early frost and that will wipe out this latest bug at least for this season.

One of the wonderful things about being a farmer in a tight knit farming community is when so many of our friends and neighbors come together to help one another out. It is silo filling time and it seems about everyone is here helping out either for help in return or in the case of a few that have no silos for a few dollars.

Elmer Brown, using his father's team of horses in exchange for my helping him.

Jon. Coveney, using T. W. Corlette's team in exchange for my helping him.

Abe Pembroke, using his team in exchange for my helping him out.

B. C. Tyler, with my own team of horses, and grateful for all the help.

P. J. Tack, working in the lot

Abe Cornelius, working in lot.

Thomas Hanagan, working in lot, I am paying him 20 cents per hour for six hours.

Jacob Tack, using his team in exchange for my helping him.

Lawrence Duffy, working in the silo and paying him 20 cents per hour.

T. W. Corlette, working in silo and I will do the same for him in exchange.

Clarence Hanagan, working in silo and paying him 20 cents per hour.

We all worked very hard, had a lot of laughs, some of Mazie's great food and we finished filling the silo in one day. Wouldn't it be wonderful if countries could work together for each other's benefit like we did rather than fighting like is going on in

Europe at the present time? I have also begun to pick up fallen apples and was paid $70.00 by Mr. McGuire for some of the pickles I delivered to him this fall. This is a partial payment only and he will pay the rest in the next few weeks.

Robert, who is living and working in Rochester for the time being, came home and attended Mr. Valentine Albright's funeral with Mazie and I. He was a close family member and we wanted to pay our respects. We would not have dared go except they have lifted the quarantine in the village because of the infantile Paralysis scare so we have started to go to church again and the twins even went to a masquerade party at the school. Mazie and I also attended a special prayer session this month praying with our brothers and sisters in faith for the epidemic to go away. The month ended up with my paying the $70.00 we owed in interest on the mortgage to George Tinklepaugh on the Griswold mortgage. Even a medical scare like Infantile Paralysis doesn't stop our creditors from collecting what is due them as is only right, unfortunately.

Here in November of 1916 I went into town, fulfilled my duty and voted for Woodrow Wilson for president of the United States. I also voted the straight Republican ticket. I am hoping that Wilson if elected will keep us out of that terrible war raging in Europe. Mazie of course isn't allowed to vote but you can be assured she told me how I was to cast my vote. The movement to give women the right to vote is gaining momentum and hopefully within the next few years an amendment to the constitution will be passed. It is certainly an archaic system when only half of the adult population is allowed to make decisions that will affect everyone. As I have said before, I am sure they would do a better job than we men have up to this point. While I was in town voting, I went and paid my subscription to the "Wayne County Journal" until February 1917 and it cost me $1.00. I also stopped and paid E. D. Brown the school tax for the year of $28.22 and to round it all off, I stopped by the First National Bank and settled up for the years fire insurance, which we buy through the Grange. I paid Willard Page, at the bank, $8.00 to cover this for the year.

I have started to feed the cows out of the silo for the first time this season and speaking of cows, we received our Oct. milk payment of $83.68 and I paid off some bills and gave Mazie her

A JOURNEY THROUGH LIFE

cow money for the cow she milks and that came to $7.85. In addition, I made a little extra money, as if there was any money that could be called extra, by selling 800 pickles to Barney Lazerson and he paid me in cash $3.20. It doesn't seem like a lot of money for bending over and hand picking 800 pickles but that is the going rate so I was happy to get it. In addition I set up a new stove in the sitting room, am cutting lots of wood in the swamp and buying lots of coal for the upcoming winter.

We did have some social activities this month when Mazie and I attended a lecture at the school hall in the evening and heard Professor Stroup talk about Yellowstone Park. That is most likely the closest we will ever get to Yellowstone and we enjoyed his lecture immensely. Henry Runterman and I also did some recruiting for the Baracca class and visited William Petty in regards to joining the group. We invited him to attend the entertainment that Henry and I are putting on for the group this month at Henry's house and he did show up along with 16 others. We all had a wonderful time.

The month ended with a great Thanksgiving dinner on the 30th and Mazie cooked two fine roast chickens, all had a great time and delicious meal. After supper the twins went to a basketball game at The Grange and the Palmyra team won.

Here in December Mr. McCleary has taken supper with us several evenings. He even came out and helped me cut wood in the swamp and haul it to the house one day and after which we all had a fine supper. We have also had the pleasure of hearing Doctor Ostrander from Lyons preach on one Sunday this month as well as Reverend Adams. Even though we think the world of Reverend McCleary, it is interesting to hear other preachers on occasion and get their perspectives on various parts of the Bible. During these Sundays, of course, our minister is preaching in one of the other churches in the area and giving that congregation some of his wisdom. We have even gone to the dedication services for the new church rooms this month. Dorothy could not make it with us as she stayed home to take care of Howdy and Helen as they both have bad colds. It seems like once one closes up the house for the cold weather, the nasty little bugs start coming around and making one or more of us sick. Hopefully this will be a relatively healthy winter season for all the Tyler family. I ended up paying up all our church accounts for 1916 and even paid the half rent on the horse shed on Church Street. B. Mitchell has given up his half of the shed for 1917 so I will be looking for someone else to share it with and split the cost.

Mazie and I also attended Mr. Aldrich's funeral and we sent flowers, which we bought from George Johnson, and it cost us 25 cents. I also settled up with E. C. Reeves for the $5.00 I owed him and left it with Mr. George Throop at the Eagle Hotel for him to pick up.

Robert decided to come home from Rochester and he has taken a job at the Garlock Packing Company in Palmyra and will be working for Mr. Fox. We are so happy to have him home. Hopefully the job will go well and he will be able to resume his education in the near future.

I sold Charles Miller 34 old hens and 14 roosters for a total of $27.50 and I gave the twins each $5.00 of this money, as they owned some of the chickens that we sold. They can use the money to buy some Christmas presents and I will use some also to buy everyone something. We all went out and bought a Christmas tree and it cost me 25 cents but it is a beauty and well worth the money we had to pay for it. The children enjoyed the adventure of going out and finding one and we found one that we could cut so they enjoyed that even more. I also dressed four chickens for Christmas and gave two to the McCleary's and of course saved two for us. We had a wonderful day and the children got lots of gifts and had a fine time. I spent part of the day cutting wood and drawing out manure but those are things that cannot wait so I did them in the morning and early afternoon and then enjoyed the time with the family later on.

The month ended with Mazie and I negotiating a new note with Lucy TeWinkel for the $500.00 she had loaned us back in early 1915. She has agreed to a new payment schedule still at the 5% rate and it will now be due in three years from Jan. 1st, 1917. Lucy is to destroy the old note and this new one will replace it. It seems like we spend a lot of time negotiating and re-negotiating loans with the family. Everyone seems to roll with this however and fortunately it has never created any rife in the family's closeness.

Chapter 11

1917

America Is Drawn Into World War 1

It is hard to believe it is 1917 already. Our lives have not changed much, for variety here in January, some days I take the manure out to spread on the fields and then cut and bring in a load of wood. Other days I do the wood first just to keep life interesting. Sometimes life can be too interesting and challenging so take the above with a grain of salt as such a mundane life can be most rewarding, especially with a loving family.

I had to find a new source of funds so I went to Judge Charles McLouth and borrowed $37.78 to pay the premium on my Aetna Life Insurance Policy which is due the 16th of the month. He was good enough to loan it to me for 90 days but insisted on keeping the insurance policy as security for the loan. That made me think a little bit more about life and death but I didn't dwell on it too long, as I was afraid I might become depressed. As it turned out, I didn't have to worry as January is butcher hogs month and that always seems to lift my spirits even though I am sure the hogs would not agree. I did end up with a bad headache here in the middle of the month and missed church, but Mazie and the children being of strong stock, marched off on foot and walked the mile both ways even in this January weather. I sold one of the hogs and kept the other meat for the family to use. The hog I sold weighed 174 pounds and Walter Brown paid me 15 cents a pound for a total of $26.10. We used this and some of the renegotiated loan from Lucy to pay for the property taxes for 1916. We have 81

JOHN W. PARSONS

acres and they are assesses at $6,318.00 total and our taxes on this came to $41.33 plus the extra 41 cents for the tax collector. We also paid the tuition bill for the second quarter to the Palmyra Classical Union School for the second quarter for Helen, Howard and Marion of $10.00. It is a great investment. The last expenditure of the month was to have little Howard's sled repaired. It cost me 30 cents and I charged it at Roy Barrett's.

Several other good things happened here in January. Mazie's cow Blossom produced more milk than any of the other cows. Also Perry had a heifer calf, Old Jersey had a heifer calf and the girls named them Violet and Midnight. You can only guess where they came up with those names. Whatever, Mazie and I approved their selections and we think they will continue to be the official calf namer's for the Tyler family. They have earned that title many times over.

We almost had a total tragedy here in the beginning of Feb. when little Helen and Howdy were chasing each other around and accidentally hit a pan of scalding water and it spilled on her and burned her face and neck. We called Dr. Chase immediately and he came right out and comforted and treated her. He said she will need a great deal of rest for several weeks and gave us some ointment to daily put on the burn areas. Mazie and I both felt terrible but it is impossible to watch all the children at all times and it reminds us how quickly accidents can happen at any time. Fortunately it wasn't more tragic and with the Lord's blessings she will make a full recovery. I would have cut off my right arm rather than have her or any of the children be injured or sick. Margaret and Marion are also ill but this time of the year it always, as I have said, seems to be the case that the illnesses starts to get to all of us. We need to have some better weather, get the doors and windows open to clear the air in the house and drive the bugs away. This unfortunately is not the time to do that however as we are experiencing the coldest, snowiest days of the winter and I am constantly kept busy keeping the fires burning, going to the coal company and buying more coal at the outlandish price of $7.50 a ton to supplement the wood that we cut and bring up from the swamp. I have been driving the children that are well to school in the bobsled since it has been as low as ten below zero and we are getting lots of snow. It seems as if Dr. Chase, bless him, has been here as much as family as Margaret has had to have her throat lanced and he prescribed some medicine for her. He is also tending to Robert as he has the grip and Marion also who is not feeling well.

This has been a busy month as far as the livestock is concerned. Blankenberg had a bull calf and I sold it even before the girls had a chance to name it. I also sold the two-year-old black and white heifer Dill to Mr. Brownell for $45.00. I have also had to pay Dr. Earle, the county animal doctor, three dollars to come out and examine our cows and make sure they are healthy and give us a certificate so we can continue to sell milk to the Brighton Place Dairy. They all passed with flying colors so we are still in the milk business. J. H. Walton also came by as he is organizing all the farmers through the Dairyman's League so that we can speak with one voice and negotiate from strength with the milk companies for a better price. I filled out the form and paid the modest membership fee and am looking forward to having a little more clout when it comes to selling our milk.

The month ended up on a high note as little Helen was finally able to go back to school after the tragic accident at the beginning of Feb. Since Helen is feeling better and everyone else seems to be healthy again Mazie and Margaret went to Rochester to have further testing done on Margaret's eyes and fit her for some much needed glasses. Mazie has had some more tooth problems so I drove her into town to the dentist and also picked up the children from school since it has been raining so hard it was tough under these conditions for them to walk. With all these expenses, I have had to borrow a few dollars from Robert since Garlock employs him and on a larger scale we borrowed $300.00 from Mazie's brother Howard for five years at 4% interest. It will be due on April 2nd, 1922.

I had the pleasure of attending a Baracca Class union banquet at the Presbyterian Church. The tickets cost 40 cents each but it was worth it, as everyone seemed to have a fine time. We also attended a Grange Meeting and it was voted at the meeting to give the Grange Hall back to Mr. Sexton who owns the building. Hopefully, a lease arrangement can be worked out with him for our continued use.

We ended the month spending some family time with Reverend and Mrs. McCleary and their children. They in turn have spent some days with us and everyone seems to get along so well and have such a great time. We even spent a part of one day fishing at the canal and caught a fine meal.

Robert decided to quit Garlock's and come to work for me on the farm full time. We agreed on a salary of $10.00 per week and he is to start immediately. We are of course all anxious here in early April as America has decided to join the Great War and has declared war on Germany. We are all concerned that Robert being 21 years old may be called up and go to the battlefront in France. Time will tell if that is the case. As it turned out, shortly after Robert decided to work on the farm he came down with what we think is the grip again and Dr. Chase has come out to tend to him. Since Robert is on the "sick list" I stayed home with him on Sunday and Mazie, the twins, Marion, Howdy and Helen all walked to church on this very pleasant April day. As it turned out, Dr. Chase felt he needed another opinion concerning Robert who is so sick that he brought Dr. Smith with him to see to Robert. It took him a good two weeks before he started to feel better and I called Dr. Smith and told him he need not come out again as Robert was on the mend.

The cultivating, plowing and planting this time of year is becoming a major task with Robert sick and my doing it myself. Hopefully I can keep up with it until he is able to work with me again. I'm sure he is also anxious to have this latest bug pass and be able to do those things that make up a regular day for those of us on a farm. It is never any fun to be ill.

We needed a little cash so I made an agreement to sell next year's calves to R. B. Chapman for $4.50 each with the understanding that I have the right to keep three heifers. He paid me a small advance on this agreement and with that money I sent Weith and Tyler a check for $9.00, which is the interest due on the loan they made us awhile back for $150.00. I also paid the $38.35 to the estate of Charles McLouth for his recent loan to us. He sadly passed away since he loaned us the money recently to pay my life insurance policy premium.

Here at the end of April we received the schedule of payment that the Dairyman's League has set for the 6-month period. It states they must pay we dairy farmers in this area as follows:

April $2.315 per 100 lbs.= 5 cents a quart
May $2.265 per 100 lbs.= 4.8 cents a quart
June $2.165 per 100 lbs.= 4.6 cents a quart
July $2.365 per 100 lbs.= 5 cents a quart
Aug. $2.815 per 100 lbs.= 6 cents a quart
Sept. $2.815 per 100 lbs.= 6 cents a quart

The standard set in the agreement between the Dairyman's league and the milk processors is that 100 lbs. is equal to 47 quarts so this will work out to our advantage. This is certainly a better price than I could have negotiated myself with the Brighton Place Dairy so the small sum of money to belong to the league is well worth it.

I re-negotiated the loan with Weith and Tyler and sent them a new note for one year for the $150.00 at 6% interest. We have several loans outstanding and it takes some juggling of the records to keep track of all of them. I wish we didn't have to borrow so often but I will say we have always paid our loans back and always paid the interest due on time or shortly thereafter. Would you believe that I was recently looking in my old memoranda booklet and came across the following entry from our days in Bellaire, Ohio? The First Presbyterian Church loaned Benjamin C. Tyler $100.00 for one year at 6% interest. I'll bet you didn't realize churches were in the loaning business but it wasn't uncommon for the church to be there in more ways than just saving souls.

Speaking of churches, we heard today that Reverend McCleary broke his wrist cranking his car to get it started. Maybe someday they will invent a means to start a car where you don't have to turn a crank, which all to often results in a broken wrist if the engine kicks back and you are not paying attention completely to what you are doing. As I have mentioned before I'm not sure when if ever we will be able to afford a car but at least when I want to go I just say giddy-up and the horses don't need to be cranked so that is one advantage to not owning a car. I am going to help the good reverend plant his garden since he is working with only one hand and Mazie is baby sitting the McCleary's babies and twins several times to help them out. Hopefully his wrist will heal soon and he will be whole again. At least it won't slow him down too much as far as his saving souls duties are concerned.

I sold the cow Perry to Bill Brownell for $72.50 and used some of the money to pay the third quarter Palmyra School tuition for Marion, Howard and Helen. I also bought a new horse and we named it Jefferson Davis after the past president of the Confederate States of America. I am trying to break him in with a biting rig and we will see how he works out. Even Howdy's heifer had a bull calf and we sold him for $4.00. I split the money with Howard since it was, he always said, his cow. I ended up the livestock work having to cut the horns off of Betty, Nancy and Howdy this month.

We did do a few things for fun this month like Robert taking young Howard to the circus in Rochester, which he loved. And also the children are spending some social time at the Y.P.S.C.E. at church. The combined Baracca class recently had a hot dog supper and I went to that and it cost me 25 cents for a fine meal with hot dogs as the main course. The reverend called and asked if Robert and I would spend a part of day fishing with him since he was so laid up with his broken wrist that he was getting bored. He didn't have to ask us twice and we had enjoyable day fishing in the canal and caught a fine catch.

This month we are also active in planning activities surrounding the 100th anniversary of the founding of the Palmyra Western Presbyterian Church. It is hard to believe that this church is one hundred years old already and had deep roots in this community. The church turns 100 and I turn 50 here on the 15th. Time certainly flies by, especially when you are busy. It is the best way to be as then one does not dwell on his or her problems. We often talk about the founding fathers and mothers who started it all and their faith, which has guided us to where we are today. As an ongoing part of this celebration we were privileged to hear Dr. Cameron and Dr. Ostrander preach on various Sundays in June and we have had several union services in other churches in the community with the most recent being in the Episcopal Church where their people congratulated our church members on our 100 years. One sad note in the community was that Mrs. F. W. Griffith passed away very suddenly here in early June. The Griffith's are a

A JOURNEY THROUGH LIFE

fine family and leaders in the community and churches and she will be sorely missed.

The Brighton Dairy paid us $131.50 for out milk deliveries in May and I gave Mazie her share for her cow of $10.00. I also paid the fourth quarter school tuition bill for Marion, Howdy and Dilly. Some of it I also used to buy more corn seed as the recent heavy rains had washed out the corn crop and it needed to be reseeded. Mazie also asked me to plant some popcorn for our home use, which I managed to do. It doesn't look like I will be planting any pickles this season as the pickle factory is slowing down and may well go out of business so I planted that extra acre in corn. I gave Howdy 10 cents as he saw something in the store that he wanted to buy for his sister, little Helen for her upcoming birthday in July. With some of the rest of the money I paid H. Runterman what we owed him on the grocery bill and then I sent Lucy TeWinkel $12.50 interest on her loan, the interest being through July 1st, 1917.

Howard McGregor and Lois and Helen, the daughters of William and Lucy TeWinkel came over from Perry to spend some time visiting with us. Howard helped me with the farm work until he had to return to New York City. All of the children and the adults went to a young peoples' social at the Crookston's home on Canandaigua Road and had a wonderful time. When Lois and Helen had to return to Perry Mazie went with them to Rochester and saw them off on the train to Perry, the twins gave both Lois and Helen some strawberries they had recently picked at Mrs. Martins and I had paid them each $1.04 for picking them. I also paid Mrs. Martin $2.70 for those that were picked. We all enjoyed them very much.

Now that Reverend McCleary's wrist is healed they had us all to supper at the manse for helping them out while he was so laid up. We had a fine hot-dog supper and enjoyed it greatly. He was careful about cranking his car and took us on an auto ride to Walworth. That was quite an experience since it had been raining quite a bit of late and I was afraid we might get stuck on some of these things they call roads. I think the lanes I have on the farm to the various fields pass more for roads than the roads they maintain around the town and county. As it was, I figured if we got stuck we could call on some dependable farmer with his horses to pull us out but alas the automobile came through with flying colors. Lois and Helen also had the pleasure of going to a social function at School No. 11 with the good reverend and he took them in his automobile. Mr. McCleary also spent part of the month switching pulpits with Reverend Creighton from Newark now that he is feeling better.

The month finished out with R. B. Chapman buying Blossoms' calf from me for $5.00. The extra 50 cents he paid was on account of the calf being an extra fine animal and we both agreed it was worth a little more money. I ended up taking Saddle to Mr. Corlette's bull for servicing and that cost me the outlandish sum of $1.00.

Speaking of outlandish costs Mazie decided that since August was already here and we were getting a lot of company from our extended family in Canandaigua and also Perry that I was to get my hair cut or she was going to do it for me. I finally agreed, fearing that I might wake up some morning without any hair, and went to the barber and the charge was 35 cents. I couldn't believe it, where did the days of the 25-cent haircuts go? Along with that I had to buy reading glasses for myself and I picked them up at Smith and Ziegler's for $4.25. Mazie also insisted on the haircut as she and I are going on a vacation later this month to my home in Haymarket, Virginia to see old friends and family and she wanted me to look presentable. This will be our first vacation in years and we are both looking forward to it. The children have been taking their vacation this summer by spending time in Perry with the TeWinkel children and they in turn are going to spend some time here for their vacation. Wouldn't it be wonderful if we had enough money to take the entire family on a long vacation someplace like Yellowstone Park? Alas it is not to be and anyway the children seem to have a great time in Perry and Canandaigua, as do the relatives' children here on the farm in Palmyra.

Howdy is now 9 years old and since Robert is feeling under the weather again Howard helped me along with Boydon, who is here on vacation to cut oats and we ended up bringing in three loads. Howard and Boydon both agreed they wanted a fishing trip for their pay so I was happy to oblige them and we all spent a very warm day fishing in Red Creek. Howard also helped me take old

A JOURNEY THROUGH LIFE

Logan to Mr. Gilfus for a shoe repair and it cost me 70 cents. I also owed him $1.40 so we agreed I would pay him 60 cents and the rest would be covered with a bushel of potatoes. Howdy and I got those together and delivered them to him. Howard also helped me deliver the bull calf that Old Blind Eye had recently that we sold for $5.00. He is a great help and a strong and willing young man.

It is already Aug. 24th and we are leaving on the 4 P.M. trolley for Rochester to catch the train to Washington, D.C. that leaves at 6:50 P.M. I had only one minor problem as I had no money to pay for our trip so I contacted Mr. Meyers at the Brighton Place Dairy and he agreed to meet us at the train station and pay me the $144.92 that he owed us on last months' milk deliveries. It was great of him to be so thoughtful or I don't know what we would have done. We arrived in Washington at 8:40 A.M. on the 25th and left for Haymarket on the 1:45 P.M. train. We arrived there at 3:30 P.M. We found everyone well except Ma who was sick in bed. Ma is now 84 years old and in failing health. We are all praying for her speedy recovery from this current illness. We attended church with family at St. Paul's in Haymarket and then we had the pleasure of being called on at the Highlands by the Whites, George Bleight, Mary Buckner, Bernard Smith, Jr. and Sr. and Lucy Brown. My brother Grayson was also there. It was great to see everyone and reminisce about old times. We spent the next couple of days visiting at the Shelter and at Stepney. We left for Washington on the 31st and arrived home Sept. 1st, tired but having enjoyed our trip and having seen Ma and the family and friends. As you realize from reading my story, I always keep good records of our expenses on this "Journey Through Life" and this trip was no exception.

Trolley fare round trip Palmyra to Rochester - $1.80
Train fare round trip Rochester to Washington - $37.12
Sleeper car round trip   - $4.00
Train fare Washington to Haymarket round trip- $4.10
Incidentals, gifts, meals, etc.   - $14.49

Total $61.51

The trip was well worth the expense and we found everyone healthy and happy when we arrived home. It was great to be home with a loving family and to sleep in one's own bed again.

It has been rainy lately and on the 2nd of Sept. we all walked to church on Sunday morning since the sun has come out. While we were in church, it started to pour so I was unanimously elected to walk home in the rain, get the surrey, drive back and pick up all the family. I somehow think Mazie rigged that vote but I didn't melt so all ended up well. I didn't even catch cold from the one-mile walk in the rain, which was a blessing.

Robert has decided to resume his college work and headed for Boston here in early Sept. Since I will no longer have his help I took the trolley into Rochester, went to the State Employment Agency and hired a 26-year-old Rumanian named Nicolas George for a two-week trial period. They told me I could pay him at the end of the two weeks whatever I thought his labors were worth and then if I wanted to keep him and he wanted to stay we would work out his pay. I bought a 5-cent cigar for the trip home on the trolley and had a great smoke out of sight of Mazie. I took the rest of the day off and went fishing in Red Creek with Howard and Helen and unfortunately while wading I cut my foot and had to have Dr. Chase lance in afterwards. We did have some luck however and caught four large suckers, which we will enjoy for supper some evening.

I tried Pete hooked up to the riding plow and he was not a happy camper at all so back to the stables he went. I then hooked up Logan and Maude to the side-hill plow and again they were not happy about that. They must have heard me talking in the barn about our association with the Dairyman's League and decided it was to their benefit to get organized for a greater say in their efforts. Needless to say I soon put a stop to that and hooked them up to the riding plow and they worked fine in that. As we left the stables I almost thought old Pete was smiling as I left him there to wile away the day. Maybe he was the organizer of the group. To round out our stock I did end up buying two six week old pigs from W. E. Spiers for $6.00 each and also a lamb from Mr. Randolph for $6.00. I thought it might pay to start raising some sheep. Only time will tell.

A JOURNEY THROUGH LIFE

Nicholas George has worked out fine so I offered him employment until December 1st at $25.00 per month plus room and board and he accepted it. The real test will come soon as we are just getting into the harvesting time, apple picking time and cutting winter firewood time so we will see how he works out over the long haul.

I found out here at the end of the month that there is an up side as well as a down side to be organized for greater bargaining power when the Brighton Place Dairy notified us that they would no longer accept our milk after Oct. 1st. I went to Rochester and met with Abe Oldenstien of the Atlantic Dairy in Brighton and he said he would take our milk at the price agreed upon by the Dairyman's League but only if it is shipped via the New York Central Railroad rather than the trolley. I stopped at the Granite Building in Rochester and told the Dairyman's League to agree to that if they could not find another dairy to take it via the trolley. Unfortunately the train is more expensive to ship the milk but it looks like that is what I will be doing from now on. When life seems to be going along fairly smooth the good Lord doesn't want to see us become too complacent so he throws some curve balls our way. It seems my first shipment of milk to the new dairy was, by mistake, delivered to the Brighton Place Dairy and instead of their sending it over to Oldenstien, they sent it back to Palmyra. By the time it took this round trip, of course it was sour and I had to dump it. I sent them a bill for it and we will see if they pay for their mistake. It's a good thing the good reverend was here to partake of supper with us when I had the milk returned or I might have said a few choice words that I shouldn't have. Between he and Mazie, I held my tongue since I knew where I would be if I let slip. I also said a little prayer to the Lord that I had learned my lesson about even thinking about a smoother life with the milk shipment going astray but He must have thought I needed an additional reminder as George Nicholas up and quit after a month of work. I paid him $12.50, bid him a fond farewell and told him I would send him the other $12.50 as soon as I got it. It seems the extra work did not fit his schedule either. To top it all off here on the 13th of October I received a telegram from George in Haymarket and he told me that Ma had passed away. I was thankful that we had seen her for the last time when we paid our visit in August. God rest her soul.

All of the neighbors are getting together and we are filling each other's silos, which has become an annual thing. After we got ours filled I drew the engine to Mr. Corbett's as his is the next one to be filled. I also hired Mr. Farrington to work for me on an as needed basis. He is willing to work under those circumstances for 22 ½ cents per hour as long as he is not tied up elsewhere. He is a good worker so this might work out rather than have a full-time hired hand.

The month ended up with Mazie and I going to a Baracca Class meeting at the manse. We do let the ladies join us on occasion, as if we had a choice. I also sent a telegram to the Brighton Place Dairy asking for the money they owed me. Only time will tell if they come through but I am not optimistic.

I have agreed to ship 15 barrels of potatoes for W. R. Beach to Syracuse and they are to pay the freight and buy the sugar barrels that they want the potatoes shipped in. They have agreed to pay me $1.35 per bushel and I can ship at my convenience. I also sold D. H. Levis 5,716 pounds of wheat, 95 bushels, and he paid me by bank draft $190.53 for the wheat. With some of this money I am paying the school tax of $37.36 to Mr. VanHall, Jr. and we are also paying the first quarter tuition for Marion, Howard and Helen's schooling. All are very worthwhile payments. Mr. Farrington has worked out well and I have used some of the funds to also settle up with him for the 78 hours worked at 22 ½ cents per hour or a total of $17.55. I also contributed $1.00 to George S. Johnson at the YMCA for the war effort. We are all praying for an early end to this madness in Europe.

I had to take the trolley to Rochester to sign a new contract with the Oldenstien Dairy for milk shipments in December of this year and January through March of next year. The price we agreed upon was not as much as I had hoped but I had little choice. I'm not sure how much good the Dairyman's League is doing the small farmer like I am. I will just have to give it more time to see.

We were headed to church with old Maude and the wagon here near the end of November of 1917 when we got to the "Flats" on our way and along came Hans and the four children in his brand new Dodge car. The rest of the family and the children went on to church with old dependable Maude and I went back home with Hans to admire his new auto. I told him how great it was but inside I was very jealous that he had a new car and we didn't. Maybe our turn will come if we can save up the few hundred dollars we need to buy one, not much chance of that however.

We recently had a vote here in Palmyra on the question of allowing a saloon to open in the village and I voted against it. Mazie couldn't of course vote but believe me my vote was Mazie's vote. Even if I had thought differently about it I had no chance of voting in any way but the negative. Mazie also saw to it that I contribute $1.00 to Reverend McCleary to help him cover his expenses to Washington, D.C. for the upcoming convention on temperance. I believe, as I have said, that this movement to outlaw the entire devils' brew is gaining strength and may well become the law of the land shortly. We also delivered to the McCleary's five pounds of potatoes as an early Christmas gift. The good reverend asked me if I would have the time and money to pay the Garlock Garage the $9.30 that he owed them for the tire chains and the five gallons of gasoline he recently bought and hadn't yet paid for. He promised to pay me back when he returns from his convention and I was happy to oblige him.

Since Ma recently passed away, myself and my brothers and sisters have inherited the Highlands. Since we are always in need of money Mazie and I negotiated a loan with the rest of the family using our share of the estate as collateral and I sent off the loan agreement to H. B. Tyler and he will send us a draft for the money. We will be able to splurge a little more on Christmas gifts for ourselves and the children with this money, pay some bills and we also had to pay George L. Clark $1.00 for the care of the cemetery plot that we purchased when little Harry passed away. We will someday join him there. It is a pretty spot in the Palmyra Cemetery.

I needed some extra help so Bernard (Bert) Bremus who is 18 years old wanted to work so I hired him for one month. I agreed to pay him $12.50 and see how he works out and maybe extend his employment after the end of the month if we both agree. He has helped me bring in the bean crop along with Mr. Harrington and I sold them all to D.H. Levis for a total of $352.20. It seems like we are rolling in money at the present but I am sure that won't last. I did pay about 8 of the people that we owed money to including Dr. Chase the $20.00 we owed him for taking care of the family. It seems now that the cold weather has arrived and the house is all shut up, the bugs are coming out and it seems that one or more of the children are sick almost constantly this time of year. Of course the weather here in late Dec. is not helping since it was 24 degrees below zero the other night and never got above 12 below all day. You can imagine how much coal and swamp wood we went through just trying to stay warm. Warm we did stay however and enjoyed our Christmas celebrations with many gifts and a fine meal. Christmas is special when it is spent with a loving family. We enjoyed the Christmas party at the church and the celebration there. The Reeves also had us to a dinner party on New Years Eve to celebrate the end of 1917 and the beginning of 1918. We all prayed that 1918 would see the end of the ceaseless slaughter of so many in this useless war in Europe.

Chapter 12

1918

World War 1 Ends
World wide influenza epidemic kills 22 million

Jan. 1918 could be called the month of isolation in the Tyler family of Maple Avenue in Palmyra. Dr. Chase has been here tending to Helen who he says has the measles so he has recommended very firmly that all the children leave the house for the duration of the illness. Robert of course is in Trenton, New Jersey trying out a new college so he is out of the picture. The twins have been offered to go to the Browns for the duration. Marion and Howard will be staying with the Whitlock's until this is over and we can all unite as one healthy family. In the meantime Mazie and I will be tending to Helen's speedy recovery, God willing, along with Dr. Chase. Reverend and Mrs. McCleary have been very helpful during this time and have had several meals with us and offered their support. None of us are making church during this time, as they have curtailed the services during the outbreak of the measles. Sadly, Mrs. T. W. Corlett died suddenly this month and the reasons are yet to be determined. It seems like there are all sorts of nasty diseases around as I have often said this time of year. The month ended with the family again reuniting under our roof with Helen feeling much better. It is good to have everyone back together and healthy. We celebrated by helping the Baracca class build a new bookcase and presenting it to Reverend McCleary and his wife for the help he showed us and other families in the community that were stricken with the measles.

Fortunately all those that had the illness survived thanks to Dr. Chase's good work, the Lord's blessing and the fact that they all come from strong stock.

Will stopped by on his way home from Canastota and told us he has taken a call at their Presbyterian Church and will be leaving Perry's pulpit soon. We all wished him the best of luck in this new chapter in his life. He has served the Perry Presbyterian Church for many a year and I am sure he will be greatly missed. We are certainly blessed also to have a wonderful man, preacher and neighbor here in Palmyra with Reverend McCleary who often comes out and works with me either cutting wood, even helping me clean the manure out of the cow barn and helping spreading it on the fields. We always look forward to the Sunday services and then the Union services at the opera house in the evening.

The government is issuing "Thrift Stamps" and encouraging folks to buy them to support the war effort and also to save for the future. I gave the children $2.25 to purchase some as they wanted to do their part in helping support this country in its fight against the Kaiser and Germany. Hopefully this madness will end soon and the boys will be brought home whole. I also shelled out $10.00 for the second term for school tuition and bought Howard a new sled for $1.75, which he is delighted with. Speaking of school, the State of New York is looking into changing the independence of common school districts and exercising more state control over each school. We had a meeting and others and I spoke out against any changes. We feel local control of schools and the education of our young people should remain a function of the communities and the state should not be involved. I don't feel however that our protests will carry much weight, as the state seems to always dictate their wants with little or no concern for the people's feelings.

I have started to order some seed for the spring planting, can't wait for spring and nice weather, and bought some leaning corn seed from Young and Sons. We are fortunate that our milk sales are running close to $200 a month so it seems we have a little extra money, at least for the time being. The month ended up with Mr. Chapman and I again signing an agreement where I would sell him all the calves we have this year at $5.00 each with the option that I could keep two of them.

We have enjoyed two Grange Socials here in March and I paid our dues to the Grange of $1.20 for the year. I also paid J. H. Walton for the $4200.00 in Grange insurance that they wrote for us on the farm. The Grange is certainly a wonderful organization in supporting the farmers, their family's interests and providing social outlets for us. I also bought a two-year subscription to the "Rural New Yorker" through the Grange and that cost me $2.00.

Marion now has come down with the measles and Dr. Chase said that her case is very mild so isolating the family is not necessary. I also have not been feeling all that well but I was only able to take a day off as the work is always there and someone has to do it. It is just as well as laying around just has a tendency to bring out some of my old demons and I sure do not need that with all the sickness around and worry about sickness, the war, the weather and all those other things that farmers constantly worry about, especially this farmer.

I went to the dairy in Rochester, Hans was here with his auto and agreed to drive me up. Mr. Oldenstien and I agreed on the price for the milk sales for the next few months and he will sign the Dairyman's League contract.

The month ended on sort of a sad note. The children's dog Blaze has been wandering into the village and I have been notified that she has threatened some of the children in town. I thought about this problem for a short time and since the dog is getting older and the Lord has given us dominion over the fish and all the animals on earth I made a decision that this could not go on. I would never forgive myself if the dog harmed someone and especially a child. I went out to Haak's, borrowed his gun and shot old Blaze so the issue is finished. The children will just have to get over it and maybe shortly we will look around for a new puppy for them.

I found out through my accounting that the Oldenstien Dairy was shorting me slightly for our milk deliveries for the past several months. I wrote them the following letter:

"Dear Mr. Oldenstien: I got your check this morning paying for the milk shipped the first half of March, but it was $2.15 short of the bill sent you by me. Please let me know where this shortage comes in. You spoke the other day about the 1 cent per 100 lbs. tax. I find in looking over my accounts that you have paid me short of my bills each month that I have shipped you. For the five months, Oct., Nov., Dec., Jan and Feb. this shortage amounts to $4.72 or an average of about 92 cents per month. Now I thought all along that part of this shortage was the 1-cent per 100 lbs. tax that you were paying to the league. Please let me know about this."

As you can tell I have always prided myself in keeping meticulous records and I am only disgusted with myself that I didn't catch this sooner. As it turned out the Dairyman's League has now told me to stop shipping to Oldenstien and start shipping immediately to O. R. Meisenzahl of Rochester. I'm not sure what is going on but as long as I have a place to ship and the money keeps coming in for our milk I am satisfied that the Dairyman's League is looking out for our interests.

Mr. Case and I were installed this month as elders in the Presbyterian Church to serve a term of three years. I found that my schedule allows me to take on this extra obligation and frankly Mazie said if I didn't she would make my life miserable so I had little choice. I am of course looking forward to this challenge and intend to give it my all. I also pledged $4.00 for 1918 to the anti-saloon league and again Mazie had a lot of influence in that decision as I have mentioned in the past.

Howard has tonsillitis and Dr. Chase is attending to him and may take his tonsils out here on the farm. Hopefully all will go well. He plans to put off that decision for a few days so Mazie and Helen left for Canastota to visit the TeWinkels for a couple of days since Howard was doing better and Dr. Chase says he will wait until they return to decide if he wants to remove them.

I sold Pete to Tom Maley for the ridiculously low price of $75.00 as he has never worked out well behind the plow and since I now have Jefferson Davis and have paid Morey Nichol of Rogers Farms $10 to break him and he is working great in a single or double harness I decided it was time to part with old Pete. I was tempted to maybe do him in but only for a fleeting moment and selling him to Tom makes more sense since maybe Tom will have better luck with him than I did. Nancy and Howdy also had calves along with Monk who had a bull calf and I sold all three for $14.50. Monks' calf was a little small so I only got $4.50 for him and $5.00 each for the other two. With this money we decided to

A JOURNEY THROUGH LIFE

purchase a $100 Liberty Bond to help out the war effort. This should return us some profit when it matures and in the meantime the government can use the cash to help prosecute the war and maybe bring it to an early end before more young men on both sides are slaughtered because of the stupidity of the leaders that still think the only way to settle country's differences are by the sword.

I ended the month buying a used Sterling Cook Stove for Mazie and Fred and I installed it in the kitchen. I also splurged and bought a new carpet for her for the sitting room. It is always good to keep on the Mrs. good side even if it cost a little money to do so.

We are celebrating Reverend McCleary's birthday here on May 4th and we baked him, or I should say Mazie baked him a fine cake and the McCleary's spent an enjoyable evening celebrating. Even Hans and the family drove over from Canandaigua and joined us for the celebration and all had a good time.

I spent the rest of the month plowing, planting and of course planting Mazie's garden with many different vegetables which we will all enjoy this coming fall and winter. George also sent us two bushels of husking corn from Manassas, Virginia, which we will put to short use. I ended the month taking the family to see the movie "The Whip" and then the next day Mr. Lamb and I went visiting members of the church, which is one of the elders' responsibilities. We discussed church life with each family and will carry back their suggestions to the full leadership in the hopes that some of the changes they brought up might be adopted.

We started June of 1918 all attending church except Marion whom is baby-sitting with the McCleary's baby while they are in church. She is very good with younger children and taking care of folks and as I mentioned before I think she would make a fine nurse someday. She is going on 15 and is a beautiful young lady. Jacob Crookston was installed as an elder at the service and Henry Runterman was installed as a deacon. The McCleary's also came out and brought some of the food and we had a fine picnic dinner on the front lawn. He also helped me after the dinner to plant some of the potatoes in the potato field.

Jefferson Davis is five years old here on the seventh of June and for a birthday present I had him shod all around and it cost me $1.80. He is a great horse and a fine animal. I also sold the heifer Patches to Charles Brownell for $85.00 and with part of that money I bought a new horse to replace Pete. The girls named the new horse Jerry and all the children are enjoying riding him, as he is very gentle. I also used a little of the money to pay J. Walton the $2.00 we had pledged to the Red Cross to help them out with all their war efforts and with the Spanish Influenza problem that we are hearing is hitting some of our troops in several of the bases around the country. I pray that both the war will be over soon and that the flu can be contained so it doesn't become a serious health threat. We also bought a war savings stamp for $4.17 to also help the war effort. Speaking of the war we are particularly concerned as Robert returned from college in Trenton, New Jersey for the summer and is going to go to Syracuse to enlist in the Naval Reserves. We pray that he will not be called up to active duty and become involved in this terrible confrontation. If Mama and Papa, I find myself referring to Mazie and I in that tense lately, had our way he would not have enlisted but he is a grown man and his destiny is in his hands and it is not to be that Mama and Papa tell him what to do anymore. You raise your children and hope and pray that you give them a good solid start in life and roots that they can always look back upon and wisdom to make the right decisions as they travel down their road. Robert has been a great help as he has helped me replant silo corn that was recently washed out with the heavy rains and also he helped me plant some poison corn to try and cut down on the number of crows and pheasants that are constantly eating and digging up the corn. He, Marion and Howard are also helping me with the hay.

As the month drew to a close I have not been feeling all that well and almost missed the twin's graduation from High School and the commencement exercises. I certainly would not miss that as it is a great occasion and they both graduated with honors for all their hard work, I gave them each a dollar as a graduation gift. Now as some would say they must face the cruel world as they are out of school and we will see what the future holds for them. Hopefully they will always walk with the wind to

A JOURNEY THROUGH LIFE

their backs and uphold the good name of the Tyler family of Palmyra.

We ended the month with my taking Howard and Dill fishing in the canal and we had a great time with Dill out catching Howard which is very unusual as Howard usually outshines us all.

It hasn't been that long since the twins graduated from high school but they are already off to visit in Bellaire, Ohio with Mazie's family for a while. They are going to check out a college in that area while they are visiting. As I often have said it is so important to have a good education that we are somehow going to manage to find the money so that all our children can go on to college to better their position in life above the struggle that Mazie and I have had. I world not give up a minute of our time together but farming is not an easy life and with advanced education we are hoping the children will find happiness, prosperity and an easier life than we have had. Hans had brought Marion home from a visit in Canandaigua and was going to pick up Boydon and take him back home but he graciously agreed to drive the twins to Rochester along with mama who went to see them off on their new adventure. Robert also went along and I'm sure he gave his sisters a lot of brotherly advise on the way up to Rochester.

Since Mazie, Bob and the twins all are gone I decided to goof off for the day and took Marion, Howard and Helen fishing in the canal. This time Howdy outshined us all with the most and the largest fish caught. We all had a grand time and had several fish cleaned and ready for Mazie to cook when she got home. When we arrived home we were surprised, as Gordon, Howard and Helen TeWinkel had come for a stay. Mazie knew about it but had forgotten to mention it to papa. It didn't make any difference as we had plenty of fish for everyone and they are always welcome at our house and at our table as are all the extended family. As it turned out they are a big help as they are all helping me cut wood in the swamp, even Helen, and draw it up to the woodshed to be able to use this winter. Mazie, Helen and I also attended a Grange Social one evening and the fine members of the Ontario Grange provided the entertainment.

Church has been hit and miss here in August as the Presbyterian Church has been closed and we are holding ecumenical services combined with other churches in the village.

With all the company, we haven't been as faithful as we should have been and we will see to it that that changes come September. I have managed to teach a couple of Baracca Classes and also led prayer meetings at the manse on several Thursdays this month.

As we move into September of 1918 we are still very concerned about the ongoing war in Europe and are hearing much more scary news about the Spanish Flu spreading throughout the country. It is mostly confined at present to military bases and there is some suspicion that the Germans may have brought it to this country as a weapon in the conflict. Whatever the case we are praying daily and in our church meetings to a quick end to the war and to the flu, either one of which is deadly to just too many people.

The children started school here on the 3rd of September and I had new shoes put on Maude all around for $2.00 at Claudia Pulver's just so she would be in fine shape to take the children to school on this first day. After today, of course, they will walk the mile or so to and from school and be the better off for it. I cannot imagine their being transported everyday to and from school and the lack of exercise and fresh air they would miss. On the first weekend of school Howdy was driven over to Canandaigua to stay with Hans and family for the weekend. Mr. Hennessey was headed that way in his car and offered to give him a lift. We picked him up however with dependable old Jefferson Davis as our horsepower on Monday so he wouldn't miss too much school.

The thrasher showed up on time here in Sept. and they thrashed with my help and Robert's 125 bushels of wheat, which I sold to Levis for $2.10 a bushel, and they also thrashed 162 bushels of oats. They charged me 8 cents a bushel for the wheat and 6 cents a bushel for the oats.

We received our first interest payment from the First National Bank on our $100 Liberty Bond and it was for $1.49 and covered the period up to Sept. 15th. We will need the money and all else we can raise as the twins have decided to enroll in college and I sent the following letter to the college on their behalf.

"Blackburn College, Carlinville, Illinois:
Dear Sir:

A JOURNEY THROUGH LIFE

I enclose for you my check on First National Bank of Palmyra for $140.00, which is in payment for board and tuition for the 1st semester for my daughters Dorothy and Margaret. The girls are at Bellaire, Ohio and will leave there for Carlinville on Monday the 16th instant. Each of them has already paid $10.00. I note in your letter that you will allow credit for all railroad fare paid in excess of $10.00. Please let me know how this will be adjusted.

Yours very truly, Ben. C. Tyler"

That most likely spells the end of my dreams to buy a new car but the choice is not a hard one. A new car never had a chance over the girls' education and anyway, our dependable horsepower will see us through as it always has.

The month of September ended on a very concerned note for the Tyler's with Robert having received a telegram to report to Pelham Bay Naval Training Station in Brooklyn. He is to leave immediately. We also notified Mazie's brother Howard at Columbia University as we are in hopes that he will watch over Robert while in that area. Since there have been no naval battles in the Great War in Europe we are not so concerned for his safety there but we are hearing more and more about illnesses, including the flu, at all the army and navy bases and that is as big or larger a concern as his possibly seeing combat. We can only hope and pray and remember that he comes from strong stock and will someday return to us whole.

As October of 1918 rolls around I was reminded to go into town and pay George Clark the $1.50 I owed him for the care of the cemetery lot that we purchased and where our dear little Harry is buried[1]. It is a very nerve-racking time at present with the school being closed because of the Spanish Influenza that is rearing its ugly head across this country and the rest of the world. The government has recommended no unnecessary gathering together until the crisis is past.

In fact, the church services have been suspended for the duration also. We are all staying as close to home as possible with

---

[1] When researching this part of my grandfather's diaries I found out that Harry had never had a marker placed at his gravesite. I purchased one from The Bronze Works of Utah and Roger Weaver the Palmyra Cemetery superintendent set it in cement to mark his grave, almost 100 years after his passing.

the exception of myself who has to keep delivering recently picked apples and other chores into town as needed to keep food on our table. We can only hope and pray that it does not strike too close to home. I had to go to the train station as we had promised to send a box of apples and also some spending money to the twins at Blackburn College. The express for the apples and the few dollars cost me 95 cents to send.

It is also silo-filling time again and without the silo filled I don't believe the cows would make it through the winter and that would most likely bankrupt us. All of the neighbors have gotten together and we are all helping each other do the filling. Everyone seems healthy enough but we are still cautious and washing up good after being around each other so as not to bring any dangerous germs into the house. We have also started to pick apples or I should say pick up apples, as I am shaking as many as possible off the trees. Since I estimate that we will have about six thousand bushel Mazie, Howard, Helen and I are all picking them up. I'm sure I could not handle this job all by myself so the help is appreciated. It also keeps the children busy since they are not in school for a while.

Mrs. Taber has passed away and we do not know if the flu played any role in her passing. We sent flowers and I bought them from Mrs. Pickering for 25 cents. Hans and the children have also come over from Canandaigua for a visit. This makes me a little nervous with the epidemic all around but then again one cannot stop being with people, especially family, even in a time like this.

I ended the month helping Pete Smith cut more corn from the corn lot for the silo. The corn lot is 40.6 rods long and 20 rods wide and he charged me $13.95 for his equipment and labor. I also decided to sell Monk and Midnight to R. Rainbow and he agreed to pay me $65.00 each for them. They haven't been producing that much milk so I am happy to be rid of them and will look around for a couple of good milk cows to replace them.

There are still no church services as November rolls around. They finally are reopening the schools here on Nov. 4th and I drove the children to school as it is raining out and I certainly don't want them to get wet and sick at any time but, particularly, the present. The schools have been closed for three weeks and two days due to the scare. I hope they are not reopening it too soon.

A JOURNEY THROUGH LIFE

Church also has reopened and one of the first services was a memorial service for Mr. Smith. I have not heard what took him, hopefully not the flu.

The church bells have been tolling as Germany has surrendered today, it is reported that they are to sign the armistice on Nov. 11th at 11 AM. (11 AM on the 11th day of the 11th month). I wondered if there was any hidden message in the three elevens. The wanton killing is over, hopefully for good. Maybe if mankind has learned anything from this slaughter of so many young men on both sides it will be that war never solves anything. Will this be "The War to end All Wars?" We are all hoping that Robert will be home soon as there is still a threat of the influenza at all the bases as well as in the general population.

I had to go into the post office and meet with tax collector Maloney and made a return showing our receipts and expenses for 1917. He will determine our tax based on the information I furnished him. Hopefully it will not be too much but with the expenses of fighting this terrible war I am sure we will be assessed something.

The month ended with Howard buying a Daisy Air Rifle for $2.50. He used the money I had paid him for helping to pick up the apples. We also bought him a new suit that cost us $10.00 and for a ten year old he looks so grown up. He is a fine handsome young man. I tallied up the total apples we had picked, picked up and delivered and it came to 52,130 pounds for 1918. We were paid $364.91 for them and the money will come in handy. Perry also had a calf and we named him December and I think we will keep him instead of selling him since we have the apple money.

December 8[th:] Howard and Marion have both become ill so Mazie kept Helen home from church as we are worried about what is going on. We thought the influenza had run its course but they are quite ill and we are very concerned. Dr. Chase came out in the afternoon to check on them both and he was particularly anxious about Marion.

December 9th: I went to town and bought a fever thermometer and Dr. Chase again came out to check on Marion and Howard but he again was mostly concerned about Marion and her deteriorating condition. We are praying constantly that it is not the deadly flu and that both of them will regain full health. We have already lost two children and I'm not sure I could survive losing another.

December 10th: Dr. Chase came out twice today to check on Marion and I drove Maude into his office to pick up some fever medicine for Helen who also is not feeling all that well. Why is this happening to us? Mazie keeps reminding me that we must have faith that the Lord will see the children through this crises and give Dr. Chase the skill and the medicines to see them well once again.

December 11th: Dr. Chase came out and brought Miss Irene Tiffany to nurse Marion. She will stay here 24 hours a day with her. We are so grateful that there are willing souls to lend a hand in a serious situation such as this is. They seem to be willing to risk catching the flu by being around those that have it but are willing to help even knowing their risks. The Lord does provide. I went into Briggs's Drugstore on Dr. Chase's suggestion and bought some anti-phlogistine for Marion to help relieve her discomfort.

December 12th: Dr. Chase brought Dr. Reeves with him to check on Marion. Howard seems to be somewhat better and the doctors are gravely concerned about Marion. They told us they were doing all they could for her and that we should pray for the Lord's help. They also brought Mr. Harold Crandall to replace Irene as Marion's 24-hour nurse. I am leading the family in prayer often.

December 13th: Dr. Chase came twice today to check on Marion. Sadly she died at 4 P.M. very quietly and apparently without pain. Mr. Crandall came out in late evening to arrange for the funeral.

We have now lost three beautiful children and my faith in God is badly shaken. Mazie said maybe Little Harry needed someone to hold his hand in heaven and Marion was whom he wanted. Maybe instead of being a nurse here on earth she will be an angel to Little Harry. Whatever the case, this is almost too much to bear. If it wasn't for Mazie's great faith and love I don't think I could go on. Mrs. Reeves and Mrs. Taber have been here most of the day looking after things for Mazie, and Lucy TeWinkel also has arrived from Canastota to help out with everything. We are grateful that Helen and Howard are both on the mend and Dr.

Chase has told us they should be fine. Who among us can explain why one goes and others are left to go on?

Just ten days before the celebration of the Birth of Christ we had a service here at the farm at 2 P.M. Dr. Henke led the service and then we took Marion to the Palmyra Cemetery and buried her next to Little Harry. Hans came over from Canandaigua to be with us but left the rest of the family home since they of course are all terrified of the flu and what it is doing to families in the entire area. We decided as well that the twins should not come home at this time from college, as the risk of being on a crowded train and in train stations is just too great. Robert did manage to get leave and was here with us when we needed family.

I have contacted Fred Guile and asked him to put our farm on the market and we are going to ask $12,000 for the farm and the 81 acres. This home holds too many a sad memory to want to stay here. We will see what comes of this decision to move on in our "Journey Through Life." I cannot function so I am giving up this journal at least until I can see my way clear to move forward. Time has a way of healing all our wounds and with time, hopefully, and with God's help Mazie, Howard, Robert, Helen, the twins and I will be able to resume our normal lives. Even though this will prayerfully happen we will always have the first Helen, Harry and Marion in our thoughts and hearts.

Chapter 13

1919

The 18th Amendment to the Constitution is passed by Congress outlawing the manufacturing, transportation or sale of alcoholic beverages

This new year of 1919 comes with a sense of sadness and a renewal of our faith that this will be a better year for the Tyler family of Palmyra. I started the year with a touch of the flu also but Dr. Chase said I would be all right as it is a mild form and not life threatening. Since I felt somewhat better I have been trying to stay busy and keep my mind occupied so that I would not fall into that deep depression that is always lurking around the corner. I have been cutting a lot of wood from the swamp and hauling it to the house. I also delivered the last of the beans to D. H. Levis and he paid me in full the $125.57 that he owed me for them. I have also had to send part of our milk production to the Macedon Creamery, as Meisenzahl Dairy cannot take all that is being shipped to them at the present time. I also have been attending church regularly as Mazie does not seem to feel she wants to attend yet. I think she is asking herself why this happened to a family that believed so strongly in the goodness of the Lord. Hopefully she will find her answers and move back into the flock of the church family, which can be so supportive in times like these. Many of the church faithful and our friends are having us to their homes often this month and it is wonderful since it takes our minds from our problems if even for a brief time. We also received a fine letter from R. C. Tyler, who is presently living in Montana, expressing his sympathies.

We were saddened that Reverend McCleary was not here when we needed him the most. I wrote to him at Paris, France, 12 Rue d' Arguesseau, c/o the Y.M.C.A. He is expecting to come home soon and we are both anxious for his guidance and steady hand. In the meantime Mazie has spent a great deal of time at Mrs. McCleary's consoling her in her husband's absence and of course the good reverend's wife has offered immeasurable support to Mazie at this time. Robert also is not going to be here to lend his support for he is leaving for Princeton, New Jersey here on January 14th.

We have heard nothing on the potential sale of the property and will just have to give it more time. I did have to shell out $55.26 to Jon VanHall for taxes for 1919 so that, at least, is paid on this property for the year. I also spent some money on buying rubbers and a pair of woolen pants for Howdy to hopefully keep him dry, warm and well.

As the month draws to a close and I am starting to heal even slightly I was again reminded of the tragedy as I had to pay George L. Clark $6.00 for digging the grave on Dec. 14th for dear Marion. I also paid Dr. Henke when we went to church as Mazie reminded me that we should pay him for conducting her service. I paid him $5.00 and he seemed to be fine with that amount.

Reverend McCleary has returned from France and he has been a great source of support for us both. He feels that Mazie should get away for awhile so that she isn't daily reminded of what we have all gone through by laying her eyes constantly on Marion's clothing, room and other things that she cherished. She has decided that she, Helen and Howard will go to Bellaire, Ohio to be with her family for a while, and is hoping as I am, that this will help. I bought some new shoes for Helen for the trip and also an overcoat for Howard. They cost me $8.50. I also took $50.00 out of the bank for them and took them to the B. R. and P. Train in Rochester and saw them off on the 7th. It cost me $11.02 for Mazie's ticket and one-half fare for Helen and Howard for a total of $22.04 plus I also bought them a sleeping birth for $2.20. It is sad to see them go but I think it for the best at this time. Now if I can stay busy so I don't become even more depressed with them gone, everything may be fine.

I shouldn't have worried about staying occupied, as I have been invited almost nightly to someone's house for supper and fellowship. The McCleary's, Whitlock's, Hannigan's, Bernhard's, Chapman's, Martins, Crookston's and Luppold's have all opened their hearts and their doors to me. What wonderful neighbors and friends they are in time of need.

Mazie and I are writing each other almost daily. They arrived safely and are settling in for some time it seems. I sent her some money and I also sent Margaret and Dorothy some money so that they would be able to travel over to Bellaire to visit Mazie and the children. I even hired Mrs. Tabor to make a new dress for Mazie and sent it to her with my love. I cannot wait for her to return although that must be her decision when she feels comfortable coming home.

I ended the month of Feb. 1919 going to a Grange dinner at Red Men's Hall and also paid my Grange dues for the year of $1.20. I also had to shell out $3.00 this month for Dr. Earl to examine and certify our milk cows so that we can stay in business as a milk provider. Fortunately, he found everything in order.

The neighbors and friends are still having me to supper on a regular basis and I can't tell you how much it helps to have such close and caring friends to help bear our burden in times like these. I cannot imagine being alone in one's grief and having no one to share it with and lean on. Mr. and Mrs. McCleary are also constantly available and offering prayer and support as only they can do. I will be forever in their debt. Mazie and I are writing almost every day and she and the children have settled in. I sent her $15 to help with her needs while she is in Bellaire. However, I imagine her family will provide all their needs while they are there. I am paying Mrs. Martin to provide my meals and do the washing while the family is away and I paid her $2.00 for the 6 dinners she provided to me and also 25 cents for the week's washing. She has been a great help and provides some grand meals when I have not been invited out. Although I will have to say, even though she is a great cook she doesn't hold a candle to Mazie.

I have been attending church each Sunday and heard the Reverend Stewart preach here early in March. He is the son of Dr.

Stewart who is the Presbyter of the Auburn Seminar. He preached an excellent sermon titled "Fellow Workers With God." I came away inspired by his talk. Also Reverend McCleary, having returned a while ago from his trip abroad, has also returned to the pulpit here in mid-March and we are all grateful for having him back full time. I have also spent some time with Mr. Whitlock in doing the every member canvas of all the church members for hopefully balancing the financial books of the church. To round out my church activities, we spent some time discussing at the Baracca Class the newly formed League of Nations, which is the brainchild of President Wilson. America has not yet officially joined the league but hopefully will. We prayed that it might be a new beginning for the world's nations to solve their problems over a bargaining table rather than sacrificing their young people in constant useless wars. We can only hope and pray that a new day is dawning.

I received word from Bellaire that Mazie, Howard and Helen are returning so I took the trolley to Rochester here on the 14th of March, met them and happily brought them home. The trolley trip cost me $2.48 cents, which I gladly paid to be with Mazie and the children again. Reverend McCleary called on us this evening and Mazie invited him to stay. We all prayed together, after a wonderful (Mazie) supper, that the healing process would continue with friends and God's help.

We are receiving a good return on our milk deliveries and most months it is coming to slightly over $250.00 so I was able to use some of this money to pay the interest on the mortgage of $2800 at 5% to April first of this year. I paid this to Romana and Covert who now hold our mortgage. I also paid $8.00 for tuition for Howard and Helen for the 3rd quarter of this school year. No matter what one does and how hard one works to keep your mind off the recent tragedy, it is impossible to get away from it even for a short while. When I paid the tuition bill I was again reminded what a blessing it would have been to pay the full $12.00 to cover not only Howard and Helen but also Marion. I pray she is looking down on her siblings from a better place and blessing them and their efforts in school.

We finished out March of 1919 with my buying a new tie for Howdy to wear to the birthday party for Huchey Williams's son and my taking Mazie to Newark to spend some time with the dentist. I never could understand how she doesn't seem to mind going to the dentist and having her teeth drilled when it is one of those necessary things in life that I so dread, but like so many other things, Mazie seems to take it all in stride.

Lots of plowing, planting and dragging are taking up much of my time here in April of 1919. Mazie and I did manage however to take some time off and go to a meeting of the Presbytery in Wolcott for one day. We enjoyed the fellowship and sharing of ideas immensely. We also stopped on the way home and bought Howard his first bicycle from J. H. Bain, which cost $18.00. He has been wanting one for some time and had agreed to pay $5.00 of his money towards it. Mazie and I agreed to pay the added $13.00 and when he saw it you would never see such a wonderful expression on anyone's face. He immediately took off down the road and waved to us as he went over the hill. We didn't worry about cars on this road as most of the neighbors, as with us, are still driving old Nelly to get where we want to go. He was not gone long however before he came back and offered to give his sister a ride on his brand new shiny bike. It's a good thing he enjoyed it for a short time as the weather has turned back to winter, is snowing and blowing and the temperature is a high of 24 degrees as this month winds down.

We have had an active month as far as our livestock is concerned with Violet and Nancy both having a bull calf. Nancy is Howdy's cow so he got the $6.00 when we sold her calf and I received the $6.00 for Violet's calf. I also decided to sell Jefferson Davis to P. Hackereman as he was very anxious to buy him and made me an offer of $115.00, which I couldn't refuse. Jeff had turned out to be a fine horse but we really didn't need four horses so I reluctantly let him go. I received the check from the dairy for the milk delivery for the 15 days of April and they docked me for 20 quarts, which they said, had been spilled at the Palmyra New York Central Station on the ninth. This came to $1.44 so I sent a bill with a note to the New York Central Railroad and asked them to reimburse me for the spilled milk.

The month ended with my turning the cows out to pasture, which will save my having to buy so much hay for them. I just paid Mrs. Corletts $71.82 for the latest hay I had to buy to keep them fed for the past few weeks. Maybe someone will invent a cow, which doesn't need feeding but still produces milk, and then all of us dairy farmers would then be rich and drive fine cars. I indulged in a little day dreaming there.

Mazie has been sick in bed for a few days here in early May and Dr. Chase and the McCleary's have spent some time with her. She is a strong women but even the strongest amongst us sometimes gets set back with a bug of one sort or another. Dr. Chase said it isn't serious and she would be up and around shortly. It didn't take long as she insisted we all go to church to hear a sermon on the evils of alcohol and she also insisted that I pledge $4.00 to the anti-saloon league for the year. I was told that a $2.00 contribution to the Salvation Army was in order and I wasn't ready to argue with her on either account.

We are lately receiving almost $250 each month from our milk deliveries and it has come in handy. I also received a check for $1.44 from the New York Central for the milk spilled back in April with a note of apology. The money will come in handy, as I have hired D. S. DeGlelike and Company to install lightning rods on our barn and silo. The project will cost a total of $72.10 but I believe it is well worth it and all the neighbors are either having them installed or are planning on them. It took the rods and 206 feet of wire to finish the job and we now feel more comfortable during lighting storms that the barn and silo will be spared if they experience any direct hits from lighting. I finished out the month white washing the cow stable to keep everything clean so it will pass the yearly inspection, and also planted a variety of vegetables and flowers in Mazie's garden including popcorn which the entire family enjoys especially on those cold winter evenings.

It is 94 degrees in the shade here in June of 1919; it is hard on all of us and also hard on the horses, as they and I have been trying to get some more corn planted. I have taken it easy in working them in all this heat but the work has to get done somehow. I have yet to wake up in all my years and find my daily work completed mysteriously without my sweat and that of the horses.

Dorothy and Margaret have arrived home form Carlinville and Mazie took the trolley up to Rochester to meet them. It is great to have them home and have all the family together so that we can lean on each other. All hands went to church and we heard the Reverend Thompson preach. There were quite a few folks from the Lyons Presbyterian Church in attendance as he is a candidate for their church and they set it up that he would preach here for those from Lyons to hear. He was a fine speaker and gave an inspiring sermon. Speaking of Lyons, it was only a short time later that I was summoned to Lyons to answer the call for jury duty. I was excused since I was a farmer and only had recently hired a man to assist me; they take pity on farmers, as the work does not get done around the farm if you are hearing a trial. I certainly didn't want to shirk my duty but it is for the best, I believe, under the circumstances. I have hired George DeLue to work for me and I am to pay him $2.00 a day or $40.00 a month, if in fact he shows up everyday for the month. It is so difficult to get dependable help that I agreed to his wanting the $40 for a month in the hopes that he will be here every day. By the way I was paid $5.12 for showing up for the call to jury duty and also paid 98 cents to reimburse the trolley fare. It sure seems like easy money; maybe I could become a professional juror if there was such a thing.

Summer is always the time for visits from family and our children going to stay with family for some time off. Hans and his family came over from Canandaigua and Virginia and Kate are going to stay for a week for a little vacation. Mazie's brother Dr. H. McGregor and Helen TeWinkel also came for a visit and we all enjoyed a picnic supper with the McCleary's. Howard and Helen will be staying for a few days and we look forward to our precious time with them.

We are really getting a full house here in the first part of July. Margaret, Mrs. McGregor, George and Eleanor have come also for a visit. We will be cramped but that is part of the fun of having the extended family with you. We all attended church on the seventh, filling up it seems about half the church and we heard a fine sermon by the good reverend. Harry has also come out from Bellaire and so we have even more company. It is a challenge for Mazie to do the cooking for everyone but as usual she came through with flying colors. All hands also went to a Sunday School picnic in the park in the evening.

I suggested that we all spend a day fishing at the canal locks for something different to do and all but Mazie and her mother decided it was just the thing for a warm summer day. We also caught our supper, which Mazie and her mother prepared for everyone. After a couple of weeks Harry, Margaret, George, Eleanor and Mrs. McGregor left for Bellaire. It was fun while they were all here but with Robert coming home for a couple of weeks from college we were just about out of room to put anyone else up. Mazie had mentioned a couple of times that one of us might have to sleep in the barn with the cows and from the tone of her voice I'm sure she didn't mean her. I was saved at the last minute although I guess I could have survived a few nights in the barn if I had to, as if I would have had any choice. It was not only great to have all the company but also beneficial to my workload as Mr. McCleary, Harry, George and I spent a few days drawing in hay and wheat. Harry and George also helped me pick out a couple of piglets I bought from Abe Vandervage. I paid $14 for the two and they were about 5 weeks old.

Time does fly by and time does also heal if ever so slowly. We all attended church here on Aug. 10th, 1919 and Mazie and I raised our subscription to 60 cents per week retroactive to the beginning of this month. We also spent an enjoyable afternoon in Pultneyville with Reverend and Mrs. McCleary. They are such wonderful friends as well as our spiritual leaders. We have not been long without company either as Mazie's brother Howard returned for a stay as well as Lois, Helen and Lucy and the children have all come to spend a couple of nights with us. Lucy and the children can only spend a couple of evenings, as they have to get back to Canastota where Will is of course the preacher.

Howdy wanted a pig so we bought him one also and he paid me $3.50 towards the $7.00 that I gave for the little fellow. He can raise him and fatten him up and then either sell him or we will butcher him for our table and pay Howdy for him. That should all work out fine if he doesn't become attached to his new little piglet. Farmers cannot afford to become attached to their livestock, as without the livestock to feed us, provide hides and income, the farmer and his family would not survive long. George DeLue and Howdy helped me pick up the piglet and get him comfortable in the pig stall. George is working out fair with him complaining one day of a carbuncle and missing about four days of work over that. He is a good worker when he is here but is not as dependable as I would like. His mother and father have asked me again to give him every chance so we shall see how he works out. George and I have been helping all the neighbors do their thrashing and they in turn will help us when the thrasher is available. George worked for a couple of days at this and then had a sore wrist so he took another couple of days off. We ended the month having the McCleary's, Mrs. and Miss Kyle, the Reeves, Crookston's, and Miss Eaton and Mrs. Eaton here for supper and all had a fine time.

September has started out on a high note with our all going to church and hearing the Reverend W. H. Landon preach and he talked on "The Roundabout Way". It was a fine sermon. In the afternoon I went with the rest of the session to School House Number 11 in Farmington and there with Reverend McCleary's guidance we welcomed nine young people into church membership. It is wonderful to see the young folks carry on the tradition of joining the church and carrying on the work that our ancestors and we have started. When one goes to church it is not surprising to see many a gray head throughout the pews so the young folks are always welcome.

Here on Sept. 12th, 1919 Dorothy and Margaret are leaving on the 2:02 PM Central Train to Carlinville, Illinois to attend Blackburn University. I borrowed $100 from the F. N. Bank here in Palmyra to help cover some of the costs and put up $150 of liberty bonds as collateral. The note is payable on demand and I hope they don't demand it too soon. It cost me $54.38 total for railroad fair for the two of them and I gave each of them $20.20 for their needs and also gave them many a hug and kiss as we are going to surely miss them especially at this time. They must however get on with their lives and schooling is so important it is time they moved on to it. I also sent Mr. M. Hudson Prest $144 to cover their college costs for the first semester.

Mazie, I, Helen and Howdy took some time off from our chores on Friday evening, the 26th and attended the Palmyra Fair of which I still hold one share of stock in. An evening was not quite enough for George DeLue however as he was gone the entire day to the fair. I think he would have spent the entire week there if he had the money. I am about at my wits ends with George as a hired hand and I asked his family if they would ask Reverend McCleary to speak to George and see if he could help him get his head on straight. I feel that farm work, as hard as it is, may not be George's calling. A few days after the fair he ran away from here and his mother brought him back. I certainly am not mistreating the young fellow and I don't even expect him to work as hard and as long hours as I do but alas on the 30th of the month he was not here, his father came for his trunk and said George had quit and they couldn't talk him out of it. I also gave him the $13.00 I owed George and wished him luck. I will need to try and find another hired hand and hope the next one works out a little better.

I started in Oct. teaching the Sunday School class that Mrs. Lines normally taught because she has given it up at least for the time being. On Sunday afternoon, Oct. 5th, Mr. Whitlock and I made a canvass of church members for the Western Presbyterian Church "Rally-Day" to encourage both financial help for the church and also to encourage being involved in the church's life. We talked to a number of people and came away with a good feeling for the future of the church here in Palmyra.

I took Maude and Logan to F.L. Guernsey for new shoes and Mazie took Howard and herself on the trolley to Newark to visit the friendly dentist, Dr. Davis. Mazie and Howdy both needed some tooth repair. I don't wish the dentist on anyone but I did say a little prayer that it wasn't me, as I would rather walk in bare feet through fire than have a dentist drill on my teeth. They both will get through it with flying colors as Mazie doesn't seem to mind it and Howard seems to take after her in that regard. Good luck to the both of them. I settled up with the blacksmith for 45 cents for two new rear shoes on Maude and two new front shoes on Logan. He would have normally charged $2.20 for the work and the shoes but I took him a bushel of potatoes and he only charged me the 45 cents. I wish I could do the same thing with Dr. Davis but I think he wants cold hard cash for his "painless?" dental work.

Mazie has also had a busy month attending dinner parties at Mrs. Reeves and also at Mrs. Riggs. These were "ladies only" dinner parties so I and the children had to fend for ourselves although Mazie did pre-prepare our supper so we wouldn't go hungry she said, as if she knew I wasn't able or willing to cook for myself and the children.

I am cutting fence posts from the swamp, picking up fallen apples and selling them. The money from the sale of the fallen apples comes in handy and is a little extra from the approximately $200 a month we are getting from our milk sales to the Rochester Dairy Company. I also sold a half-bushel of hickory nuts to Mrs. Sanders and made $2.40 from that sale. Maybe if I had another 100 years to live I could plant the farm with all hickory trees and be a hickory nut farmer, but alas, I think they grow too slowly for a farmer my age to make a living off that idea.

It is silo-filling time and the Duel brothers are working this area and are here in mid- October to fill ours. Many of the farmers get together to help each other as I have said before and this time is no different with Peter Brown, F. Martin, C. Hanagan and Mr. Duffy working in the silo. T. Hanagan and A. Martin are on the wagons and J. Martin, Elmer Brown and Jeffrey and myself bring up the remainder of the crew. With so much help it goes pretty fast and it is also fun to be with so many fine neighbors and friends who help each other out. It cost me $17 for the Duel brother's equipment and time but it was well worth it as we now have a full silo of cow feed for this coming winter.

We finished out the month having four new shoes put on Jerry for $2.40 and I also took Liberty Loans to E. Jeffery's bull. Saddle also blessed us here at the end of the month giving birth to a heifer that the girls promptly named Victory Loan. A suitable name for a decade that saw a deadly war start, be fought and be won by America and her allies, even at a terrible cost in human suffering. The last war I pray.

I hate to say it but I am beginning to feel a little down here as November rolls around. I think it has to do with the transition of going from outside work to inside work, that the weather is changing for the worse and I do not look forward to that in any way especially that I now am in my early 50's it seems to get harder every year. In the spring, summer and early fall I am always so busy I don't have the time to feel sorry for myself but this time of year, that old enemy depression seems to stick its ugly head out and get into my thinking. I imagine I will give up on my diary at least for a while until I can get my head back on straight again. I plan on spending some time with the good reverend but I hate to admit to him, Mazie or anyone else that I am in anyway weak and cannot handle that which life throws my way. God only knows the sadness that has come our way in now having lost three precious children, the first little Helen, Baby Harry and our beautiful daughter Marion.

I dug the diary out again here in mid-December as Christmas is right around the corner and it certainly isn't fair to the family if I am not 100% myself this holiday season. I managed to go to the Dairyman's League State meeting at the Post Office and I had a fine time, chatted with several of my friends and fellow farmers and shared our ups and downs. I felt better after that meeting and finding out that I was not alone in the trials and tribulations of family and farming and went home refreshed and took Mazie shopping so that we could buy some Christmas gifts for Lucy and Will and the children in Canastota and get them in the mail so they would arrive there by Christmas. I hope the Lord blesses my family and myself with high spirits and loving caring for each other this season and all seasons.

Chapter 14

1920

*The 19th amendment to the constitution gives
women the right to vote*

It has been great to have Robert and the twins here for a while in between their semesters at college. Here in early January of 1920 Robert took the New York Central train back to Amherst College to resume his studies and he bought a new suit so he would look the part of an up and coming lawyer that he intends to be. We all pray for his success in this endeavor, it certainly would be a lot easier life than being a farmer, especially this time of year. I paid the $35.00 for the suit since I owed him quite a few dollars for all his help here on the farm. He never wants to take anything for the work he does but since I have no hired hand at present his strong back and willingness came in very handy. While we were buying his suit I also bought myself a pair of drawers for $1.50 and some much needed suspenders for 40 cents. The twins have also gone back to Blackburn College and I paid the $104 tuition for them for the second semester. We will surly miss them all but wish them God speed. I decided to take a one-day vacation to keep my spirits up so Howard and I took the trolley into Rochester and spent some time there, shopping, eating and taking in a movie. Howard now going on 12 years old always enjoys our brief journeys into the big city.

Lots of church activities this month. We all went to the communion service on the 11th and Mazie also went to a missionary meeting at Mrs. J. DeVoist's home. I had to drive her there and go pick her afterwards with the surrey since we have so much snow this month. She also attended a ladies meeting at Mrs. VanHlstynes so she has been a very busy lady and I have been busy transporting her around. We also attended the funeral service for Miss Eleanor Kyle held at the church manse. A sad time for that family. Mazie also has spent a couple of afternoons with Mrs. McCleary and that was certainly time well spent. While she was doing all this visiting Mr. Brown and I spent several hours each day for about 4 days shoveling the road out front here and in front of the Jeffrey house. I wonder someday if they will have something besides strong backs to clean out the roads, it sure isn't a fun job but everyone pitches in the best that they can to try and keep the road relatively open. I should charge the town for my shoveling as they just sent me a bill for our taxes and it came to $56.46 for 1920 and I sent a check to Mr. VanHall. I am not sure what they use all that tax money for but that is the way of politicians and most likely will never change and probably get worse with time. I also paid Tuttle and Co. $234 for the new furnace and installation and I had to pay $10 for the 2nd quarter tuition for Howard and Helen. Lord knows I would have willingly paid $15 if it had included our lovely daughter Marion.

Lucy is here from Canastota for a short visit and while she was here she attended church with us. We all were able to go except Helen who has a cold so I stayed home with her and the others drove the surrey into church. Mazie came home and said she had seen Mr. Chapman's little boy in church and she wondered if it wouldn't be nice if we gave the children's hobbyhorse to him. Of course we had to get Howard's and Helen's permission but they agreed they had outgrown it and were happy that it was going to some other youngster that would enjoy it as they had. Mazie, the children and Lucy even took in a moving picture downtown and all saw the film "Little Women" which they enjoyed.

It seems the rest of the month besides taking Violet to Jeffery's bull and having Dr. A.Y. Earl examine our cattle and give them a passing grade was made up of taking some money in and almost as fast paying it out. I was paid $1010.16 from Aetna Life Insurance Company for a matured policy and this came in very handy. I had to pay 19 cents at the bank for them to cash the check. It doesn't quite seem fair that I should have to pay them to cash my checks since I deposit some of the money which they earn interest off of. I realize however that I have little choice than to be nickeled and dimed if I want the checks cashed. I gave Mazie $10.00, Howdy and Helen each $1.00 and also took the family to a Grange dinner at which time I paid the 1920 dues of $1.20. I also sent the twins $5.00 each and paid the telephone bill of $4.00 for Dec. and January.

It is census time again so we invited George Harrison to supper along with Reverend McCleary as George was doing the local census and we thought it would be nice to ask him to dine with us.

I ended the month taking Lucy to the New York Central Train station to catch the train home to Canastota and we will surely miss her. Mazie will miss her most, as she has been a great companion and supporter during the past few months.

What can I say about February 1920 except it is colder than a well diggers ass and we have plenty of snow on the ground and more to come. I have had to buy lots of coal for the stove and the furnace and I just got 400 lbs. of peanut coal and 480 lbs. of egg coal. The peanut coal cost me $2.00 and the egg coal cost me $2.52. With this weather I will have to replenish the supply shortly especially as the month has started off and remains below zero. We seem to go through the coal ever so rapidly in this extremely cold weather. I have even had to drive the children the mile plus to school and home due to the cold weather and the buildup of snow on the road. We have had so much snow that T. Hanagan and I spent the better part of a day shoveling snow out of the culvert on the West Shore Railroad so the trains could get through. Seems I spend a lot of my time in the winter either shoveling out the road or the railroad track. It is helping out my fellow man however so I guess it is worth it. It has been so stormy and cold that we have not been making church on a regular basic and Howard even decided one Sunday to walk in alone and he got about half way and was forced to turn around and come home. The weather is not fit outside for man or beast.

We have had some social outings however and they have helped keep "Old Man Depression" from my door. When the weather is so bad I spend most of my days working around the barn and house and frankly have too much time to think so I build my mind with all my problems. We did all attend a Grange dinner and then a few days later Mazie, Howard and Helen walked in for the Valentine Social at the Grange and enjoyed it very much. I was not feeling very well, mind and body, so I decided to stay at home and rest up.

Mazie attended the Ladies Aid meeting at Mrs. Stoddard's house near the end of the month and the weather had improved enough so I could drive her in with the surrey and go and pick her up. I also stopped and delivered a bushel of potatoes to the McCleary home and also took them a bottle of Virginia Dare wine. Now you may be wondering as you read Chapter 13 that this country had passed a law, prohibition, so that no one could buy or sell or legally consume alcohol. Let us just keep this between us and say that the bottle is for communion purposes, which for all I know, the McCleary's may use it. Fortunately I have a few more bottles hidden away so I can lift my spirits through Virginia Dare on occasion.

I ended the month buying a subscription to the Wayne County Journal for a year and it cost me the exorbitant price of $1.75, but at least it keeps us up on the happenings in the county. The last purchase of the month was a new sled for Helen, which I bought from Lawrence Brothers and it was well worth the $1.00 it cost me to see the smile on her face when she saw it with a big red ribbon on it. Now she has her own so when she and Howard go sledding down the hill to the North of the house they don't have to share sleds anymore.

March has started out just like February except instead of being cold and snowy it is snowy and cold. I would even be happy to begin to draw manure to the fields if this terrible weather would moderate a little. Working just in the barn can sure get boring day in and day out. Mazie seems to roll with the punches much easier than I and she has spent some time in the village going calling with Mrs. Still. She also told me that I was going to the schoolhouse to attend a prize-speaking contest put on by the upper grades. We all attended and Howard and Helen seemed to enjoy it very much and both said they hope to enter the competition when they are old enough. We are sure they will both do very well.

Mazie took a trip into Rochester to hear a lecture by Sir Oliver Lodge, the famous scientist and believer in the after-life.

Sir Oliver has announced that he will prove there is an after-life by reappearing after he passes on. He need not try and convince Mazie and I of a more beautiful place to go after we break the bonds of this earth because we know that Little Helen and Harry and of course Marion are all with God in that beautiful place. She decided to go anyway as he is world-renowned and she wanted to see him and hear him in person. I did not attend but went over to see Dr. Chase and got some cough medicine from him, as I seemed to have a persistent cough that won't go away. Maybe with Mazie gone for the day I may try and spend a few moments with Virginia Dare and see if that helps get rid of my cough. Believe me I am not one to indulge much, but on brief occasions the spirit moves me.

I butchered two hogs with T. Hanagan's help and they weighed in at 183 and 168 pounds. I sold most of it to Mr. M. Darling and received 18 cents a pound or a total of $63.18 for them. I also took Saddle to E.D. Jeffrey's bull and it cost me $1.00 to have her serviced. She will be due Dec. 26th of this year and I have marked that on my calendar. I used a little of the hog money to get a much needed haircut which cost me 35 cents. I can't believe the price of some of the things we must get today and then I stopped at the bank and deposited $15 in the account of Robert so he could draw on it as needed at the college.

We ended the month as social butterflies going to a father-son banquet at the church and Howard went to a young men's supper at the church and took along my contribution to the supper in the form of two gallons of milk. We also had the McCleary's to dinner and I drove Mazie in to the ladies meeting at the manse. All of us went to the Grange Social in the evening and it cost me $1.00 for us to attend but it was well worth the money as we all enjoyed ourselves. The weather is also starting to break some and I can now spend some more time outdoors especially spreading manure. I never thought I would look forward to that job but anything to get me out in the fields and away from being cooped up is a pleasure. I feel like a bird that has been released from a cage this time of year.

It feels great here in April to be able to start the trimming of the orchard, put the cows out to pasture and start the plowing to get everything ready for this season's planting. I even ordered three-quarters of a bushel of medium Clover seed, one bushel of Timothy, one quarter of a bushel of Alsike and one quarter of a bushel of Alfalfa for the planting and had to pay the New York Central Railroad 52 cents for the freight charges. I ordered it from E.F. Deubble from Honeoye Falls and I am so happy to get it I would have paid almost anything for it knowing that I can get out in the fields and work with the sun warming my back and neck. What a great feeling that will be. On top of all this, several of the cows had calves this month with Nancy having a heifer, Howdy had a bull calf, and Dandy Jim and Betty also both had a bull calf. We sold them all to B. Chapman for $6.50 each and he gave me his check for $26.00. With some of the money I bought Howard a new pair of shoes and they cost $4.00. We got them from J. Congdon and they are fine shoes. I also paid the "painless" dentist, as Mazie has had to go twice this month. I even bought a new pair of gold-filled bowed spectacles from Ziegler and they cost me the exorbitant price of $7.50 but I guess that is cheap to help a fellow see better. Mazie always said take good care of your eyes and your teeth and we seem to be doing that lately. I sent Robert $15.00 and the twins $10.00 each and then Mazie insisted that I buy some wallpaper for the dining room, the kitchen and the upstairs unused room. It cost me about $9.00 for it all and of course the time to put it up. Mazie will help me however so it will go along much faster as she is a great taskmaster. I was even paid $3.12 by Mr. Young for shoveling snow out of the road. I had done it along with many of our neighbors just to keep the road open and didn't realize we would be paid, but the extra few dollars comes in handy.

Even with so much going on we have not neglected our church responsibilities, as they are the cornerstones of our lives. We had the good reverend out for supper on two occasions this month and we also have all attended both the morning and evening services each Sunday. I have gone to the prayer meetings and session meetings as they have been scheduled and we all attended the annual meeting of the church on April 8th at which time Mr. McCleary's salary for the year was set. He is to be paid $200 for the year and he is well worth every penny of it. We would be devastated to see him leave and I hope he is here as long as we are. We also had a joint meeting of the session and the trusties and the McCleary family served us all a fine meal at that meeting. Mr.

Whitlock and I also prepared the list for the various session members to call upon for the every member canvas and we spent an entire Sunday afternoon in that endeavor covering our list. We were warmly welcomed into each and every home by fellow church members and I believe I can speak for Mr. Whitlock as well as myself in saying the canvas was a success. The month was finished out with Mazie and the children going to the church for a social for Miss Jackson's Sunday School classroom.

H. Feldman stopped around on his swing through the neighborhood to see if we had any junk we wanted to sell him and I found two old stoves and 24 lbs. of old rags which we could part with. He paid me $1.75 each for the stoves and 48 cents for the rags. We were happy to get rid of them and hopefully he can make a few cents on them also. On top of that money the Rochester Dairy paid me $116.12 for the milk delivery for the last one half month and it is considerably more than the cows produced in the winter. I guess even the cows can have the winter blues. I put $15.00 of it in First National Bank in Robert's account so he can draw upon it as needed while he is at college. I also used some of the money to buy all the seeds for Mazie's garden, which as you may well remember she takes credit for and I do all the planting. That is the way of things and I'm sure not going to complain to her or I will be planting a garden twice the size. I planted about every imaginable thing including potatoes, 200 strawberry plants and even some popcorn. Even though I complain a little bit I still enjoy the wonderful meals she makes with all the harvest. I don't have a hired hand at present so I hired Mr. Martin to help me plant all the corn lot and paid him 30 cents per hour or a total of $1.35 for his time. It is a much easier job when two people do it. We also sold one of our cows, Baker, to Mr. Brownell for $65.00 and it makes one feel like we might finally be getting our heads above water with all this money flowing in. Lest I should become over confident Mazie will certainly bring me back to earth quickly.

We ended this month with Hans and family coming over to spend some time with us and we all went to church and heard the Reverend Mr. Nichols from the Auburn Seminary preach while Mr. McCleary was attending the General Assembly in Philadelphia. He gave a fine sermon and we were so inspired we decided to take the afternoon off and go fishing. We all went out to Red Creek and fished for awhile but didn't have any luck, even Howdy couldn't catch one so we went down to the canal and I had the biggest catch, an eleven pound carp.

It is a great time of the year for a number of reasons. One of the most important is that the family is all together for the first time in awhile. The twins came home from college here on the 4th of June and Mazie went to Rochester to meet them. As it turned out, the train was very late getting in so Mazie came on home and the girls took the trolley later, finally arrived, and were most warmly greeted. Robert also came home from Amherst and plans on working on the farm this summer by helping me out. With the twins helping Mazie and Robert helping me, things should be somewhat easier around the old farm. Also Howard and Helen are looking forward to the summer off and that will be starting vacation soon. I did get the bill for their tuition for the next two terms and had to shell out $20.00 to cover it. It of course, as I have often said, is well worth the money even though I had to go to the First National Bank and borrow $25 for 30 days to cover it since we are a little short of cash at present. I'm not so sure that is anything out of the ordinary for us but we always seem to manage and land on our feet even though the struggle sometimes seems overwhelming.

This is a busy time of the year for the farm work. As I Mentioned I sold Baker to Mr. Brownell for $65.00 since she was not producing the milk quantity that I require. Dandy Jim and Betty also paid a visit to Mr. Jeffrey's bull. Robert and I have finished planting the corn and unless we get heavy rain, hopefully we will not have to replant it, which often happens. I have been cutting the poles also for the Kentucky Wonder Beans for Mazie's garden and planting a few other items there for her. We are also drawing in hay this month and we have managed to draw in 23 loads in all, which finishes it up. The good Reverend McCleary also helped us draw it in for several days and we had the pleasure of his company at dinner for a couple of night.

Rochester Dairy paid us $116.24 for the milk for the first 15 days on this month and the payment was $2.24 short of what I had billed them. They claimed I was short some gallons but I do not make errors in my count and I have asked them to recheck to make sure they didn't credit it to someone else's account. I need

A JOURNEY THROUGH LIFE

the full payment as the cistern piping broke down and it also needs to be re-plastered so Robert cleaned it all out and I paid Mr. Jeffrey $2.00 to fix it and re-plaster it. I also attended the Dairyman's League meeting with Mazie and was moved to purchase 5 shares of stock in the company at $5.00 each. We are to pay $10.00 by Oct. 1st and the remaining $15 by Jan. 1st 1921. I hope it is a good investment and will make us some money in the future.

I finished out the month being a pallbearer for Mr. F H. Reeve's funeral. We also paid the bank back the $25 we had borrowed and since we paid it back within the 30 days they didn't charge us any interest. Mr. Brownell picked up Baker and paid us the $65.00 he owed. I gave the twins $25 and they and Mazie went to Rochester on a shopping trip. I will say the ladies sure like to shop even thought I could do without it. Mazie doesn't make me go often which is just as well. I also spent $3.00 for Mrs. Taber to make a new dress for Mazie and she looks pretty sharp in it. I married a pretty lady and I consider myself very lucky.

The last of the month and the first of July finished out with Hans, Jennie, the boys and Kate all coming over from Canandaigua for a little one day's vacation and we all went fishing at the locks on the canal. We caught 18 fish; mostly bullheads and we will have a fine bullhead meal tonight.

I just finished paying off the First National Bank the $25.00 we had borrowed and already we are cash short so I had to again hit up our friendly banker and borrowed another $80.00. I owed Robert $40 for his help so I paid him that as he was taking a trip to Minneapolis for a week and needed the funds. I also gave Mazie $5.00 and drove she and the children over to Canandaigua for the festivities that were being held on the lake. I came home to do some chores and then went back over in the evening to pick them up. They were all excited about the entertainment that was put on by Canandaigua and want to do it again sometime if we can spare the money.

We have had a busy July in Church with a Sunday School picnic on the 15th. and going to regular Sunday School on the 18th and the 25th. Reverend McCleary is on vacation so there is no regular church service so we are attending the Sunday School and also we went to the park one evening to hear a fine speech by Mr. Sheldon. We also attended a Grange picnic in Pultneyville and we had the pleasure of going to and from the picnic in the back of Cady Riles truck. He only charged me 75 cents for all of us to ride in the truck and it was a lot easier than hooking up one of the horses for the round trip. I envy those fortunate enough to be able to own these fancy cars and trucks and still hope we will find our way clear someday to join their ranks.

We finished out July with another great fishing trip. Liberty Loan had a bull calf that we sold for $6.50 and the Rochester Dairy paid me $103.14 for the last half of June, which included the extra $2.24 for one can of milk which contained 32 quarts. They had credited that can to another party and found the error after I asked them to check.

Mazie informed me that time was running out to paint the house before fall so I ordered ten gallons of paint and started scraping and painting. I'm sure with all the other work I have to do that this project will take me almost up to winter. If I want to be fed however I'd best get to it and Mazie will make sure I do a fine job. Robert is here to help with the chores so I should be able to spend some time on it. I had just about gotten started and Hans came over from Canandaigua and asked me if I wanted to go with him back to Prince William County and attend Mr. Skinner Day at Hickory Grove. Mr. Skinner, being one of the early settlers of that area and having attended in the past when I lived in Ben Lomand House with Mother and Dad I was anxious to go back and attend and visit family. Mazie said I could go as long as I gave her money to go to Canastota and visit with Will, Lucy and their family while Hans and I were off in Virginia. I agreed and left on the 12th via the train and we arrived in Haymarket on the 13th. I stayed with family at the "Shelter" the first night and went to Hickory Grove on Sat. the 14th to Mr. Skinner Day and had a wonderful time. I saw many of the Virginia family, many an old friend, had some wonderful conversations and caught up on old times with family and friends. A wonderful meal was served and I hope, God willing, I can make it again next year. It is so great to get away from the grind of the farm life if even for a few days. None of us being able to afford a fancy vacation, this must suffice but this get together with old friends and family beats a fancy vacation any day. Hans had to start back on Saturday evening but I decided to stay a few extra days. I stayed at the "Shelter" until

Monday afternoon and then went on to the "Highlands" to spend a few days there with our relatives. I finally managed to break away from the area of my childhood and so I headed out on the morning train on Wednesday the 18th for Washington, D.C. and I arrived back home in Palmyra Thursday afternoon. I had a wonderful time but it is always great to come home no matter how grand a time one is having. Home is where the heart truly lies. Mazie is expected home on the 26th so I better get back to scraping and painting the house as she will inspect it and either give me her approval or that look that I can easily interpret.

The children also wanted to take some vacation time so Hans drove over to get them and they are going to stay with the Canandaigua Tyler's for a week, which will be their outing. I am painting and Robert is drawing out manure so I'm having a hard time trying to decide which of these two tasks is the most fun and rewarding. I will most likely go to my grave still trying to figure that one out along with a lot more questions of a much more serious nature.

September is a happy and sad time. Robert is shortly going to head back to Amherst and I have decided to pay him $90 for all his hard work. It will help him get a good foothold in his advanced studies this year. I had to hit up our friendly banker First National for a loan of $100 to help me take care of paying Robert and of course giving the twins each some money for their trip. Dorothy is also leaving on the milk train for Brocton and Margaret is going to follow her shortly. Margaret wanted to stay at home for a little while longer as she wanted to be here when Mazie's brother Howard comes up for a visit from Columbia University. She will be leaving shortly also and we will be a much smaller family here on Maple Avenue in Palmyra.

We did all manage to spend some time in church before they left hearing the Revered Dr. Landon preach on "Why Has Thou Sent Me" and it was a fine sermon. We also spent an enjoyable evening in Pultneyville at a hot dog roast put on by the combined churches and we had a good time. Reverend McCleary, Mrs. McCleary and their children all spent an enjoyable evening with us before the family scattered and we had a great Mazie meal.

I have talked to a number of our neighbors and it is thrashing time and silo-filling time again so we are all going to get together to help each other out. It is hard to believe it is already September and we must again face the fact that old man winter is right around the corner with all his surprises to throw our way. It seems like just yesterday that I was able to get out in the fields, feeling the warm sunshine on my back and feel like I had been reborn again. Life is certainly fleeting and we should make the most of every day.

It is October of 1920; myself and about eleven of my friends and neighbors have started working to fill each other's silos for this coming winter. Some of us are working the wagons, some are inside the silo working and others are out in the fields. It is hard work but wonderful to see the comradeship of so many helping each other.

Chapter 15

1921

*First Radio program transmitted, station KDKA
in Pittsburgh, PA.*

Chapter 16

1922

Irving Berlin writes "APRIL SHOWERS"

*This is a difficult time for myself as author of this chronicle
of the lives of Benjamin and Mary Tyler. There is either a period
of time when Benjamin stopped keeping his diaries from October
of 1920 to Jan. of 1923 or possibly the diary was kept only to be
lost by the family over these past many years. I had thought I
might try and make up this period and "wing" it but that would not
have been accurate and for such a fine family I do not think it
would have done justice to them. During this missing period they
sold the farm and moved into the village of Palmyra and lived at
120 West Jackson Street. It is not known why they stopped farming
and sold the farm, it could have been that Ben was in his 50's and
found the farm life to physically demanding or it could have been
that Mazie decided it for them. Whatever the case it is written in*

the Thomas Cook book about the history of Palmyra that they moved in 1921 to the house on Jackson Street where I lived for a time with my grandfather and grandmother. As I stated in the introduction I was three years old when Benjamin passed away at the age of 68 and I unfortunately cannot remember him. Mazie lived many more years at the home on Jackson Street and I remember her well. We will pick up the story in Jan. of 1923 from the last of his diaries. It is interesting also to note that during this time The Reverend McCleary and his family left the ministry of the Palmyra Presbyterian Church and Reverend Tighe was called to the pulpit.

Chapter 17

1923

Enrique Tiriboschi is the first to swim the English Channel (16 hours and 33 minutes of swimming)

I bought this new journal from Smith and Ziegler that I am resuming my diary in and paid them 50 cents for it. I charged it. I am working in the office of the West Shore Railroad, which is part of the New York Central Railroad system, and this line is used mostly for moving freight. I am being paid $93.50 per month for my labors. Seems it is a lot easier than getting up at dawn and milking the cows and working at the farm work until dark or sometimes afterwards. I would not want to leave one with the impression that we didn't love the farm with all its great and sad memories it just was becoming hard for both Mazie and I so we got a good price for it and decided to move into the village and go to work from 8 to 5 each day. One of the advantages of course of being a farmer was that I was my own boss however it became increasingly difficult to find and keep good help since the work was so demanding and this way as Mazie says, I don't have to worry myself to death over all the problems. The memories of our farm life on Maple Avenue in Palmyra will always be with us and can never be erased.

Here on Jan. 19, 1923 Mazie and the children went to the movies and when they came home Mazie had a severe pain in her side. She was sick all night and in bed for several days. Dr. Chase came out and treated her and left some medicine, which we all hope will help. The Reverend Tighe also has paid a visit to Mazie and that helped lift her spirits. We truly miss our great friend and minister, Reverend McCleary, but if anyone could fill his shoes it has been Mr. Tighe. We are truly blessed to have him here in Palmyra.

With my steady income I am able to save a little bit of money at the State Bank of Palmyra and maybe with a little luck we might even be able in the future to buy one of those fancy automobiles since we no longer have the horses to transport us faithfully wherever we need to go. One advantage of living in the village is that you can walk to most everywhere you need to go even though we often walked the mile plus from the farm into the village. As Mazie often reminds me we aren't getting any younger. I also gave Mazie her $10.00 for the household expenses for the week.

The month ended up with a touching letter received from the McCleary's and we took the opportunity to call on the Reverend and Mrs. Tighe in the evening. Church is the most important part of our lives after family; nothing will ever take the first place of family as the Lord has blessed us.

Speaking of the church, here in February we have all gone to church each Sunday and then to a Union Service in one of the other four churches on the corner each Sunday evening. I have attended the Baracca Class faithfully and we also went to J. Lines in an evening for a Philanthropy supper. Along with all this we have attended prayer meetings at Henry Runterman's home on several occasions. Topping it all off, I taught Sunday School two Sundays when Frank Granger was not feeling able to teach them. I think Mazie, the family and I have fulfilled our religious obligations in thanking the Good Lord for all the blessings he has bestowed upon us.

We decided here in February of 1923 to subscribe to the Democrat and Chronicle newspaper as we now have as I have said a steady income and hopefully can afford it. It cost me 65 cents per month or as I paid it up front $1.30 for a two month subscription. We also paid the taxes on our house and lot at 120 West Jackson Street and it came to $27.69. The house and lot are assessed at $3300 and the rate is $8.31 per thousand dollars assessment. We also had to pay 1 percent to Mr. VanHall for

A JOURNEY THROUGH LIFE

collecting of it. As I have often said I can't figure out what our politicians find do to with all this money they are collecting. Maybe someday they will fix up the roads in the village that need it so badly.

Mazie has received a telegram from Margaret that their mother has pneumonia. She is very concerned for her mother and contacted Harry and he told her she should take the next train to Bellaire, as her mother was getting worse. We telephoned Lucy in Canastota and she and Mazie are taking the same train out to Ohio. I asked P.A. Green at the South Shore if I could have a pass for the New York Central train and he happily gave me one. It did however cost me 65 cents to telephone Lucy in Canastota. However, we did save the train fair. As they say pneumonia is often called the old person's friend as it takes those of us whose time has come and are ready for another life. In this case it is no different, as Mazie has sent me a telegram that her mother, Mrs. McGregor passed away from here on the 28th of February. She was 79 years old so she lived a long, happy and prosperous life and will be sorely missed by her beloved family.

Dorothy received a letter from Mazie saying that she would like to come home by way of Oberlin & Wooster if we could spare her. We sent a telegram as follows and it cost me 43 cents to do so. "Getting along all right. Go Oberlin Wooster sure. Take your time, Dorothy." I'm not at all sure why Mazie didn't ask if I was getting along OK but I'm sure she knows I can take care of myself or she realizes that Dorothy was taking good care of me as Mazie does when she is around. As it turned out I am feeling a little under the weather. I got some Camphor Pills from Dr. Chase and I also took a hot mustard foot bath to see if that would help get rid of the cold I seem to be coming down with. Most likely my feeling poorly is just my missing of Mazie not being around to comfort me in my illnesses. After all these years I need her more and more everyday.

ROBERT ALEXANDER MCGREGOR
BORN 1835
DIED MARCH 03,1906

ROBERT ALEXANDER MCGREGOR IS THE FATHER OF MARY BLANCHE (MCGREGOR) TYLER [MAZIE] AND WAS MARRIED TO LUCY (WATTERSON) MCGREGOR. THEY WERE MARRIED IN 1871 AND LIVED IN BELLAIRE, OHIO. HE WAS BORN IN ROCK HILL, OHIO AND DIED IN BELLAIRE, OHIO. HE IS BURIED IN THE GREENWOOD CEMETERY IN BELLAIRE.

BROTHERS: JAMES JR.: MARRIED LUCRETIA W. SHEETS

SISTERS: JANE (MCGREGOR): MARRIED JUDGE A.W. ANDERSON
ELIZABETH (MCGREGOR): MARRIED JOHN TARBET
LUCINDA: NO INFORMATION
MARGARET AMELIA (MCGREGOR): MARRIED JOHN
ALLEN OR ALLERS

LUCY (WATTERSON) MCGREGOR
C. 1910 EST.

As it turned out she wasn't gone that long and she and Lucy came in on the 1 AM train from Ohio and Lucy left the next morning on the trolley for Canastota. The Reverend Tighe and his family paid a visit to us to express their sympathy for the passing of Mazie's mother and we all shared in a prayer for her soul. Mazie's brother Howard has also come from New York City after going to Bellaire and is planning on staying through Easter with us. We all look forward to having him here. The expenses are building up a little but I did get a small raise from the railroad and I am now making $50.43 for a half-month's work. This comes in handy as I gave Helen and Howard each $1.00 to add to their bank accounts. I also treated the entire family to the movies and we saw a great movie. The title of it was "When Knighthood was in Flower."

Our church obligations have also flowered this month as Hans and Boydon came over from Canandaigua. We all went to church and in the evening the Tighe family called on us and we all had a wonderful Mazie meal with great conversation. Reverend Tighe asked me to lead us all in prayer before supper as I always do and we all joined hands. Later in the month we attended the evening union service at the Methodist Church, heard the Reverend Tillman preach and he gave a fine sermon. We finished out the month having a union service at our church. All four ministers preached and a variety of topics were preached upon. We all went home full of the spirit and moved by the wonderful talks of Reverend Tighe and the other ministers.

April of 1923 started the same as March ended with Dr. Chase and I leading the prayer meeting as the good reverend is out of town. If I do say so myself we both did exceptionally good jobs. Dr. Chase is not only a fine doctor but also a good Christian and a fine leader. We even spent an evening in the Reform Church for an ecumenical service and found the message inspiring. When Reverend Tighe did return later in the month he used the new Bible for the first time that has been given to the church by Agnes, Ruth and Charles Drake in memory of their dear departed mother. His sermon that day was " The grass withered, and the flower thereof falleth away, but the word of the Lord endureth for ever." The word was inspiring.

Mazie has informed me that even though I am no longer a farmer that does not mean that her garden is not to be planted. I have started working on "her" garden and am planting early cabbage seeds, onion seeds, peas, lettuce, radish and corn. She is giving me plenty of direction as to how it should be done and believe me I do not take issue with her over this project. After planting the entire garden she did allow me to join Arthur Barnhart and six of our other friends to go to entertainment at the Baptist Church in Newark. All eight of us rode down to Newark in Arthur's car and needless to say it was a bit crowded. I am still waiting for out first car but if driving around with 8 people in a four-seater car is the norm I think I will wait even longer.

Mazie and I ended the month going to Rochester on the trolley. It cost me $2.54 to listen to a lecture from that famous author Sir Arthur Conan Doyle on spiritualism. We went to the Convention Hall and it was packed to the rafters for his lecture, which we enjoyed immensely. Mr. and Mrs. Griffith were also there and they were kind enough to offer us a ride home in their fine motorcar, which we enjoyed.

I often pine for the farm and think about all out great and sad times we spent there over the years. I found myself out walking here at the end of the month and decided to walk out to the farm. As I approached I had many thoughts wash over me, thoughts of little Harry and beautiful Marion and thoughts of all the great times we had there with our friends, family and especially Reverend and Mrs. McCleary and their family. I realize one cannot turn the clock back so I turned around and just as quickly headed back into town and away from the mixed messages that flowed over me.

I started May out paying for the gas and electric bill and it came to $1.93 for gas and 40 cents for electric. Seems like a lot but then everything is going up. We also decided to increase our church pledges and increased the church support part of the pledge to 80 cents per week and left the benevolence to 65 cents per week as it has been for all of last year. After all these big decisions I decided I needed to rest my mind so the children and I went fishing down at the aqueduct and caught a fine skillet of fish.

It is as I mentioned pledging time for the Palmyra Western Presbyterian Church. Mr. Whitlock and I are spending several weekend days and evenings visiting all the parishioners and trying our best to answer their questions and drum up support for the growing church. We also went to a prayer meeting in which Miss Easton led us and I even attended a Baracca entertainment put on by H. Chapman and Wilbert Scheels at the Chapman home. It was a fine night and I thoroughly enjoyed it.

Mazie has asked that I talk to Mr. Green at the West Shore and see if I could set up my paid vacation time for this coming summer. We would like to have the six-paid vacation day's start on July 9th. He readily agreed and I also asked him if he would give me a couple of railroad passes to Bellaire, Ohio and to Manassas, Virginia so we could visit our families in both of their homes. Mr. Green, being the fine fellow he is, agreed to everything and will set aside the passes as the time draws near.

Reverend Tighe has indicated an interest in learning more about the Mormon religion so he and I went to A. Lawrence's home one evening and read Pomeroy Luckens book on the History of Mormonism. It was very interesting and possibly somewhat slanted as are all books. I also agreed to attend a Mormon service at Red Mans Hall and tell him my impression. It was that they are fine folks, true believers in a higher power and a great benefit to this community. We ended the month on Memorial Day visiting the cemetery to pay our respects. Mazie, Miss Eaton and I spent considerable time visiting the gravesites and as it was when I walked out to the old farm many emotions overtook me. I prayed to thank the good Lord for the time we had to share on this earth with those that had gone before.

I hired Robert and young Tuttle to scrape and paint the entire house, I believe it will be a big job and take them most of this month of June 1923. It needs it and I am sure they will do a great job, particularly as Robert is in charge and as I am, he is a tough taskmaster. Robert told me, this tough task manager, that since he would be working every day on scraping and painting that he thought it only best that he take Howard over to Sodus Point to do a little fishing to relax and prepare himself for the work ahead. Now who could argue with that reasoning? They came home with a fair catch and Mazie cooked a fine fish dinner for us all.

Church has been a little hit and miss this June with Hans and family coming over from Canandaigua to visit on two Sundays

A JOURNEY THROUGH LIFE

and Mazie's brother Howard coming from New York City to spend some time with us. Also Margaret has returned from Wooster, Ohio and George has come from Bellaire to spend some time with us. It is a crowded household but so wonderful to be with the immediate and extended family. We did manage to take supper with the good Reverend Tighe and Leslie one evening and had a fine time. We also attended the service where Mr. Tighe preached a fine sermon to the Palmyra Classical Union School graduating class of 1923. I think it will be a good reminder to them all as they go through their "Journey through Life." We also attended a meeting at the Methodist Church on temperance enforcement where Mazie told me in no uncertain terms that I was to pledge at least $8.00 for the cause. Believe me I did not argue with her. This would not qualify as doing one's duty on behalf of the church but Mazie and Dorothy also went to see the movie, "The Little Church Around The Corner", and they said they thoroughly enjoyed it. It has been around for a few years but they had not yet seen it.

I paid the electric bill for May of $1.00 and also paid the gas bill of $1.50. It seems high for these modern conveniences but necessary and Mazie certainly enjoys them and it makes her life easier. I also paid the water rent of $4.97 for the quarter ending this month. We decided to buy a three-burner gas stove and I also got four feet of gas line from Bird and Flynn to connect it up. This way it will be easier for Mazie to cook her wonderful meals.

I am putting up a fence between the neighbors, Hucksley's and ourselves, as I am a firm believer in the fact that fences make good neighbors. It will also keep the neighbors dog out of Mazie's garden where I have already had to replant some early vegetables. I am not sure that neighborhood dogs were the cause but why take any chances.

At the end of the month Robert and Tuttle finished the house painting, we all went to a children's' day service at the church. As it was a beautiful Sunday afternoon I decided, without telling anyone, to walk down again to the cemetery to pay Marion and little Harry another visit. Of course my thought also returned to the first little Helen who is laid to rest in Bellaire.

Author's note: Since the same journal was being used by Benjamin for the period beginning in January 1923 until now and again being picked up by him in October of 1923 it is assumed since the months of July, August and September are not recorded that he chose to stop keeping his journal. Whatever the cause, if it was depression or just making a conscious decision to stop keeping it, we will again pick their story up in October of this year. The fact that he spent a number of days visiting the gravesites of Marion and little Harry leads me to conclude he may have been weighed down with some depression again and that may be the reason for the gap.

It is now October of 1923 and things are normal again or as normal as they ever get in my life. I'm sure most other folks feel the same way but sometimes things just become overwhelming and it is hard to reach down and pull oneself up by one's shoelaces so to speak. I am managing to get things back together however and if I could just get the dates to all fall in place when money was coming in and then had to go out it would help. I had to borrow $75.00 from the State Bank of Palmyra for 30 days so that I could pay Mrs. Alice L Ballow the $75.00 interest that we owed her on the $1500 mortgage on our home. I am expecting from John DeSeyn the $93.00 interest he is due to pay on the mortgage we hold on the farm of $3100 but it won't be paid in time for my obligations. I also had to borrow $50 from the First National Bank of Palmyra to help pay our school taxes. As you will note I like to spread my borrowing around to give all the banks an opportunity. In reality most likely the State Bank might not have seen fit to loan me another $50 on top of the other loan. However they all know that Benjamin and Mary Tyler always pay their obligations and always will as difficult as it might be. When John DeSeyn did come through here in Dec. of 1923 he also paid $100 on the principal amount leaving $3000 as his obligation under the 6% mortgage.

I did find a little time between my hours at the West Shore Railroad and the other tasks to go to Lyons and be accepted in the Railroad Clerks Union and be elected Chaplin to this fine organization. I was proud to be elected Chaplin as it shows my roots in the church and my belief in our good Lord. Mr. Green also told me I could take every other Saturday afternoon off from

A JOURNEY THROUGH LIFE

my labors at the railroad since I have been such a dependable employee.

Our church activities in these winter months have been limited. As the weather permits, we make every effort to get out. We paid $1.00 to the Civic League early in the month when we went to church and heard the Rev. Greene speak. I also paid my church pledge of $1.35 and my Sunday School pledge of 30 cents. We also attended a prayer meeting where the poem, "Pippa Passes" written by Robert Browning was the subject of Reverend Tighe's talk. You may recall the famous line from this poem: "God's in His heaven- All's right with the world." We enjoyed the talk and the conversation with our neighbors and friends. I ended our religious duties by attending a session meeting at Henry Runterman's store.

As 1923 rolls to a close, I gave Mazie some money to buy the family some Christmas gifts and also paid the State Bank of Palmyra $25 on the $75 note. It was due a couple of days ago but they give their customers a three day grace period which I took advantage of. I also paid the First National Bank the $50 that we owed them and the 25 cents interest that was due on the loan. Christmas day was a bright beautiful cool day. We exchanged gifts and had a wonderful Mazie chicken dinner and blessed the Lord for all that he has granted us.

Chapter 18

1924

The first Winter Olympics is held in Chamonix, France

Howard will reach 16 this year and has been asking for some new gumshoes and a new suit. We decided he certainly deserved them and we bought him the shoes at Foster Shoe Company for $1.40 and the suit at LeBreeht's for $13.50. I don't remember ever having paid that much for a suit but times are changing. We also bought him a new pair of pantaloons for $2.00 so he will be fully decked out in his Sunday finest. He wore them for the first time when he and I went to a men's supper at the Tighe's and he certainly looked great. What a handsome young man he is. Since we spent all this money on Howdy I could only afford to have my shoes re-soled and re-heeled at R. J. Tilling's and that cost me the tidy sum of $2.00. Howard and Helen even talked me out of a $1.10 each so they could go to a supper at school and watch the basketball game. The supper cost 60 cents and the ball game cost 50 cents. It was well worth it as they thoroughly enjoyed them both.

Here in February, the family is on the move. Dorothy is leaving on the 12:09 AM train out of Rochester for Urbana, Illinois and Mazie, Margaret and Mrs. Tighe all went to Rochester with her to see her off. I think the ladies wanted to see Dorothy off but they also wanted a day of shopping and site seeing in Rochester. Robert also came home from Leonardsville here in New York and I took the opportunity this time to go to Rochester myself and spend some time there before meeting his train.

Expenses never seem to stop and this month is no exception with taxes coming due. I paid J. VanHall, who of course is the tax collector, $33.17 on our property on Jackson Street, which is assessed at $3500. I keep hoping each year that the taxes will go down but that never seems to be the case as the life blood of politicians is money, money, money. I also paid Session Coal Company for another ton of stove coal and I was disappointed that this coal was about the worst they had ever sent us, as it was full of slate. Usually their coal is of the highest quality. We decided to renew our subscription to the "Wayne County Journal" and paid the $1.00 necessary for the year. We were also charged 50 cents for our month's use of gas and $1.00 for the electric needs for January.

Mazie said she needs some time off so she left for Canastota on the 5:17 PM New York Central Train to visit Lucy and family. It was only about a day after she left that I started to feel like I was coming down with something. Margaret is taking care of me and went to Briggs Drug Store and bought me some White Pine cough syrup. It is helping some but this is the heaviest cold I have had in quite some time and it is really getting me down. I need Mazie's loving tender care when I feel like this. Margaret also sent for Dr. McPherson and he prescribed some tablets and a different kind of cough medicine. I think it is one of those early spring colds that just has to run its course. I did call Mazie in Canastota and she told me if I got out and started to plant her garden I would most likely feel better. I'm not sure if that qualifies as tender loving care but I did it anyway and put in some Alaska Peas and a few other vegetables of her choice. Amazingly it did seem to help me shake the cold and depressed feeling so I guess she knows what she is doing.

April of 1924 is a milestone in the life of the Tyler's of Palmyra. We have purchased, between Robert and I, a 1924 Model T Touring car and we paid $959.48 for it. We are going to pay it off a little at a time. It sure is a beauty with its shinning black paint and fabulous seats. I did get a chance to drive it for a few days before Robert, George and Gordon left for Canastota and also a stop in Leonardsville to show off our new automobile. I don't think I ever believed we would be fortunate enough to be able to afford a fine car like this one but with a friendly banker and a fine son who is contributing to it we did manage to make a deal. Mazie asked me if I would drive her to Urbana, Illinois to visit Dorothy at college but I told her I thought it would be easier, not knowing what the weather might bring to take the train so she reluctantly decided that was for the best. While she was gone and Robert was gone with the car I did manage to attend a Railroad Lodge meeting, by trolley unfortunately, in Lyons where I officiated as Chaplin and also paid my dues of $3.00. Mazie sent a card from Indianapolis and it was mailed in Champagne. I sent her one back to ask her to tell Eckland about an opening in Palmyra for a science and chemistry teacher as he is a friend of Dorothy's at college and wishes to find a teaching job possibly in this area. He seems like a fine chap and I believe he may be a little sweet on Dorothy.

I have missed Mazie terribly and she finally got home on the 7th of May from Urbana. It sort of depressed me so I am going to stop keeping my journal for a while.

Here it is already September of 1924 and if someone were to ask me where the summer went I don't think I would be able to tell him or her. I am back, as fit as a fiddle and started this month with Hans, Jenny, Boydon, Kate and John all coming over from Canandaigua. We all went to church and Sunday School and heard the Rev. J.J. Edwards preach as Reverend Tighe is away at Endicott. It was a fine service and lifted my spirits. I even pledged $1.00 per month for Near East Relief for a year. Mr. DeSeyn paid us the $90.00 he owed us on the mortgage less $1.00 for a load of manure we had bought from him for Mazie's garden. This pays the interest from Dec. 1st, 1923 to June 1st, 1924. With some of this money I hired J. W. Thomas and Co. to put in a new hot water boiler in the kitchen. With all these new fangled gadgets, our water and gas and elect. bill just keeps going up. I paid $4.14 for our elect. usage in Aug. and $1.80 for gas and also $5.18 for water rental of 1477 cu. Ft. I never could figure out why they call it water rental as we don't use it and return it but they tell me that is the correct term and who am I to argue with them. If I ran the world I think I would tell them to call it water usage, which seems more appropriate.

This is a big month for me as I have decided to leave the employment of the West Shore Railroad and go to work for

A JOURNEY THROUGH LIFE

Sessions Coal Company. They offered me $30.00 per week for a six-day week. Mr. Green could not match that so I reluctantly left and I think I will find the new job interesting and we can particularly use the extra money. I used some of my advance to buy Helen a few used books as she loves to read and I also loaned Robert $20 for his auto trip to Lansingburgh. One of the books that Helen bought was "Prose and Poetry" which she loves. I even treated Mazie, Dorothy and Mrs. Tighe to a trip to Rochester via the trolley to see the show "Thief Of Baghdad" at the Eastman. They were very excited about it and talked about it for a couple of days afterwards. Douglas Fairbanks played in the movie and they thought he was quite the handsome swashbuckler.

While all this excitement was going on, we did have some bad happenings when Howard broke his left leg just above the ankle playing football. Dr. Nesbitt put it in a cast and Eckland and I carried him upstairs to the spare room on a closet door and then I went down to Briggs Drug Store and bought him a bedpan, as I believe it will be sometime before he is up and moving around. Mazie and his siblings are taking great care of him and with so much attention we did feel free later in the month to spend a little time at the Palmyra Fair. I gave Mazie a dollar to spend and I also bought a few cigars for myself for 15 cents. Cigars I may add, that Mazie usually tells me are to be smoked outdoors and I don't argue with her about that even thought I thoroughly enjoy a fine cigar on occasion. As I am sure you can tell by my rambling on that I am feeling much better lately both in body and mind.

Since Eckland is teaching in Palmyra presently, and he is also the football coach, I have been going to some of the football games. Palmyra beat Newark on the 3rd of Oct. and then we lost to the freshman team from the University of Rochester 19-0 a week later. I even contributed $1.00 to the High School Athletic Association to help them out as I am enjoying the games so much. Howard misses the games but his leg is still healing from the break so he can only get the information second hand for yet a short time.

Here on Oct. 9th, it is the twin's birthday and I gave them each $1.05 to go to the movie and for ice cream with Mazie. I also set out a row of rose bushes for Mazie along the fence line. She calls them "**her**" rose garden, which is similar to "**her**" vegetable garden.

Mr. and Mrs. Tighe and the Whitlock's spent an enjoyable evening with us and we also went to the Whitlock's at the end of the month for a Halloween party in which everyone dressed up and we had a fine time. Rev. Tighe is also beginning his series of lectures on preparation to teach about the Bible this month which Mr. Whitlock and I attended to prepare us for our Sunday School classes.

I ended the month visiting my friendly banker and borrowing $75.00 from the First National Bank of Palmyra with an "on demand note" at 6 percent. I used the money to send a check to Alice Ballow in Rochester to cover the interest at 5 percent on our mortgage on the $1500 loan. This covers the period from Nov. 1st, 1923 to Nov. 1^{st,} 1924. I will have to be thrifty to save this much to pay the bank back before they demand the money. I am sure they trust us as we have always paid them back the many loans we have taken from them.

We all went to church here early in November to celebrate the first day that Howdy was able to get out and hobble around from his recent broken leg. We even had the pleasure of all going to the Tighe's in the evening for a banquet put on by the Tighe's, Grangers and the Stoddard's. Everyone had a fine time.

Here as 1924 comes to an end I again think of all the good times and the sad times Mazie and I have been through these many years. I paid Mr. Clarke $1.50 for 1924 for the care of the cemetery plot where some of our memories are laid to rest. I also paid the school taxes of $49.03. I would have gladly paid more if those that have gone before us were here to attend. The Lord grants each of us a brief time on this earth and hopefully if we live our lives as He desires we will then move on to a more beautiful place. What we do with the brief time we have here is up to each of us. I have been truly blessed to share it with Mazie and our wonderful family and I thank the Good Lord for that privilege.

Who of you by worrying can add a single hour to his life?

THE END

Epilogue

I wish to take this opportunity to thank my wife, Lois for her kind correction of my spelling and punctuation in this book over the past several years. I also wish to thank my sister Dorothy Ann for her constant guidance and sharing of her knowledge of the family history during this time. My heartfelt thanks also to Howard Tyler's daughter, my cousin, Barbara Tyler Ahlfield for her assistance and the design and drawing of the cover for the book. She is an extremely talented artist and in producing the cover has shared some of that talent with the family. My son-in-law, Ken Romano also was of great assistance in formatting the pictures and text on a computer discs for submission to the publishing company and I am in his debt. I am saddened that my younger sister Linda is not here to enjoy the entire book as it is finished. I did share with her some of the early pages and we often discussed the book, but in the time between my starting and finishing she has passed from this life.

I have taken liberties, as most authors of course must do, with the writing of this book. However the facts as they unfold down through the years are as my grandfather wrote them in his diary. It is sincerely hoped that members of the family will enjoy knowing a little more about their ancestors and in some way this work will enrich their lives.

Benjamin Chinn Tyler lived the rest of his days on Jackson Street in Palmyra with Mazie and many of the extended family including, as I have mentioned, myself the author of this book of their lives. His autopsy report partially reads as follows. "This

A JOURNEY THROUGH LIFE

patient had been in good general health until Jan. 6th, 1936. In the evening of that day he slipped on ice while carrying an empty coal bucket. The bucket struck him over the right malar region and caused a rather superficial abrasion about 3 centimeters long." Over the next few days his temperature soared, his face became reddened and swollen and he became irrational and dysphonic and somewhat cyanotic. He passed away from this at 3:05 P.M. on Jan. 1st, 1936.

Author's note: As someone who has been told by doctors today that I have an inherited immune deficiency which came down through the family I often wonder if this was also Benjamin's problem but of course then little was known of this type of ailment. Today I receive monthly infusions of gamma globulin to support my immune system. Before the days of anti-biotics, if he in fact had this condition his chances of fighting off an infection however slight would have been difficult.

Mary Blanche McGregor, affectionately known as Mazie lived for many more years on Jackson Street in Palmyra along with myself, my sisters and Uncle Howard. In those days, shortly after the great depression when good jobs were hard to find it was not uncommon for extended families to live together. She passed away in 1956. She was a devout Christian woman with a strong personality and a major influence in our lives.

Author's note: I remember many an evening meal around the formal dining room table when the supper started with a prayer and Spanish Rice was served since it was a very reasonable meal to prepare at that time. My current passion for Spanish rice is extremely low on my priority list of meals from this experience, however we never went hungry for a caring or a devoted family.

Robert Benjamin Tyler married Evelyn O'Briant who was from Jackson, Mississippi. He was a lawyer in a New York City law firm for many years and had three children. Robert later in life developed Parkinson's disease and finally succumbed to it in March 1963.

Margaret Tyler married James D. Anderson, Jr. and they lived in Avon, New York and they ran a successful farm there for many years. They also had three children. She passed away on February 2$^{nd.}$ 1970.

Dorothy, Margaret's twin sister married Carl Eckland who is referred to in the book. He was from Colorado. They had two children, the younger of the two tragically died in a car accident rather early in his married life. They lived for many years in Floral Park, Long Island, New York where Carl taught school. She passed away in 1980 having moved with her husband to Geneseo, New York several years earlier.

Howard Alexander Tyler married Mary Estelle Storms and they had one daughter, Barbara, who as I mentioned, is responsible for our wonderful cover. For many years he worked for General Railway Signal Company in Rochester, New York. He was a graduate of Oberlin College. He passed away in June of 1992 and is buried at Riverside cemetery in Rochester with his beloved wife.

Helen Watterson Tyler, my mother, married John Merrill Parsons and had three children. She worked for many years as a secretary to several lawyers in Palmyra and passed away in 1978, a few months after my father passed away.

Last but certainly not least, I mention the first little Helen who died early in this history of their lives, my mothers brother Harry who passed away at a very young age and of course Marion who succumbed to the flu pandemic in 1919.

It is a family that I can say
I am proud of being a member of.

Mary (Mazie) Tyler
C. 1884

Top left & right: Lucy, Mary & Margaret McGregor
Center: Dr. J. H. McGregor ----- Mazie
Bottom: Robert Tyler, Dorothy-Margaret

**Perry, New York
The farm on Maple Avenue in Palmyra**

Printed in the United States
204897BV00002B/1-24/P